12·99

Cultural Revolution?

Are the cultural upheavals of the sixties just a media myth? The Summer of Love with its ambience of marijuana and sitar music, the glitterati of Swinging London and student protesters battling with the police, evoke a period of material prosperity, cultural innovation and youthful rebellion. But how significant were the radical aspirations and utopian ideals of the sixties? And what is the legacy of the social, political and cultural transformations which characterized the decade?

In an interdisciplinary collection of specially commissioned essays, the contributors to *Cultural Revolution?* uncover the complex economic and political contexts in which these changes took place. Covering a wide variety of art forms – drama, television, film, poetry, the novel, popular music, dance, cinema and the visual arts – they investigate how sixties culture became politicized, and how its inherent contradictions still have repercussions for the arts today.

Cultural Revolution? will be an important resource for students and teachers across social science and arts disciplines, especially those involved in cultural, media and communications studies.

The editors: Bart Moore-Gilbert lectures in English at Goldsmiths' College, University of London. John Seed is Senior Lecturer in History at the Roehampton Institute of Higher Education.

Cultural Revolution?

The challenge of the arts in the 1960s

Edited by

Bart Moore-Gilbert
and John Seed

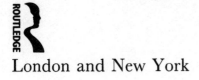

London and New York

First published 1992
by Routledge
11 New Fetter Lane, London EC4P 4EE

Simultaneously published in the USA and Canada
by Routledge
a division of Routledge, Chapman and Hall Inc.
29 West 35th Street, New York, NY 10001

This collection © 1992 Routledge; individual chapters © 1992
individual contributors

Typeset in 10 on 12 point Baskerville by Intype, London
Printed in Great Britain by Clays Ltd, St Ives plc

British Library Cataloguing in Publication Data
Cultural revolution?: the challenge of the arts
in the 1960s.
I. Moore-Gilbert, Bart II. Seed, John
700.941

Library of Congress Cataloging in Publication Data
Cultural revolution?: the challenge of the arts in the 1960s/edited
by Bart Moore-Gilbert and John Seed.
p. cm.
Includes bibliographical references and index.
1. Arts. British–Themes, motives. 2. Arts, Modern–20th century–
Great Britain–Themes, motives. 3. Arts and society–Great
Britain. I. Moore-Gilbert, Bart II. Seed, John.
NX543.A1C8 1992
700'.1'03094109046–dc20   91–37597

ISBN 0–415–07824–5
    0–415–07825–3 (pbk)

Contents

Notes on Contributors

Dave Harker teaches cultural studies at Manchester Polytechnic. He has written widely on 'folk' and 'popular' music from Britain and the USA, including *One for the Money* (1980), and remains a revolutionary socialist. His next book will be called *Two for the Show*.

Stuart Laing was a senior lecturer in the School of Cultural and Community Studies at the University of Sussex and is now based at Brighton Polytechnic. Previous publications include *Representations of Working-Class Life 1957–64* (1986), and he co-authored *Disorder and Discipline: Popular Culture from 1550 to the Present* (1988).

Jane Lewis is reader in social administration at the LSE. She is the author of numerous articles and books on the history of women and of social policy, including *The Politics of Motherhood* (1980), *Women in England, 1870–1950* (1984) and *Women and Social Action Since 1860* (1991).

Alf Louvre teaches English and cultural studies at Manchester Polytechnic. He has published articles on the theory and practice of cultural studies and on working-class writing. He was co-editor of *Tell Me Lies About Vietnam* (1988).

Judith Mackrell is dance critic for *The Independent* newspaper and has contributed regularly to *Dance Theatre Journal, Literary Review* and *Vogue*. She is the author of *British Dance Since 1968* (Dance Books, forthcoming).

Bart Moore-Gilbert lectures in the English Department at Goldsmiths' College, University of London. He is the editor of *Literature*

viii   Notes on contributors

and Imperialism (1984) and author of *Kipling and Orientalism* (1986) and a forthcoming study of the postwar British novel.

Martin Priestman lectures in the English Department at the Roehampton Institute of Higher Education. He is the author of *Cowper's 'The Task': Structure and Influence* (1983) and *Detective Fiction and Literature: The Figure on the Carpet* (1990).

Jeffrey Richards is professor of cultural history at Lancaster University. Among his books are *Age of the Dream Palace* (1984), *Thorold Dickinson: The Man and His Films* (1986) and *Mass-Observation at the Movies* (1987). He is general editor of Routledge's *Cinema and Society* series.

Jeremy Ridgman lectures in the Drama Department at the Roehampton Institute of Higher Education. His published work includes articles on television drama and on contemporary British and Australian theatre in *Australasian Drama Studies*, in *Contemporary Australian Drama* edited by Peter Holloway (1987) and in *Theatre, Politics, Political Theatre* edited by Graham Holderness (1991).

John Seed teaches history at the Roehampton Institute. His publications include essays on social theory and on English history in *Economy and Society, Social History, The Historical Journal* and in Janet Wolff and John Seed (eds) *The Culture of Capital: Art, Power and the Nineteenth-Century Middle Class* (1988). He is review editor of the journal *Social History*.

Robert Sheppard is the author of several volumes of poetry, including *Daylight Robbery* (1990). He has published a number of articles on contemporary poetry and poetics, and has reviewed for *The New Statesman* and *The Times Literary Supplement*. He is also co-editor of an anthology of new poetry from London, *Floating Capital* (1991).

Stuart Sillars divides his time between writing and teaching for the University of Cambridge Board of Extra-Mural Studies. He is the author of *Art and Survival in First World War Britain* (1988) and *British Romantic Art and the Second World War* (1991).

Acknowledgements

The editors would like to warmly thank the following for all their help on this project: Sue Bilton, Sarah Dann, Claire L'Enfant, Alex Potts, Peter Humm and Sally James.

The editors and publishers are grateful to the following for permission to include in this volume material from the sources indicated: André Deutsch Ltd for Daniel Cohn-Bendit, *Obsolete Communism* (1969); Faber & Faber Ltd for Philip Larkin, *Whitsun Weddings* (1964); HarperCollins Publishers Ltd for Lee Harwood, *Crossing the Frozen River; Selected Poems* (1988) and for Tom Raworth, *Tottering State: Selected Poems 1963–1987* (1988); David Higham Associates Ltd for Anthony Crosland, *The Future of Socialism* (1956); Oxford University Press for Roy Fisher, *Poems 1955–1987* (1988).

Chapter 1

Introduction

Bart Moore-Gilbert and John Seed

'The sixties' in Britain is a construct with varied and contested meanings. The earliest and perhaps most persistent derives from a composite of media-constructed images evoking material prosperity, cultural innovation and youthful rebellion: the 'Swinging London' of *Time* magazine's special April 1966 issue, with its King's Road boutiques, Mayfair art galleries and fashionable glitterati; the enamelled butterflies of the summer of love; the hippie cult with its vocabulary of love and peace, its ambience of marijuana and sitar music; or protesting students battling with police outside the US Embassy in Grosvenor Square.

The central aim of this collection of essays is to penetrate beyond the conventional emblems of the sixties and to begin to elaborate a much more complex and precise history of what occurred in some of the central spheres of cultural life in Britain during these years. In this introduction we will, necessarily, be talking at an over-generalized level about 'the cultural opposition', 'cultural radicals', the 'counter-culture'. But the thrust of the volume as a whole is towards recognizing differences and contradictions within the cultural practices of the 1960s. Thus it needs to be stressed at the very beginning, and this too is part of the work of demythologizing, that there was in these years no single monolithic counter-culture or cultural opposition with a coherent programme. There were diverse attacks on official culture (and that too was a more fissured and de-centred formation than the very term suggests), but in myriad locations – not only within the academy, within arts institutions of all kinds, within publishing, but also within more dispersed spaces around issues of gender, class, race and generation. Greater specificity about the chronology, location and often problematic interrelationship of these engagements is crucial to any adequate

interpretation of the changes, the incorporations and the marginaliz-
ations of the cultural politics of the 1960s.

This is particularly important in the context of the New Right's
attempt in recent years to establish its own politically charged
reading of the 1960s. For Mary Whitehouse, for instance, the 1960s
was 'an illiberal decade' in which all but a minority of unrepresent-
ative voices were silenced: 'The avant garde flooded our culture
and our society with its dirty water, churning up foundations, over-
turning standards, confusing thought and leaving in its wake an all
too obvious trail of insecurity and misery' (quoted in Tracy and
Morrison 1979: 152). Concern about the alleged damage done to
Britain's cultural institutions by the infiltration of counter-cultural
values and personnel into the BBC, the education system, even the
Church of England, has provided a rallying point for the New
Right. Whitehouse's obsessive harrying of the BBC throughout the
1960s was an augury of what was to become in the 1980s a much
more pervasive and state-sponsored *kulturkampf* (see Whitehouse
1972). Norman Tebbit, former cabinet minister and from 1985 to
1987 chairman of the Conservative Party, has frequently pronounced his anathemas upon 'the insufferable, smug, sanctimoni-
ous, naive, guilt-ridden, wet, pink orthodoxy of that sunset home
of the third-rate minds of that third-rate decade, the Sixties'. His
1985 Disraeli Lecture blamed what he perceived as the current ills
of Britain – violence, crime, above all 'personal irresponsibility' –
on the 'Permissive Society' that overturned traditional values in the
1960s:

> The permissives scorned intellectual standards. Bad art was as
> good as good art. Grammar and spelling were no longer impor-
> tant. To be clean was no better than to be filthy. Family life
> was an outdated bourgeois concept. Criminals deserved as much
> sympathy as their victims. Many homes and classrooms became
> disorderly – if there was neither right nor wrong there could be no
> basis for punishment or reward. Violence and soft pornography
> became accepted in the media.
>
> (quoted in Eccleshall 1990: 247)

Mrs Thatcher herself contrasted 'Sixties culture' with 'the old-
fashioned . . . clean and orderly' 1950s:

> Permissiveness, selfish and uncaring, proliferated under the guise
> of the new sexual freedom. Aggressive verbal hostility, presented

as a refreshing lack of subservience, replaced courtesy and good manners. Instant gratification became the philosophy of the young and the youth cultists.

(quoted in Sinfield 1989: 296[1])

Malcolm Bradbury's *The History Man*, first published in 1975 and then shown twice as a television series in the early 1980s, provided a powerful and influential picture of the sixties as destructive of intellectual and educational values by popularizing negative images of a new university sociology department at the end of the decade. The novel's anti-hero, Howard Kirk, is cynical and meretricious in every aspect of his life. His intellectual work is superficial, carefully tailored to the fashionable market for radical chic. As a teacher he is demagogic, self-indulgent and biased. In his personal life he is manipulative and devious, sexually predatory, emotionally cold, devoid of personal loyalties or principles. Kirk's colleagues and students are simply two-dimensional caricatures. Nevertheless Bradbury's novel has been taken as an authoritative representation of the state of at least some parts of higher education in Britain in the late 1960s. According to a reviewer in the *Sunday Express* it was 'horribly accurate' and the *Financial Times* thought it was 'possibly the most effective picture of academic life since Mary McCarthy's *The Groves of Academe*'. In many ways this picture of the 1960s as a phase of cultural trivialization, of superficial but sinister radicalisms, 'trendy lefties', self-indulgent and immature psyches, gratuitously destructive of order and tradition, devoid of any meaningful project for constructively transforming the real structures of social life, has become part of contemporary 'common sense'.

The success of the New Right in generating an influential political orthodoxy about the sixties has been reinforced by disillusioned reaction to the decade from very different cultural and political perspectives. John Lennon's 1970 interview with *Rolling Stone*, for instance, was forthrightly negative:

The people who are in control and in power and the class system and the whole bullshit bourgeois scene is exactly the same except that there is a lot of middle-class kids with long hair walking around London in trendy clothes and Kenneth Tynan's made a fortune out of the word 'fuck'. But apart from that, nothing happened except that we all dressed up. The same bastards are in control, the same people are running everything, it's exactly the same. They hyped the kids and the generation . . . there has been a change and we are a bit freer and all that, but it's the same game, nothing's really changed.

(quoted in Wenner 1972: 11–12)

Disillusion and antipathy also pervade several of the most substantial academic studies of the cultural politics of the decade. Daniel Bell's *The Cultural Contradictions of Capitalism*, first published in 1976, provides a sophisticated sociological account of the failure of the counter-culture. For Bell – who describes himself as 'a socialist in economics, a liberal in politics, and a conservative in culture' (1978: xi) – the ultimate exhaustion of the modernist dream is evidenced in the emptiness and nihilism of much of the art, the cultural values and the radical politics of the 1960s: 'All that there was, was the pathetic celebration of the self – a self that had been emptied of content and which masqueraded as being vital through the playacting of Revolution' (144). Or, as he put it in the foreword to the second edition:

> The so-called counter-culture was a children's crusade that sought to eliminate the line between fantasy and reality and act out in life its impulses under a banner of liberation. It claimed to mock bourgeois prudishness, when it was only flaunting the closet behaviour of its liberal parents. It claimed to be new and daring when it was only repeating in more raucous form – its rock noise amplified in the electronic echo-chamber of the mass media – the youthful japes of a half-century before. It was less a counter-culture than a counterfeit culture.
>
> (Bell 1978: xxvii)

Bell's focus is primarily on the United States, though its ramifications are considerably wider. In *A Sociology of Contemporary Cultural Change*, Bernice Martin develops often parallel kinds of arguments about Britain. She argues that the radical movements of the 1960s were particular instances of a long-term historical conflict between the individual and social order, which she terms 'the expressive revolution' developing out of romanticism. The late 1960s counter-culture, she argues, 'was always an impossible Utopian dream' (Martin 1981: 235). Its ideals were impossible to realize as a total way of life and, as a consequence, 'that missionary generation' suffered major casualties. Martin does acknowledge that the 1960s brought significant change. An older culture of control was decisively undermined: 'much that was only "lurking irreality", or unspeakable in the 1950s is now the stuff of daily cultural consumption' (237). Out of the cultural contests of the 1960s there emerged a new synthesis of structure and anti-structure – a widening, in other words, of the whole cultural repertoire. But the essential thrust of her argument is that such transformations indicate the ease with which the challenges of the cultural opposition were absorbed and contained.

Martin's overall thesis, and especially her stress on the subsequent incorporation of the radicalisms of the 1960s, converges with Regis Debray's sardonic comments on the significance of May 1968 in France. 'A modest contribution to the rites and ceremonies of the tenth anniversary' deflates radical nostalgia. 'May '68 was the cradle of a new bourgeois society. It may not yet realize this, but it is time someone told it so' (Debray 1978: 46). Or, as he puts it later, 'The sincerity of the actors of May was accompanied, and overtaken, by a cunning of which they knew nothing . . . they accomplished the opposite of what they intended' (48). For Debray the May events brought about the transformation of a regime and a culture that were increasingly incompatible with a dynamic capitalism; the superstructure was brought back into line with the base, the relations of production with the forces of production. The targets of French radicals – the cult of work, the patriarchal family, a narrow patriotism, the dead weight of tradition – were increasingly obsolete. 'Capital's development strategy required the cultural revolution of May' (49). These three critics of the cultural significance of the 1960s, despite differences of emphasis, share a sense of the cultural opposition as naive, dupes of history, unconscious of their real effects and comfortably assimilated into the dominant formations.

In Britain, disillusionment with the sixties has been particularly marked in relation to the decade's impact on the arts. Amongst the earliest voices to dissent from the counter-culture's own estimation of its significance in this respect was Bernard Bergonzi. He commented that Britain had 'few cultural achievements to offer the world apart from the strident trivialities of the pop scene' (Bergonzi: 1970: 57). Triviality and an obsession with the private sphere are charges commonly laid against much artistic practice in Britain in the 1960s. Thus Martin laments the period's 'penchant for the exploration of essentially private states . . . and the relative neglect of (and even contempt for) issues and experiences which involve public behaviour' (Martin 1981: 98). Yet others hostile to the decade accuse it of the very opposite. Swinden caustically compares the vogue for Patrick White with the neglect of Barbara Pym, whom Cape ceased to publish in 1961. This, he opines, reveals the characteristic pretentiousness of the cultural values of the time: 'Obviously a novel about a crucified Jew [*The Riders in the Chariot*] was bound to be ten times better than one about two old ladies who don't know what to do with a milk bottle' (Swinden 1989: 267). Several commentators have argued that just as the most revolutionary political initiatives occurred elsewhere – in the United States, in France, in Germany, in Italy, in Czechoslovakia – so too Britain was largely untouched by, or merely parasitic on, the most challenging cultural innovations being developed elsewhere. In his book on experimental fiction, for example, Robert Alter (1975) found only one British novelist – John Fowles – worthy of comparison with continental and American writers engaged in revolutionizing the genre.

A recurrent charge against the 1960s avant-garde is that it attempted to destroy the very categories of art and culture. Symptomatic of this vandalism were: the erosion of the status of the individual artist, for instance by stressing group collaboration or the obliteration of the distinction between performer and audience, whether in theatre, poetry readings or 'happenings'; the blurring of the status of the artwork by the use of 'found objects' and collage in the visual arts, found texts and cut-ups in writing, or the use of everyday gestures in dance; the instrumental use of art in agit-prop; and, at the other end of the spectrum, the interest shown in chance and random occurrence as constitutive elements in composition; and finally, at its most extreme, the exploration of auto-destructive art. Swinden has been particularly critical of two of the most striking directions taken by the avant-garde: the erosion of distinctions between politics and art, and between 'high' and 'popular' culture. The former tendency, he argues, led to a vast overrating of new dramatic voices like Mercer, Bond and Potter, whose 'combination of theatrical sensation and political naivety failed to produce plays that merited more than passing attention' (Swinden 1989: 271). 'Cultural decline', as he calls it, was also apparent in the widespread interest in the uses of 'popular' forms. He complains of the 'frightful philosophical vacuity that is typical of the popular culture of the period' and alleges that its influences on traditional 'high' cultural practices simply 'exerted a pressure towards the juvenile, the irresponsible' (264). Bernice Martin, by comparison, locates the threat to the distinctive identity of art in the avant-garde's increasing subordination of practice to theory. The latter, she says, 'becomes almost more a work of art than the art works themselves. The Word is thus infiltrating arts whose essential codes are not verbal at all' (Martin 1981: 91 – though, paradoxically, she dismisses rock music as a serious art form precisely because of its failure to theorize itself).

This book does not casually dismiss the force of some of the critical views surveyed above. Nevertheless the 12 essays gathered here do provide a critique of some of the emerging orthodoxies about the 1960s in Britain. Four recurrent areas of debate can be briefly noted. In the first place these essays suggest that the question of the alleged self-absorption or provincialism of British culture in these years needs to be reconsidered. In a range of cultural practices, from fiction and poetry to dance and pop music, foreign influences – especially American – were marked. Equally, however, in pop music, the visual arts, theatre and cinema at least, Britain's international reputation was high. A number of foreign figures were attracted to Britain in these years, precisely because of the vitality and cosmopolitanism of its cultural scene – in cinema, to take one example, Polanski, Losey and Antonioni. In any case, the capacity to respond to foreign influences indicates a decisive shift away from the cultural introversion that characterized much of the British cultural establishment in the 1950s.

A second emerging orthodoxy about the 1960s, which this volume questions, concerns the apparent ease and speed with which the decade's cultural radicalisms were absorbed into the Establishment they so vociferously opposed. First, that assimilation did not occur without a good deal of political counter-pressure. The state intervened directly to contain a range of challenges. Bookshops and galleries were prosecuted for the promotion of 'obscene' material – including work by Aubrey Beardsley. Publishers such as John Calder were involved in lengthy court cases over the publication of books like Trocchi's *Cain's Book* and Selby's *Last Exit to Brooklyn*. The underground press was harried by the police, contributing to the closure of *Oz* and *International Times* in 1970. Particular pop songs were excluded from television and radio. Peter Watkins' important film *The War Game* was banned. More subtle pressures – selective distribution of government subsidy by the Arts Council, for lack of which projects such as Arnold Wesker's Centre 42 withered away – also served to deflect or undermine elements of the cultural opposition, filtering out what was deemed disruptive. This trend was already in evidence during the 1960s, but became much more marked after the accession to power of Heath's Tory government in 1970. The new minister of the arts expressed in parliament his unhappiness at the Arts Council's use of public money to support 'works which affront the religious beliefs or outrage the sense of decency of a large body of tax-payers'. The Council's clients were subsequently sent a 'reminder' (Hewison 1986: 227). It would, of course, be absurd to exaggerate or over-dramatize the subtle repressions experienced in Britain in the 1960s; nevertheless it is shortsighted not to see the real political antagonisms that were in play in the field of culture.

It is also careless to forget the values and the work of many oppositional figures and groups who continued to remain outside, and opposed to, the mainstream after 1970 – whether poets, musicians, dramatists, artists or academics. Indeed, Perry Anderson (1990) has recently noted the paradox that in Britain in the 1980s 'a regime of the radical right part confronted, part created an overall cultural drift to the left'. Since the 1950s successive waves of radicalized intellectuals have preserved an oppositional culture crystallized in a range of journals, conferences, networks and venues.[2] To quote Anderson again: 'While an authoritarian populism was redrawing the electoral contours of the country to the advantage of capital, in this domain the hegemonic legacy weakened' (Anderson 1990: 47).

In any case, so far as one does accede to the proposition that substantial elements of the counter-culture were subsequently assimilated within the mainstream, this can be interpreted as testimony of its success rather than its failure. The spectacular transformation of styles of dress, of relations between the sexes, of attitudes to authority, of the whole content and style of many radio and television programmes, of the output of journals and publishers, of work within major sectors of the academy, of the marked internationalization of debate within intellectual culture and the arts by the 1970s, may not have amounted to a political revolution. Nor did it realize the amorphous utopias of the counter-culture. In fact in many ways it was precisely the groups who seemed to be finding a voice in the 1960s – young people, women, blacks – who have suffered the worst effects of economic recession and political reaction during the 1970s and 1980s. Nevertheless, in all kinds of ways, the political ramifications of cultural change in the 1960s were undeniably significant.

Looking at the 1960s only in terms of what came after, and not also in terms of what went before, can obscure that significance. Focusing more precisely on the dominant values and cultural formations of the 1950s produces a different set of emphases, in understanding the subsequent decade, to those provided by Bell, Martin, Debray and others. It was precisely a sense of the exhausted potential of central institutions, practices, canons and definitions in sphere after sphere of cultural life that animated much of the activity and dissension of the 1960s.

Third, the volume reassesses the charge that much of what claimed to be most radical and challenging in the arts and the wider culture was in fact obsessively private and narcissistic in its concerns – 'a pathetic celebration of the self' in the words of Bell (1978). The cultural activities we are looking at here – from theatre to the counter-culture press and political argument, from cinema to the novel or dance – were varied in their point of attack on established values. Clearly there was in the 1960s some exploitation of violence and sex because of their ability to attract a paying audience. But there is, of course, nothing unique to the 1960s about this; nor was it, by any means, merely the prerogative of the cultural opposition. The new frankness in dealing with sexuality or violence can be read, in carefully specified instances, as genuine attempts to confront hitherto suppressed (or at least embattled) areas of social experience. The alleged preoccupation with private experience was not then necessarily a withdrawal from the public sphere but a recognition of the institutionalized narrowness, both of what was conceived as public and of who was permitted to have access to it. Hence the concern to explore the boundaries between public and private, to insist sometimes that 'the personal *is* the political', to redefine the very nature of what was political. As feminists were beginning to argue by the end of the 1960s, those boundaries ensured the invisibility of key forms of women's oppression. The Gay Rights campaigns of the late 1960s were making a parallel case. This privative and elitist (though 'public') institutionalization of discourse also marginalized and de-politicized other areas of social experience and certain largely unquestioned facets of Britain's official self-image. A play like Bond's *Saved*, for instance, could surely earn notoriety only in the context of a deep complacency about the conflict-free and consensual character of British society

– represented as late as 1970 in Bergonzi's proposition that 'the English are a remarkably innocent people, who scarcely know what violence, crime or civil disorder is' (Bergonzi 1970: 60).

More recent perspectives on issues of gender, sexual identity and race have identified some of the profound limitations of 1960s radicalism. Though the left-wing paper *Black Dwarf* was one of the first to bring feminist issues before a wider readership, declaring 1969 'Year of the Militant Woman' and publishing a number of pioneering articles, it is clear that throughout the 1960s the New Left was largely 'gender-blind' (see the contributions of Benson, Wedderburn and Segal to OUSDG 1989: 107–16). The New Left, David Caute comments, was 'a movement of male captains and female corporals' (Caute 1988: 267). The evidence of Green (1988) is more damning, clearly indicating that the counter-culture reproduced – indeed sometimes exaggerated – the sexual exploitation that suffused the wider society. Nor would it be difficult to document the limited critical perspective of much of the 1960s cultural opposition on issues of race or other kinds of marginalized social identities – not excluding social class. Yet too present-minded a view of the period has its own costs in terms of understanding and analysis.

Fourth, in contrast to Martin's claim that much of the decade's innovative activity was little more than the vehicle for the self-definition of a new cultural elite, some of the contributions to this volume look at varied attempts to democratize access to, and conceptions of, culture. There were, for instance, transformations in the material base of cultural production – the expansion of higher education, the inauguration of the Open University, the broadening of the role of the Arts Council after 1967. There was also the emergence of 'alternative' spaces to house drama, dance, poetry readings and so on. Redefinitions of the role of the artist, which stressed the involvement of others in the making of the artwork, the weakening of the boundary between performer and audience, the raids on popular culture, all helped to demystify art and undermine discriminatory distinctions between 'high' and 'low'. Such developments encouraged a wider and more confident access to the arts.

Neither blanket condemnation nor nostalgic celebration of the sixties is now very useful. We argue that it is now time for a more searching and discriminating rethink of the central issues involved. Dominant representations of the 1960s too often fail to make careful analytical distinctions or to identify the precise discourses and institutions where specific contestations were occurring at specific times.

This rethinking is essential, even at the basic level of chronology. When did the sixties begin? As Robert Hewison notes, the media myth of the sixties is in fact largely based on the years 1964–7. Hewison himself proposes that 'the Sixties did not really begin until about 1963, and that they do not fade away until 1975' (Hewison 1986: xiii). A number of chapters in this book indicate different moments of transition in different fields. The chronologies of change in these years were extremely complex and not reducible to some central and pivotal moment or some *Zeitgeist* simultaneously inhabiting the diverse spheres of British life.

If we need to recognize the horizontal complexities of chronology we have also to be attentive to vertical tensions within particular art forms and genres. No art form or genre was an undifferentiated bloc. Generalized statements about, say, pop music in the 1960s need to be grounded in fairly precise mapping of the different variants available – and the differences within particular oeuvres or even specific LPs. Was *The Sound of Music*, which Dave Harker's essay (chapter 12) shows outsold the Beatles and the Stones, precisely the same in its cultural meanings and effects as *Sergeant Pepper* or *Beggar's Banquet?* Clearly not. Similarly the 1960s novel includes C. P. Snow and Angela Carter, B. S. Johnson and Ian Fleming, Muriel Spark and David Storey – all significantly different, even contradictory, in their cultural implications. These essays include this necessary focus on changes and internal differences within specific spheres of cultural production, and thus transcend simplistic and premature totalizations that serve only to short-circuit empirical analysis.

Equally central to the whole book is exploration of some of the links between culture in its more traditional sense – as 'high art' – and in the sense that emerged out of the work of Leavis, Hoggart, Raymond Williams and E. P. Thompson – as the ways in which social life is structured and experienced. It is, ironically, precisely a recognition of this dynamic and politically charged intersection of art, institutional structures and the culture of everyday life that was registered in Thatcherite interventions in the sphere of culture throughout the 1980s – whether in pressure on, and sometimes outright censorship of, the BBC and other television companies; in systematic attacks on higher education, and especially some of the more critical sectors of the academy; in stereotyping of 'the chattering classes'; or in the encouragement of private patronage of the arts in preference to state support. This, and the anathemas that pour forth on the 1960s from the likes of Tebbit, Whitehouse, Levin and other pundits, testifies to the increased politicization of the cultural sphere since the 1960s. Hence our focus on the politics of culture.

These essays make no claims to be anything other than inquiries into certain key aspects of cultural production in Britain during the 1960s. Essays on topics of equal importance – architecture, classical music, fashion, sport, photography, many aspects of popular and youth cultures, and so on – could have been usefully included. However, the essays that are included do attempt to contribute to a wider project: to understand the present by bringing it into a critical relationship with the recent past, making intelligible the various histories that shape our present identities and present crises.

NOTES

1 It is worth noting a common rhetorical strategy underlying neoconservative attacks on cultural change in the 1960s. The economic and social determinants of the problems they deplore – dependence on social welfare, rising crime figures, marital breakdown, widely-expressed discontent and scepticism towards traditional authority – are blatantly ignored. They are the responsibility of the cultural radicals, favourite targets being 'permissives' inside the BBC, progressive schoolteachers and social workers, polytechnic lecturers, especially sociologists. No attention is paid to the impact of capital's almost untrammelled restructuring of British society with all its disruptive consequences: unemployment, declining living standards among significant sections of the population, housing shortages, disintegrating urban infrastructures, the under-resourcing of education at all levels.

2 See for instance Crozier and Longville (1990) for an anthology of a generation of poets that began to coalesce during the 1960s and has remained outside the self-regarding metropolitan literati. See also Kenner (1988) for sardonic comments on the latter from J. C. Squire and Lascelles Abercrombie to their contemporary epigones Motion, Raine & Co.

BIBLIOGRAPHY

Alter, R. 1975. *Partial Magic: The Novel as Self-Conscious Genre*. London: University of California Press.

Anderson, P. 1990. 'A culture in contraflow – I'. *New Left Review*, 180.

Beer, S. H. 1982. *Britain Against Itself: The Political Contradictions of Collectivism*. London: Faber & Faber.

Bell, D. 1978. *The Cultural Contradictions of Capitalism*. New York: Basic Books.

Bergonzi, B. 1970. *The Situation of the Novel*. London: Macmillan.

Caute, D. 1988. *'68: The Year of the Barricades*. New York: Harper & Row.

Crozier, A. and Longville, T. (eds) 1990. *A Various Art*. London: Paladin.

Debray, R. 1978. 'A modest contribution to the rites and ceremonies of the tenth anniversary'. *New Left Review*, 115.

Eccleshall, R. 1990. *English Conservatism Since the Restoration: An Introduction and Anthology*. London: Unwin Hyman.

Green, J. 1988. *Days in the Life: Voices from the English Underground 1961–71*. London: Heinemann.

Hewison, R. 1986. *Too Much: Art and Society in the Sixties 1960–75*. London: Methuen.

Kenner, H. 1988. *A Sinking Island: The Modern English Writers*. London: Barrie & Jenkins.

Levin, B. 1970. *The Pendulum Years: Britain and the Sixties*. London: Pan.

Maitland, S. (ed.) 1988. *Very Heaven: Looking Back at the 1960s*. London: Virago.

Martin, B. 1981. *A Sociology of Contemporary Cultural Change*. Oxford: Blackwell.

Marwick, A. 1982. *British Society Since 1945*. London: Allen Lane.

Morgan, K. O. 1990. *The People's Peace: British History 1945–1989*. Oxford: Oxford University Press.

OUSDG (Oxford University Socialist Discussion Group) 1989. *Out of Apathy: Voices of the New Left Thirty Years On*. London: Verso.

Sinfield, A. 1989. *Literature, Politics and Culture in Postwar Britain*. Oxford: Blackwell.

Swinden P. 1989. 'Literature at home'. In Pearce, S. and Piper, D. (eds), *Literatures of Europe and America in the 1960s*. Manchester: Manchester University Press.

Tracey, M. and Morrison, D. 1979. *Whitehouse*. London: Macmillan.

Wenner, J. 1972. *Lennon Remembers: The Rolling Stone Interviews*. London: Penguin.

Whitehouse, M. 1972. *Who Does She Think She Is?*, revised edn. London: New English Library.

Williams, R. 1985. *Towards 2000*. London: Penguin.

Williamson, B. 1990. *The Temper of the Times: British Society Since World War II*. Oxford: Blackwell.

FURTHER READING

The most useful introductory survey of the arts in the 1960s is probably Robert Hewison's *Too Much* (1986). Alan Sinfield's *Literature, Politics and Culture in Postwar Britain* (1989) is wide-ranging and thought-provoking, though somewhat Byzantine in organization. Two sceptical sociological accounts that we have referred to in this introductory chapter are Bell (1978) and Martin (1981). David Caute's *'68: Year of the Barricades* (1988) provides a comprehensive and reasoned account of perhaps the key year in the decade. Both Jonathon Green's *Days in the Life* (1988) and Sarah Maitland's (ed.) *Very Heaven* (1988) offer stimulating perspectives on the

1960s via memoirs, which, if personal, are by no means uncritical. There is much relevant material in recent histories of the postwar period such as Marwick (1982), Morgan (1990) and Williamson (1990).

Chapter 2

Hegemony postponed: the unravelling of the culture of consensus in Britain in the 1960s

John Seed

'The class war is over and we have won it', Macmillan pronounced in 1959. Within a few years that hubris had gone. The unexpected occurred: the Conservative Party lost successive general elections in 1964 and 1966. Indeed they were subsequently to govern for only four troubled years until Mrs Thatcher's election victory in 1979. Hegemony postponed indeed. Yet, if Labour were in government for much of the 1960s, they too – in the face of economic disruption, industrial militancy, student protest, and wide-ranging radical challenges to the traditional order of things – experienced failure, loss of confidence and a major weakening of support among important social constituencies. The ideological initiative – whether expressed in anti-Vietnam War protest and the student movement, in an uncontrollable surge of union militancy, in the counter-culture or in the intellectual influence of such radical dissenters as E. P. Thompson, R. D. Laing, Raymond Williams and a host of others – was seized by groups outside the established political formations.

What happened? It is not, of course, my intention in this essay to construct a full history of social, political and cultural change in Britain during the 1960s. Rather, the aim is to sketch in how Conservative and Labour parties each suffered significant crises of authority – the former in 1962–3, the latter after 1966. These crises were multi-determined and their ramifications were complex and far-reaching. But their effects, I will argue, were to break down established assumptions of what was 'political' and thus to open up, for a period, the whole field of civil society and everyday life to a widely-diffused contestation of authority and tradition.[1]

THE CRISIS OF CONSERVATISM, 1961–4

The Conservative Party presided over a long period of boom in the 1950s. Output increased by over 35 per cent between 1951 and 1961. Real average earnings rose by around 2.7 per cent per annum in the same period. Profits were good. Unemployment was low. A prosperous capitalist economy could finance what was generally assumed to be a humane and enlightened welfare state while maintaining satisfactory levels of profit, rising standards of living and more or less full employment. But Britain's rate of growth was outstripped by many of its western rivals in these years, and from the late 1950s overall share of world exports began to plummet. Growing international recognition of Britain's industrial frailty led to spells of speculation against sterling in financial markets. This in turn provoked packages of deflationary measures in 1955 and 1957. Unemployment began to edge up, reaching 2.3 per cent in 1959, the highest since 1948. At the same time, from the mid-1950s there was a steady increase in the number of strikes and the numbers of working days lost. Voices began to be raised about Britain's gathering economic difficulties. Andrew Shonfield pointed out in 1958:

> Because our wealth grows more slowly than the wealth of other countries, our prices rise faster; industrial relations have grown strained, and now many people have come to be positively afraid of full employment. The Government's policies both in home and external affairs are constantly constricted by penury; the balance of payments is like a raw and exposed nerve: with the first breath of adversity the economy is wracked and convulsed. It is bad for the spirit of any country to live with so little room for manoeuvre.
>
> (Shonfield 1958: 51)

These problems culminated in a major balance of payments crisis in 1961, the most serious since the war – widely ascribed to mismanagement by a series of six economically illiterate chancellors. A pay freeze, public spending cuts and a hike in interest rates followed. Gaitskell and the Labour Party moved ahead in the opinion polls for the first time since the 1959 election (Wybrow, 1989: 63).

Economic problems were only one factor in the increasing difficulties of the Conservative Party in the late 1950s. Delusions of Britain's status as a 'first-class' power – and with it a sense of the Tory leadership as statesmen on the world stage – persisted within governing circles in the 1950s. This required a substantial military presence in Europe and the Far East and considerable investment in developing an independent nuclear capability. Thus high levels of military spending were incurred – around 9 per cent of GNP. This was more than double that of Britain's main competitors, and a significant drain on resources, contributing to the financial strains on the economy (Chalmers 1985). These delusions were punctured by the 1956 Suez crisis. For sections of the Tory Party the steady dismantling of empire, especially after the appointment of Iain McLeod as Colonial Secretary in 1959, further exacerbated British decline as a world power (Gamble 1974). So too did a series of expensive military and aerospace projects that were dismal failures, sometimes cancelled before completion.

The impossibility of continuing to finance an independent nuclear capability was finally recognized in 1961. Policy shifted to purchasing directly from the United States, with all the dependence and subordination that that implied – a policy disapproved of by seven out of ten people, according to a 1962 Gallup Poll. The Cuban missile crisis in the autumn of 1962 further exposed British impotence; unilateral action on the part of the United States could clearly draw Britain into a nuclear war (Mander 1963). The last of a series of humiliations in the international sphere was the rejection of Britain for Common Market membership in 1963. The after-effects of de Gaulle's resounding 'Non' are succinctly summarized by Middlemas: 'Apparently for nothing, Commonwealth sensibilities had been outraged, the old Tory right revitalized, and the party split for a time into three. An enormous sense of loss and disillusion ensued, at all levels of the party' (Middlemas 1990: 80).

'The Right is acutely aware', Peregrine Worsthorne noted in 1959, 'that the kind of Britain it wishes to preserve very largely depends on Britain remaining a great power' (quoted in Gamble 1974: 62). A significant part of the Tory Party's electoral appeal was, thus, its 'close association with national greatness'. It represented church and queen and empire, the armed services, Land of Hope and Glory, tradition and patriotism, Elgar and the rolling green hills of England. The Conservative party was, in other words, the embodiment of a particular culture that imagined itself at the centre of the nation, even of the world. The royal enclosure at Ascot, the senior common room at Balliol or All Souls, a box at Covent Garden, the Carlton Club, the board room of a merchant bank, Henley Regatta, were some of the interconnected spaces that constituted the inner world of 'the Conservative Nation'. Thus the Conservative Party was not merely an instrumental political organization. It was also one of the inner scaffoldings of a structure and a consciousness that fused together the social and the national in a single identity: 'England'. Suez, the dissolution of empire and the aborted reorientation towards Europe, all undermined the identity of Tory government and international prestige in the late 1950s and early 1960s. Undermined at the same time was a sense of social authority; as Worsthorne had gone on to observe in 1959, 'Everything about the British class system begins to look foolish and tacky when related to a second-class power on the decline'.

(Gamble 1974: 62).

Another essential facet of this Conservative identity and authority was broken open in the early 1960s – its role as guarantor of moral order. A series of scandals – the Vassall, Philby and Profumo cases – seemed to indicate a deep moral rot within the establishment. Especially after the Profumo case – with its rumours of much wider sexual licence in high circles – that guardian of public morals and Christian ethics, the Tory Party, was widely seen to be morally discredited. Macmillan's 'England' began to look like a pornocracy. In *Private Eye* (June 1963) Timothy Birdsall represented 'The Last Days of Macmillan' in a Roman bath; Nero-like, Macmillan stretches corpulently and bleary-eyed on a couch; one naked woman fans him, another holds a glass to his lips. Around him court politicians in togas whisper and plot; others chase naked women around the pool, beneath the sign 'Nymphs (deleted) Models disporting themselves with famous names' (Walker 1978: 165). According to the *Washington Post*, 'a picture of wide-spread decadence beneath the glitter of a large segment of stiff-lipped society is emerging' (quoted in Young 1963: 36). The after-effects of the Profumo case were certainly damaging electorally, at least in the short term. 'At present the Conservative Party is a shambles', the *Daily Telegraph* wrote (quoted in Young 1963: 33). A Gallup poll, immediately after Profumo had admitted to Parliament that he had lied, found that support for the Tories had dropped 7 per cent in a couple of weeks and Labour's lead was over 20 per cent. 'A great party is not to be brought down because of a squalid affair between a woman of easy virtue and a proven liar' Hailsham pronounced on BBC television (quoted in Young 1963: 34). But this liaison and its subsequent ramifications did cause the Tory Party significant harm.

A deeper crisis of authority became evident in the early 1960s as questions began to be asked about the moral health of the nation as a whole under Macmillan and the Conservatives. There was growing unease about a crisis in the family, with rising figures for divorce, illegitimacy, children in local authority care. This – and the increasing number of working mothers and 'latchkey kids' – was in turn linked to rising crime figures and increased hooliganism. At the same time London was fast outstripping Paris and Amsterdam as the vice capital of Europe. A *Times* leader thundered in June 1963 that government policy had brought the nation spiritually and psychologically to a low ebb' and equated affluence with moral bankruptcy (quoted in Tracey and Morrison 1979: 24).

A series of substantial studies published in the early 1960s expressed a sense of national crisis and tried to anatomize the problems – especially economic and political – confronting British society. *The Stagnant Society: A Warning* by Michael Shanks, published as a Penguin Special in 1961, posed the alternatives: growth or stagnation. The latter – 'a slow slide towards impotence and failure' – offered what in retrospect seems almost utopian: 'A lotus island of easy, tolerant ways, bathed in the golden glow of an imperial sunset, shielded from discontent by a threadbare welfare state and an acceptance of genteel poverty' (Shanks 1961: 232). With the exasperated innocence of his class (public school, Oxford) he wanted to know 'Why WON'T our workers work harder?' In many traditional and working-class communities there was, he claimed, 'a sheer lack of awareness of the new horizons opened up by the affluent society' (65). Such inward-looking communities with their 'us' and 'them' attitudes were, however, being steadily dissolved by the new culture of affluence. The greatest barrier to 'an expanding dynamic economy' was, inevitably, the trade union movement, with its bloody-minded resistance to technical innovation and more effective use of labour. 'The unions', he argued, 'are too often proving themselves the natural allies of the forces of stagnation and conservatism in industry' (93).

Suicide of a Nation?, a special issue of *Encounter* edited by Arthur Koestler in July 1963 and brought out as a book within months, was also based on the assumption 'that Britain is in the course of a crisis which, if it is not overcome within the not very distant future, will lead to her permanent decline' (Koestler 1963: 48). From left, centre and right, contributors pointed to outdated attitudes, especially towards social class, and a deeply ingrained resistance to change. On the one hand were the representatives of the Establishment – a gentlemanly, backward-looking, amateur elite deeply averse to change of any kind, incapable of utilizing new scientific and technical knowledge, and guilty of mismanagement at every level. On the other hand were the working class, especially trade unionists, who clung to outmoded class resentments, resisted innovation in industry, engaged in frivolous and fratricidal strike action and in general constituted 'a massive inertial resistance' to change.

Perry Anderson gave a Marxian inflection to the argument in 1963 in his 'Origins of the present crisis'. 'British society is in the throes of a profound, pervasive but cryptic crisis, undramatic in appearance, but ubiquitous in its reverberations' (Anderson 1965: 11). Inveighing against British backwardness – 'a sclerosed, archaic society', 'a torpid economy, a pinched and regressive education, a listless urban environment, a demoralized governing class, a wretched cultural provincialism' (47) – he traced its roots to the premature English revolution of the 1640s. This led to the dynamic agrarian capitalism of eighteenth-century Britain, over which a landed aristocracy presided. An emergent industrial bourgeoisie briefly challenged aristocratic predominance in the early nineteenth century but subsequently compromised, becoming infected by the virus of traditionalism, amateurism and nepotism. For Anderson, British history was thus a series of failures. The industrial bourgeoisie failed to revolutionize and rationalize British capitalism in the nineteenth century. In turn 'a supine bourgeoisie produced a subordinate proletariat'. Hence the lack of radical vigour in British society in the early 1960s.[2]

Others crowded to the patient's bedside (Davenport 1964; Chapman 1963; Hartley 1963; Hill and Whichelow 1964). Whatever their political stance or intellectual approach – and whether their primary focus was on large-scale managerial incompetence, trade-union obstructionism, the narrow unworldliness of the civil service or the elitism and conservatism of the educational system – there was a common emphasis: British backwardness, traditionalism, parochialism and the threat of steady economic decline. The choice of the 14th Earl of Home to succeed Macmillan at the end of 1963 seemed to confirm the icy grip of the past in governing circles. As Anderson put it, 'the party obeyed its oldest and deepest instincts and chose as its leader a caricature of its past aristocratic eminences (Anderson 1965: 51).

Yet it would be wrong to see Macmillan's government as merely the indolent representative of a crumbling *ancien régime*. At the beginning of the 1960s a number of important government enquiries were set up to investigate key institutions: the Newsom committee on secondary education; the Robbins committee on higher education; the Trend enquiry into science; the Pilkington committee on the future of broadcasting; the Beeching enquiry into the railway system; and the Buchanan enquiry into roads and traffic. The National Economic Development Council was set up by government in 1961. Its report of 1963, *Conditions Favourable To Growth*, recommended greater investment in science and education, and put forward policies for economic growth. The government was positive in its response and at the same time approved regional development plans for various parts of the country. But the image of backward-looking old men stuck to the government. The dramatic loss of the safe seat of Orpington to the Liberals in March 1962 was a sign of rebellion even within the comfortable suburban heartlands of Tory support. A small back-bench faction of anti-Macmillan Conservatives sometimes barracked the prime minister and on occasion voted against the government. The purging of one-third of the cabinet in July 1962 – 'the night of the long knives' – caused bitter, and very public, resentment. Conservative Party morale plummeted. The Profumo affair further exacerbated Tory gloom and Macmillan's isolation. The appointment of Home to replace him in October 1963 left the party in disarray. Leading members of the government – notably Butler and Hailsham – were publicly humiliated. Six cabinet ministers refused Home's invitation to join his new government, though only two – Enoch Powell and Iain McLeod – stuck out. Strained relations and bickering within the upper echelons of the party persisted throughout much of 1964 (See Churchill 1964; and McLeod's review of it, reprinted in Hutchinson 1980). According to one Conservative, 'You couldn't really get anything done during that period. We had to get the party straight first' (quoted in Butler and King 1965: 84).

The political party that throughout the 1950s had seemed to be a smooth and efficient political machine representing all interests within the nation and maintaining Britain's role as a world power was, by 1964, ramshackle and conflict-ridden, widely perceived as guilty of economic mismanagement and cynicism, presiding over a demoralized society, a declining economy, a fading empire. This manifold crisis of 1962–3 culminated in Conservative defeat in the general election of 1964. The margin was narrow and the election result was extremely complex. Labour had 317 seats compared to the Conservative's 304 and Labour's overall majority was a mere four. Yet, if Labour had not enjoyed a sweeping victory, the Tories had suffered a serious defeat. Their share of the poll was 6 per cent down, the biggest drop of any party since the Tory defeat of 1945. Six ministers lost their seats, including Barber, the Minister of Health. The Home Secretary, Henry Brooke, suffered a swing against him of over 10 per cent, barely holding on to his previously safe Hampstead seat.

The Conservatives were to win only one out of the next five elections and were to govern for only four years out of the next 15. For a political party that saw itself as a national party and the 'natural' party of government – and that had been in power for a clear majority of the years since the 1867 Reform Act enfranchised the bulk of the working class – this marked a considerable period of failure. Labour's overall majority increased in the 1966 general election to 97 – the largest in the Labour Party's history. The demise of 1950s Toryism was complete.

AFFLUENCE, COLD WAR, CROSLAND AND THE NEW LEFT

The situation looked bleak for the Labour Party at the end of the 1950s. They had suffered defeat in three successive general elections, their share of the vote falling from 49 per cent in 1951 to just over 43 per cent in 1959. The Conservative Party majority had increased from 26 seats to 107. Profound shifts in British society seemed to be undermining traditional working-class loyalties. Rising standards of living, an improved quality of life and a whole new culture of affluence were dissolving old class identities. People were no longer, it seemed, divided between rich and poor, the haves and have-nots. Now it was a matter of the haves and have-mores. 'Must Labour lose?' a study commissioned by *Socialist Commentary* asked in 1960. The answer seemed to be 'yes', unless the Labour Party radically adjusted itself to the new classless culture of affluence (Abrams and Rose 1960). Prominent voices inside the Labour Party concurred. Gaitskell himself observed that 'the changing character of labour, full employment, new housing, the new way of life based on the telly, the fridge, the car and the glossy magazines – all have had their effect on our political strength' (quoted in Hall *et al.* 1978: 230).[3]

The impact of rising standards of living was significant. Unemployment was extremely low throughout the 1950s, varying between 1 and 2 per cent. Wage levels rose steadily, on average by over 20 per cent between 1951 and 1959. And in almost half the families of Britain there was more than one wage earner. At the same time there were shifts in the occupational structure: white-collar jobs expanded as the number of manual workers declined; more and more working-class families owned cars, televisions, washing machines, and could afford holidays and minor luxuries – there were, for example, 300,000 televisions in Britain in 1950 but 10,500,000 by the end of the decade (Halsey 1972). The experience of Arthur Seaton's father in *Saturday Night and Sunday Morning* (1958) spoke for many at the end of the 1950s. Unemployed during the 1930s, he and his family had struggled through years of poverty; 'And now he had a sit-down job at the factory, all the Woodbines he could smoke, money for a pint if he wanted one, a holiday somewhere, a jaunt on the firm's trip to Blackpool, and a television set to look into' (Sillitoe 1958: 29). This relative affluence was widely perceived as radically transforming the character of the working class. Life was less focused around social and public spaces – the local pub, cinema or fish-and-chip shop. The private sphere – home, with its new facilities and comforts – was becoming more important. Changes in housing patterns undermined traditional neighbourhood solidarities; between 1948 and 1958 one family in every six moved into a new house or flat. The old terraced houses, enshrined in Coronation Street, survived; but increasing numbers of working people had moved out to new council estates on greenfield sites, often with limited public facilities, and some were now buying their own houses. Similarly a car opened up new horizons for private leisure, far beyond the local community.

This image of British society as a set of classless individual families consuming in private was represented in the Conservative Party's poster campaign in the run-up to the 1959 general election. In one a photograph of a modest but comfortable interior shows a mother and two children sitting around a table plentifully stacked with food. The mother smiles benignly as her children eat. In the background the father is switching on the television. In another poster the picture is of mother, father and son washing the family car. Again the affluence is modest – the car is an Austin A35. Another smaller boy is playing on his tricycle in the background. Both posters announce 'Life's Better with the Tories', 'Don't Let

Labour Ruin It'. The images in each were delicately calibrated to mirror the broadest strata of the modestly affluent, whether bank clerk or schoolteacher, white-collar or blue-collar worker.

Of course, the social realities of Britain in the late 1950s were a good deal more complex than this sanguine image of 'the affluent society' suggested. There was extensive poverty, bad housing, dilapidated schools, low wages, appalling working conditions, inadequate health care. Afro-Caribbean and 'new Commonwealth' immigrants were especially vulnerable to all of these, and often suffered vicious racial discrimination as well. Such problems were not just a matter of the disadvantaged – marginal groups, numerically limited, who were represented as the unfortunate (even self-appointed) victims of an overall success story: they were part of the lived experience of substantial numbers of the population. And they were structural, effects of the very essence of the British polity. As a number of important contemporary studies demonstrated with empirical precision, Britain remained a society in which social class determined access to the benefits of increasing social wealth, and where palpable inequalities, regardless of the welfare state, serenely persisted. In a series of lectures and essays during the 1950s, Richard Titmuss punctured complacent assumptions about the effectiveness of the welfare state in reducing poverty and inequality. Real social needs were being neglected while in crucial respects the middle classes were benefiting more from the welfare state than were the working class (Titmuss 1958). He went on in a further study (Titmuss 1962) to demolish, quietly and patiently, widespread claims that a massive redistribution of income had taken place since 1945 (see also Atkinson 1972). A number of other studies in the early 1960s demonstrated the extent of poverty and inequality. Townsend and Abel-Smith, for instance, calculated that those in poverty had increased from under 8 per cent of the population in the early 1950s to over 14 per cent by 1960, affecting around 7.5 million people (Abel-Smith and Townsend 1965; see also Coates and Silburn 1970; Westergaard 1965; Kincaid 1973).

Significant forces within the Labour Party in the 1950s nevertheless accepted the fiction of the affluent society. The key political text here is Anthony Crosland's *The Future of Socialism* (1956). Published some 18 months after the Labour defeat in the 1955 general election and less than a year after Gaitskell took over as Labour leader, it was a timely and influential intervention in national political debate. Essentially Crosland argued that capitalism had been transformed. No longer was society characterized by a structural antagonism between labour and capital, between worker and employer. An increasingly stable and prosperous economy was capable of financing a general rise in living standards and a humane and generous welfare system. Socialists had won the essential battles. Now the task for organized labour was to ensure continuing economic growth and at the same time move towards a more equal and meritocratic society via specific reforms. A fairer education system, better relations between workers and managers on the shop-floor, better welfare provision for the disadvantaged, more liberal policies towards censorship, abortion, divorce and sexuality – these were essential steps to a more egalitarian social order (Crosland, A. 1956). Of course Crosland was expounding views that were more widely held within the Labour Party (see for instance Socialist Union 1956). But *The Future Of Socialism* was a substantial and subtle book that filled an ideological vacuum for the centre-right of the party and that was to provide a doctrinal focus for an influential group of younger MPs, consolidated in the Campaign for Democratic Socialism formed in 1960 (Crosland, S. 1982: 100–1).[4]

The early and mid-1950s marked a profound nadir in socialist thinking in Britain. This was not only a matter of coming to terms with a revitalized capitalism and a supposedly affluent working class. Nor was it only a matter of the marginalization of the left within the Labour Party. More significantly disabling was the international context. The Cold War's division of the world into two dominant blocs seemed to construct a stark political choice: Communism or anti-Communism; Washington or Moscow. As the first editorial of *The Universities and Left Review* put it in 1957:

> The post-war decade was one in which declining political orthodoxies held sway. Every political concept became a weapon in the cold war of ideas, every idea had its label, every person had his place in the political spectrum, every form of political action appeared – in someone's eyes – a polite treason. To recommend the admission of China to the U. N. was to invite the opprobrium of 'fellow-traveller'; to say that the character of contemporary capitalism had changed was to be ranked as a 'Keynesian liberal'. Between the high citadel of Stalinist Russia and the 'welfare state – no further' jungle of the mixed economy, there seemed nothing but an arid waste.
> (quoted in Oxford University Socialist Discussion Group 1989: 17, hereafter cited as OUSDG)

The conjuncture of Suez and Hungary immediately and decisively abrogated this ideological straitjacket. Suez, as Stuart Hall recalled, 'underlined the enormity of the error in believing that lowering the Union Jack in a few ex-colonies signalled "the end of imperialism" ' (OUSDG 1989: 13). It led to the first mass political demonstrations of the 1950s. At the same time, the invasion of Hungary by Soviet tanks demonstrated the constricted possibilities for democratic change in eastern Europe; some 10,000 members of the Communist Party of Great Britain resigned in its aftermath. To quote Hall again, ' "Hungary" and "Suez" were . . . "liminal", boundary-marking experiences. They symbolized the break-up of the political Ice Age' (OUSDG 1989: 13).

Out of this conjuncture emerged the New Left, in the form, initially, of two journals, *The New Reasoner* and *The Universities and Left Review*. The former was established in the first place as *The Reasoner* in 1956 by E. P. Thompson and John Saville, to provide a focus for dissent and debate inside the Communist Party. Suspended from membership, both then resigned and established *The New Reasoner* as an independent socialist journal. *The Universities and Left Review*, first published in the spring of 1957, originated among a diverse group of left-of-centre Oxford University students. Coming from quite different, if sometimes overlapping, political traditions, belonging to different generations and separated by the experience of the Second World War, nevertheless these two constituencies shared a common stance and project: to open up a 'third way' between the rigidities of Stalinism and the pragmatism of right-wing social democracy. An essential starting place for this New Left was a conviction that British capitalism in the 1950s was in some sense new and required new critical analyses. However valid Old Left arguments were that capitalism was always capitalism and that the class struggle was as pertinent as ever, the fact was that social structure, political consciousness, the culture of everyday life was undergoing significant change. Analysis of the new realities required the rejection of the simplistic and reductionist base-super-structure arguments of traditional Marxism and the development of new concepts and new approaches. If there was a degree of convergence here with aspects of Crosland's analysis, the New Left remained sharply critical of Labour Party revisionists and remained committed to a radical transformation of economic, social and political structures. Abandoning the rigidities of an exhausted and inflexible Marxism-Leninism, they were nevertheless still interested in developing aspects of the Marxist tradition, turning to such diverse sources as the newly-available 1844 *Economic and Philosophical Manuscripts* of the young and humanist Marx, the writings of the American radical sociologist C. Wright Mills and the work of philosophers of the French left such as Sartre and Merleau-Ponty. The common ground between these two strands of the New Left led to the fusion of the two journals at the end of the 1950s in the *New Left Review*, the first number being published in January 1960.

The New Left of the late 1950s and early 1960s was not only a group of left intellectuals gathered around a couple of journals and a theoretical project. It also saw itself as a political movement, though one of a distinctive kind; not a formal and bureaucratic organization but open-ended, participatory, spontaneous and thus immediately responsive to people's changing experiences. A coffee bar and library – the Partisan – were set up in Soho. Here and elsewhere in London public meetings, discussion groups, exhibitions, conferences, often attracting hundreds of participants from diverse political backgrounds were held. Forty or more other associated clubs were established throughout the country. There was also direct political involvement. In 1958 members of the New Left were involved in anti-racist action in Notting Hill and Kensington in the aftermath of the race riots there. Calling it the strategy of 'one foot in, one foot out', there were various attempts to influence Labour Party policy, including agitating at Party conferences via cyclostyled daily broadsheets, and even an exhibition, for delegates. It intervened extensively in party debates, contesting party publications and proferring alternative analyses and policies. *A Socialist Wages Plan*, drafted by Ken Alexander and John Hughes and published in 1959, laid down guidelines for a new kind of alliance between the trade unions and the Labour government in the transition to a planned and socialist economy. Perhaps the most significant political commitment of the New Left in this period was to CND. As befitted a movement that originated in the conjuncture of Hungary and Suez, the role of Britain in the consolidation of global politics into two hostile camps was of central importance for the New Left. They were involved from the first in the organization of the Aldermaston marches and played a significant role in influencing sections of the Labour Party towards a unilateralist stance, culminating, of course, in the unilateralist triumph at the 1960 Party conference in Scarborough. As the opening editorial of *New Left Review* stated:

What we need is a living movement of people, battering away at
the problems of socialism in the mid-twentieth century, pooling
their experiences, yet, at every point, breaking back into the
Labour Movement, thrusting forward like so many uninvited
guests into Constituency Parties and Trade Union branches,
pushing within CND.

(quoted in OUSDG 1989: 51)

This first New Left, however, 'flourished hectically before entering
a fatal decline', according to Peter Sedgwick, an early participant
(Sedgwick 1964: 15). He dates the decline very precisely to the year
1961 and writing three years later, pointed to evidence of the depth
of that decline. The Partisan coffee bar and associated club had
been closed, and there remained only the office from which *New
Left Review* was published. Most of the clubs elsewhere had also
disappeared. In London the crowded meetings and thriving
discussion groups had gone. 'The largest assembly that can be
mustered under the New Left banner is a literary discussion group
that meets at a London pub' (Sedgwick 1964: 16). What went
wrong? Several factors can be indicated. There were manifold tensions within the core group editing the *New Left Review*; after Stuart
Hall's resignation Perry Anderson took over the editorship and
quickly introduced radical shifts in policy, abandoning the New
Left as a social movement and concentrating instead on the need
for the development and dissemination of a rigorous Marxist theory
in Britain. This break up of the original project of the New Left
was itself, however, symptomatic of the movement's weaknesses. Its
polymorphous structure and refusal to formalize organizationally
meant that concerted political action was difficult, and even financial survival often uncertain. At the intellectual level openness could
easily turn into an empty eclecticism, even opportunism. Sedgwick
stressed this diffuse inclusiveness of the early New Left, perhaps
too severely: 'It had become little more than an image-conscious
disc-jockey of political and cultural L.P.s cut outside its own ambit,
its heterogeneity rationalized by a listing of the various "audiences"
and "concerns" in which it was supposed to have a footing' (Sedgwick 1964: 20). With an overwhelmingly metropolitan and academic
ethos, the New Left's social constituency remained fairly narrow:
predominantly students, schoolteachers and academics, social
workers, people working in the arts or the expanding media. Indeed,
Mike Rustin has gone so far as to argue that the New Left was the

expression of a new class fraction of intellectual and cultural workers who, of course, were highly concentrated in London (OUSDG 1989: 122–6). Certainly its links to the labour movement were fragile, and confined in practice to a scattering of rank-and-file militants and full-time officials. These social characteristics of course were also shared by CND (Parkin 1968).

THE CRISIS OF THE LABOUR GOVERNMENT, 1966–70

Another factor contributing to the fading of the New Left was the apotheosis of Harold Wilson as leader of the Labour Party. 'Modernization' had been the talisman both of the Labour right and the New Left. They shared a sense of being forward-looking and iconoclastic, enemies of the stuffy traditions of Macmillan's crumbling *ancien régime*. And the Labour Party in the early 1960s, noting the relative numerical decline of its traditional constituency among manual workers in the industrial heartlands of the north, began to target as sources of support precisely the groups that the New Left had found receptive – younger members of the professions, scientists, administrators. Harold Wilson not only formulated a highly-effective rhetoric of modernization, convergent with the interests of such groups, but in his very person seemed to embody it. As an editorial in *International Socialism* commented in 1963, 'In the portly lineaments and plummy accents of the late Gaitskell the world could detect more than a mite of that amateur, gentlemanly, public school tradition which Labour is so dedicated to combatting'. But Harold Wilson, his successor, looked and sounded quite different. While Macmillan and Home posed as Edwardian gentlemen on their grouse moors in plus-fours, Wilson was a pipe-smoking northerner, a self-proclaimed supporter of Huddersfield Town with traces of a Yorkshire accent. Far from being a landed gentleman, he was the son of an industrial chemist. Wilson shrewdly exploited these assets. Still seen as something of a man of the left within the Labour Party, his rhetoric of modernization, of scientific revolution, of technological innovation, of efficient central planning for a leap into modernity, swayed both left and right. Crossman, Wilson's campaign manager in the campaign for the leadership, wrote of how this stress on science and technology reunited the party after the bitter struggles under Gaitskell: 'we realised that here was the new creative Socialist idea needed to reconcile the Revisionists of the Right with the Traditionalists of the Left: Harold Wilson succeeded where Hugh Gaitskell failed' (quoted in Bogdanor and Skidelsky 1970: 107). This rhetoric was also utilized to attack the disintegrating power base of Macmillan's Tory grandees and his struggling successor, the 'elegant anachronism', Sir Alec Douglas-Home:

> We are living in the jet-age but we are governed by an Edwardian establishment mentality. Over the British people lies the chill frost of Tory leadership. They freeze initiative and petrify imagination. They cling to privilege and power for the few, shutting the gates on the many. Tory society is a CLOSED society, in which birth and wealth have priority, in which the master-and-servant, landlord-and-tenant mentality is predominant. The Tories have proved that they are incapable of mobilising Britain to take full advantage of the scientific breakthrough. Their approach and methods are fifty years out of date'.
>
> (Wilson 1964: 9)

This is worth quoting as a sample of Wilson's rhetoric. The sentences are short and punchy, reminiscent of the editorial style of the *Daily Mirror*. The distance between, on the one hand, the Tory government – an obsolete Edwardian elite of privileged and wealthy landowners ('shutting the gates' is cleverly evocative) – and, on the other, the forward-looking, 'the jet-age', 'scientific breakthrough', 'imagination', 'initiative', are hammered home in a rapid sequence of images. On a January night in Birmingham Town Hall the Tories are even convicted, subliminally, of the winter weather ('freeze', 'petrify', 'chill frost'). The power of this rhetoric in the run-up to the 1964 election was undeniable. It produced standing ovations and emotional conviction among thousands of Labour members and supporters. It even seduced the press (Foot 1968: 152–3).[5]

Labour's victory on 15 October 1964 was anything but a landslide; in fact fewer people voted Labour in 1964 than had done in 1959. Instead, 13 years in opposition came to an end through a major collapse in the Tory vote. Though all kinds of problems began to accrue from the beginning, Labour's first 17 months in power were based on a tiny Commons majority, and all sections of the Labour Party maintained support for Wilson. In the words of Paul Foot, 'Scepticism and gloom about his leadership and Labour's wholesale support for it were confined, this time exclusively, to "satirists and sectarians" ' (Foot 1968: 169). It was after the sweeping electoral victory of March 1966 that the Labour government began to run into major difficulties on a range of issues, and experienced a major crisis of support.

From the beginning the new government energetically set about creating the institutional conditions for industrial modernization, incorporating both trade unions and employer representatives. Frank Cousins, radical union leader, became minister of the new Ministry of Technology. A new Department of Economic Affairs was established, fronted by George Brown, and a number of industrialists were brought into its Industrial Policy Division. The leadership of the unions had committed themselves to 'a planned growth' in wages in return for a parallel restraint on profits and prices and government undertakings to improve social welfare; employers' associations had undertaken to cooperate via voluntary price restraint. In December 1964 government, employers and unions signed a *Joint Statement of Intent on Productivity, Prices and Incomes*, leading in 1965 to the creation of the Prices and Incomes Board. This consensus seemed to provide the institutional basis for non-inflationary economic growth. The *National Plan* emerged from Brown's DEA in September 1965 and projected a 25 per cent growth in the economy by the end of the decade – and with it rising investment, rising productivity, rising exports and a rising standard of living.

Things turned out differently. The actual growth rate was only 14 per cent, barely half the original projection and significantly less than under the Tories prior to 1964. The second half of the 1960s was marked by permanent economic crisis – balance of payments deficits, runs on sterling, a squeeze on profits, strikes, rising unemployment. The precise causes of these economic difficulties are complex and subject to much dispute. Certainly of central significance was the utter failure of the Department of Economic Affairs. By 1966 the *National Plan* was dead and buried and the DEA soon followed; 'The story of the D.E.A.', according to its supremo George Brown, 'is the record of a social revolution that failed' (Brown 1972: 87). It failed because it was systematically undermined by the Treasury:

> Once the heady first days had gone, and the novelty had worn off, the Treasury began to reassert itself, and with its absolutely superb mastery of the government machine gradually either filched things back or – more to the point – made it rather difficult

for us to effect the grand design we had in mind so that a coherent
and continuous economic policy could emerge.

(Brown 1972: 92)

Behind this were two deeper structural weaknesses in Labour's
strategy. First, the central axis of the Treasury, the Bank of England
and the City were simply not included as participants in the modernizing strategy, and their independent operations outflanked the
government and limited domestic policy options. Second, both
the TUC and the Confederation of British Industry (itself formed
only in 1965, at the government's insistence, out of a number of
employers' associations) possessed limited power to enforce national
agreements on their membership. The result of this double
structural weakness was to reduce the government's modernizing
strategies to impotence (Ingham 1984; Overbeek 1990). The
Treasury-City-Bank of England nexus enforced deflation whenever
the pound came under threat. 'Stop-go' policies were the order of
the day, not planned growth. Industrial decline began to accelerate.
The UK's share of world exports fell and import penetration
increased. Britain compared badly with competitors in terms of
productivity growth, investment levels and the quality of its techno-
logically advanced products (Blackaby 1978).

Especially after the inflation that followed devaluation of the
pound in November 1967, organized labour at the shopfloor level
refused to accept 'wage restraint' – frequently a synonym for more
work and less pay. By 1968 the TUC itself was in formal opposition
to the government's incomes policy. Strikes multiplied; there were
around 2,000 strikes a year between 1965 and 1968, but over 3,000
in 1969 and nearly 4,000 in 1970. Over 2 million trade unionists
were directly involved in strike action in 1968. The number of
working days lost spiralled, from between 2 and 3 million in the
years 1964 to 1967, to 4½ million in 1968, nearly 7 million the year
following and almost 11 million in 1970. The government's response
was to establish legal controls over shopfloor militancy. The Dono-
van Commission was established soon after the 1964 elections; its
report, published in 1968, identified an informal system of shopfloor
organization that provided a base for militancy beyond the union
hierarchy's control. It did not recommend direct intervention, but
in the worsening climate of industrial relations in the late 1960s its
diagnoses seemed to point that way. The government's White Paper
In Place of Strife was published in January 1969. Mutiny ensued.

The TUC rebelled. The Parliamentary Labour Party and even the Cabinet was in disarray. The government was forced to abandon its legislation (see Jenkins, P. 1970). Its last desperate attempt to control the economy had failed, and in the process the Labour Party's bedrock of support had been bitterly alienated.

The humiliating failure to fulfil its ambitions to modernize the British economy was not the only source of the Labour government's crisis of support in the late 1960s. Foreign policy was also important. Throughout the 1950s the Labour leadership had been in agreement with the Tory government on the basic issues of foreign and colonial policy. It had been vigorously anti-communist and pro-Cold War. The American alliance was sacrosanct and their right to expand their military bases, with a nuclear capability outside the control of a British government, went largely unchallenged. Nor was British involvement in a series of violent colonial engagements – in Aden, in Cyprus, in Malaysia, in Kenya and elsewhere – seriously contested. After 1964 Wilson's government retained its military commitment east of Suez and threadbare pretensions to world-power status. Its compromises with the regime in South Africa and its refusal to take punitive measures against the white rebels in Rhodesia, in contrast to its rapid use of military force to suppress native independence movements in Aden in 1965–6, raised questions about the degree of its contamination by imperial ideologies. So, too, did some of Labour's policies on immigration. A strand of popular imperialism took on an increasingly racist tone from the late 1950s. Anti-immigrant riots in Nottingham and Notting Hill, as well as many more localized outbursts of violence, set the context for the 1962 Commonwealth Immigration Act. Though the Labour opposition disapproved of this legislation, its own 1965 White Paper on immigration policy was extremely restrictive and provoked opposition, especially via the recently-established Campaign for Racial Equality. Labour's 1965 Race Relations Act, aiming to outlaw racial discrimination, was weak and ineffective. The immigration from 1967 of growing numbers of the 100,000 Kenyan Asians carrying British passports brought racial tensions to the fore. Powell's notorious 'rivers of blood' speech at Birmingham in April 1968 attracted considerable public approval. London dockers marched in his support. According to polls, three out of four people agreed with Powell's message and two out of three thought that Heath was wrong to sack him from the shadow cabinet (Wybrow 1989: 87). The Labour government rushed through its shameful Commonwealth Immigrants Act in 1968, abrogating the citizenship rights of the Kenyan Asians – though this was a dead letter from the beginning. These compromises with racism again alienated sections of Labour support, though the Race Relations Act of October 1968 went some way towards reaffirming Labour's commitment to genuine racial equality within Britain (Foot 1965).

The support of the Wilson government for American policy in Vietnam stopped short of sending troops, though Australia and New Zealand complied. Nevertheless there was discontent within sections of the Labour Party from 1965 as the war escalated. Initially CND took the lead in organizing demonstrations in 1966 and 1967, though with limited impact. In 1968 the Vietnam Solidarity Campaign became a major force in coordinating opposition. Perry Anderson describes it as

> the most important single political mobilization of the British Left in the 60s, which at its height commanded mass demonstrations equal to those of CND in numbers, and surpassing them in militancy. . . . Opposed as adventurist by the British Communist Party, belaboured by the police at the behest of the British Labour Party . . . it was the VSC which rallied a major popular force in the streets.
>
> (Anderson 1980: 151–2)

By the end of the 1960s the Labour Party was experiencing a major crisis of support. Hilary Wainwright recalls:

> between 1966 and 1970, thousands left the party; when Harold Wilson came to office in 1964 there were 66 constituencies with a membership of over 2,000, when he left office in 1970 there were 22. Party branches in effect closed down; trade unionists talked of contracting out; some of their leaders threatened to disaffiliate; constituency parties even debated – but rejected – proposals to disaffiliate from the national party. The party's electoral machine, which depends on the commitment of the party members, came almost to a standstill in some areas.
>
> (Wainwright 1987: 27)

By the summer of 1968 polls were showing Labour, at 28 per cent, with the lowest level of support of either major political party in the postwar period. The local elections in the same year wiped out Labour control of a succession of councils, especially in London. In these years they lost a series of by-elections, including a number of formerly safe Labour seats. Finally the Conservative Party returned to power in the 1970 general election. The result was close, yet the 42.9 per cent of the electorate who voted Labour was the lowest proportion in postwar Britain (Butler and Pinto-Duschinsky 1970).

'1968' AND AFTER

Six years of Labour rule had seen the utter failure of its modernizing project; wage restraint and rising unemployment; embittered industrial relations; systematic attacks on the trade union movement; uncompromising support for the US in Vietnam. As Lewis Minkin puts it, 'rarely in modern times can a parliamentary leadership have appeared as impervious to the policy preferences of its extra-parliamentary supporters as the Wilson government did in the late 1960s' (Minkin 1978: 317). Yet a series of important reforms and initiatives were carried through between 1964 and 1970. In areas like the rights of tenants, redundancy rights, state support for education at all levels, divorce and abortion, gay rights, state support for the arts, the weakening of censorship, there were substantial gains. The economic balance sheet is more complex. The standard of living of any population is difficult to assess with precision. Certainly more people owned cars, washing machines, refrigerators, televisions in 1970 than had done so in 1964. Within an overall increase in incomes, however, there were quite divergent experiences within different sectors of the workforce and different parts of the country. Poverty persisted, as did bad housing, harmful working conditions and a pervasive structural inequality. Nevertheless, despite the international economic pressures, the overall share of national income going to working people in the form both of wages and social expenditure was rising under the Labour government. At the same time the share of profits fell. This was, of course, not a matter of the socialist commitment of the government. On the contrary, it was often a result of active resistance to erosion of wage levels and social spending in sometimes bitter and protracted struggles in the workplace and in all kinds of other settings and institutions – sometimes even within Parliament itself. Close scrutiny of the effects and outcomes of the Wilson years reveals, then, a complex picture in which the gains in material terms and in social rights, however uneven, were real.

How then to explain the evident discontent, the rising industrial militancy, the radical alienation of many younger people, the general sense of disenchantment with both the government and the wider status quo by the close of the 1960s? Crosland's valuable reassessment of the Labour government's record (Crosland, A. 1974) was apparently oblivious to these wider and profounder discontents and aspirations. His answer was more efficient administration of social policy, higher social expenditure and, yet again, faster economic growth. Thousands and hundreds of thousands of trade unionists, students and many other groups had recognized that there were deeper issues to be contested and other alternatives to be realized. Focusing on labour militancy first: inflation is experienced as a direct and daily loss of spending power, even if that loss is periodically compensated for by wage increases. The experience then is one of a series of stepped declines. Moreover, the compensating increases have often to be vigorously fought for and, if at all, are grudgingly conceded. For millions of people, that experience in the 1960s generated a widespread sense of injustice and grievance – especially against the major employer, the state itself. Long-term gradual, if uneven, rises in real incomes may be observable in tables of figures and graphs, but these do not express the experience of inflation, or begin to explain the roots of industrial militancy. Also in these years something more was occurring than a struggle over wages; issues were often to do with working conditions, the rights of the shopfloor worker (male and female), redundancies and plant closures (see especially Beynon 1973).

This brings us again to the central theme of this chapter. *The May Day Manifesto* in 1968 made the following point:

> No coherent analysis of capitalist power, no movement of socialist education and propaganda, no authentic ideology of social change, has emerged from the institutional Labour party for two decades. Whatever has emerged (like the New Left) has been the initiative of individuals working outside the party's institutional framework, who have improvised their own organizations, and who have been regarded by the officialdom of Labour with distrust or (as in the case of several initiatives among the young socialists) with actual proscription. Everything in fact has been subordinated to a single purpose: the building and management of a popular electoral machine.

(Williams 1968: 156)

The disintegration of the ideological stasis of the Cold War in the later 1950s and the crisis that overcame the Tory government in the early 1960s helped create a context in which the boundaries of political culture fragmented and opened up. The inner circles of the great and the good in their well-appointed offices, London clubs and Oxbridge senior common rooms were no longer accepted as the arbiters of wisdom, policy or taste. For a brief moment Wilson's rhetoric of 'the new Britain' captured popular support and provided some kind of direction for this repudiation of the old order. It quickly dissolved. Subordinated to the City-Treasury-Bank of England nexus and to the American alliance, lacking a coherent and radical ideology or the agencies to intervene in the wider cultural spheres of the period, the Labour Party soon began to look as creative and innovative as the local Methodist chapel.

Instead the diverse radical energies that had been released, challenging authority, tradition and convention, found expression in new movements and practices across the whole field of civil society. Dissent emerged in a thousand forms, especially in the last few years of the 1960s. Organizations to the left of the Labour Party proliferated and expanded as never before: the Solidarity Group (1960), the International Socialists (1962), the Radical Student Alliance (1966), The Vietnam Solidarity Campaign (1967), the International Marxist Group (1968), the Revolutionary Socialist Students Federation (1968), the Institute of Workers' Control (1968). New kinds of community politics emerged: campaigns against homelessness in Notting Hill, Southwark, Ilford and other parts of London; squatters groups such as the London Street Commune; Claimants' Unions, and so on. Within higher education there were sit-ins, occupations, periodic disruptions, notably at the Hornsey College of Art, the London School of Economics, the Universities of Essex, Hull, Birmingham and Warwick. In February 1968 an Anti-University was set up in East London with support from R. D. Laing and David Cooper, Jeff Nuttall, the poet Bob Cobbing, the Marxist composer Cornelius Cardew and others, though it barely survived the year. A new alternative press emerged – *International Times* (1966), *Oz* (1967), *Black Dwarf* (1968), *Friends* (1969) – with its roots in a radical rejection of the dominant political culture. 'Only the scum of a society could bother to fashion a career so ruthlessly opportunist, so intellectually parasitic, so spiritually unrewarding', *Oz* commented on politicians of all parties in 1967 (quoted in Nelson 1989: 69). Major events like the Dialectics of Liberation conference at the Roundhouse in Camden Town in the same year provided some kind of focus for these disparate, if often overlapping, groups, the opportunity to find a shared intellectual perspective, however incoherently and provisionally. Fundamental redefinitions of the culture of politics and the politics of culture circulated, as the Labour government imploded.

Many of the radical ideals and projects that emerged in Britain in the 1960s failed, degenerated or were marginalized. The opening out of political culture was arrested and, in part, closed down again in the 1970s. But if, as John Lennon sang, 'the dream is over', we have to begin to analyse precisely why and to what extent. Industrial militancy persisted and expanded after the defeat of the Wilson government. The 11 million days lost in strikes in 1970 rose to over 13 million in 1971 and reached a staggering 24 million in 1972 – the highest figure since 1926 and the year of the General Strike. The NUM, with wide popular support, seriously damaged Heath's government in the strike of 1972, and the strike of 1974 contributed to the collapse of the Conservative regime in a year of profound hegemonic crisis. These strikes and a range of other industrial actions by organized labour in the early 1970s, spectacularly the UCS work-in on Clydeside, demonstrated new radical strategies and demands. There were hundreds of factory occupations between 1969 and 1974.

The counter-culture proved more evanescent. It disintegrated rapidly after 1970. Its newspapers faded and closed down. Some of its elements moved up-market. Others disappeared. Fragile connections broke down. Yet too dismissive an attitude to the counter-culture of the 1960s is now of limited analytical value. Thompson commented sardonically in 1973:

> From Paris to Berkeley, from Munich to Oxford, the 'West' offered a supermarket of avant garde products . . . Posters of Che Guevara, juxtaposed against mini-skirts, 'Mao tunics', and military leather jackets, decorated the most modish, swinging boutiques, in the King's Road and in Royal Leamington Spa.
>
> (Thompson 1978: 99)

Of course there was a great deal about the counter-culture that was trivial, vacuous, merely bizarre – and in some of its 'Swinging London' manifestations certainly was 'a rich kid's revolutionary farce' (see especially Potter 1967: 403–4). Yet there was more to it than that, as Thompson himself half-grudgingly concedes. The vast majority of those involved in the student movement, in the Vietnam Solidarity Campaign, inhabiting dimensions of the counter-culture,

were not rich kids; indeed, quite a number were from working-
class families and often the first generation with access to higher
education. In the pages of the alternative press in the late 1960s
can be found a rich, complex, often contradictory, mix of genuine
radical critique – often influenced by the likes of Marcuse, R. D.
Laing and, especially, CND – and self-indulgent waffle. If it sometimes bordered on a mindless and childish hedonism, aspects of the
counter-culture did challenge traditional repressions, and both in
theory and practice provided a cultural environment where nonconformity in sexual matters, for instance, was accepted. The depth of
its withdrawal from the dominant culture is glimpsed in the moves
towards communes – a quite literal withdrawal to an alternative
society, and one informed by readings of Owen, Fourier, Kropotkin,
Winstanley. Even the apparent superficialities of dress sometimes
directly contested dominant discourses of masculinity and the
unquestioned right of those in authority to impose particular forms
of dress or behaviour in public space. Much of the counter-culture
was in fact about redrawing the line between the public and private
spheres and widening the autonomy of the individual – not without
significant political implications, as the Womens Liberation Movement was to show throughout the 1970s.

Turning back to the New Left, in July 1966 Raymond Williams
renounced the Labour Party and launched the idea of a political
manifesto at a London meeting of some of those who had withdrawn
from the *New Left Review* and had subsequently lost touch with each
other. Williams drafted a first edition that was privately published
in 1967. A much larger second edition, with major contributions
by E. P. Thompson and Stuart Hall and a number of other figures
from the first New Left, was published by Penguin in May 1968
(Williams 1968). This was a major political intervention, engaging
with a whole range of pivotal questions. The aim, in line with the
aspirations of the New Left in 1959–61, was to influence directly
the labour movement as a whole and generate some unified strategy
among the diverse and scattered forces of the British left. A National
Convention of the Left gathered in 1969 with considerable support.
However its call for the establishment of new socialist organizations
to be set up nationally in opposition to the Labour Party ultimately
came to nothing. Sectarian animosities undermined unity. In the
run-up to the 1970 election, Left Labour people, the Communist
Party and some other socialist groupings refused to oppose the
Labour Party electorally. The movement splintered and the

Convention never reassembled (Williams 1979: 373–5). Meanwhile the *New Left Review* and expanding Trotskyite groups such as the International Socialists and the International Marxist Group tended in the late 1960s to centre their strategy, rigorously Leninist in impulse, on the student movement and the campaign against the Vietnam War. Despite undeniable successes, their impact on the wider political culture was marginal and, after the collapse of the Vietnam Solidarity Campaign at the end of 1969, tended to fade.

At the end of the 1960s, then, the multiplying forces to the left of the Labour Party remained fragmented. Despite the crisis of support experienced by the Labour Party, the New Left itself had a severely restricted political impact. It is facile to ascribe this merely to the inadequacies of the New Left – in particular its isolation from a broader social constituency. Its numbers and resources were always limited. The fragility of the New Left's immediate political influence was not, it hardly needs saying, a result of its prose style, its jargon, its use of big words. Its intellectual influence within the humanities and social sciences, especially in historical and literary studies, has been substantial (see Anderson 1990: 42–5). The successive introspective polemics of the 1970s did in part undermine confidence in some of the central coordinates of 1960s New Left theory – its emphasis on agency, on culture, on class consciousness, on the centrality of social experience, on an open, critical and humanist Marxism. But too narrow a focus on intellectual divisions within the Left can divert attention from, and obscure the reality of, countervailing and coercive power. The unavoidable – because historically determined – conceptual limitations of the New Left are now less important than the political realities that reconstituted a new hegemony during the 1970s.

The New Left, and some of the other critical dimensions of the 1960s cultural opposition, did not merely fail. They were defeated. A highly-resourced and exceptionally flexible cultural apparatus, radiating from the BBC, the 'quality' press, the universities and their varied academic platforms, discreetly rigged agenda, laundered and sanitized radicalism for a colour-supplement readership and systematically excluded critical issues from the 'public sphere'.[6] The Parliamentary Labour party, and its less subtle apparatus, interlinked with the former at crucial points, performed a similar function within its own spheres. A counter-reaction on the outer flanks of this Establishment – the Festival of Light, Mary

Whitehouse's National Viewers and Listeners Association, the *Black Papers*, the neo-liberal Institute of Economic Affairs and so on – was already beginning to coalesce before the end of the 1960s, with resonances inside the Conservative Party. Margaret Thatcher's Conservative Political Centre's party conference lecture at Blackpool in October 1968 already began to articulate this paradigm (the full text is printed in Wapshott and Brock 1983: 270–81). But Enoch Powell identified himself as the man of destiny at this moment. He embodied that confluence of free-market liberalism in the economic sphere, a deep nationalism with racist connotations, a vigorous assertion of traditional values in the private sphere, which subsequently crystallized as a political force in the mid–1970s. He broke cover too early, in 1968, and was consigned to his own kind of wilderness. Jesus Christ to his John the Baptist, Margaret Thatcher soon materialized as the nemesis of all that the militant wing of organized labour, the counter-culture and the New Left represented, in their disparate but intersecting forms.

NOTES

1 Rebecca Bunting, John Davies, Simon Gunn, John Lucas and Peter Weston made helpful comments on an earlier draft.
2 For more detailed discussion of this seminal essay see Johnson (1976) and Nield (1980).
3 Laing (1986) provides an excellent survey of the social and cultural contexts of these debates.
4 *The Future of Socialism* overshadowed the theoretically much more interesting *Contemporary Capitalism* (1956) by John Strachey, an unjustly neglected classic of British Marxism.
5 Tony Benn had an important role in the writing of these speeches and in the whole media presentation of Wilson at this time (see Jenkins, R. 1980: 98–100).
6 Some of the *Scrutiny* essays of F. R. and Q. D. Leavis provide a useful starting place for analysis of this cultural establishment; see section six of Leavis 1968.

BIBLIOGRAPHY

Abel-Smith, B. and Townsend, P. 1965. *The Poor and the Poorest*. London: Routledge.
Abrams, M. and Rose, R. 1961. *Must Labour Lose?* Harmondsworth: Penguin.
Anderson, P. 1965. 'Origins of the present crisis'. In Anderson, P. and Blackburn, R. (eds). *Towards Socialism*. London: Fontana.

Anderson, P. 1980. *Arguments Within English Marxism*. London: Verso.

Anderson, P. 1990. 'A culture in contraflow – 1'. *New Left Review* 180, March/April.

Atkinson, A. B. 1972. *Unequal Shares: Wealth in Britain*. London: Allen Lane.

Bacon, R. and Eltis, W. 1976. *Britain's Economic Problem: Too Few Producers*. London: Macmillan.

Beynon, H. 1973. *Working for Ford*. Harmondsworth: Penguin.

Blackaby, F. 1978. *British Economic Policy 1960–74*. Cambridge: Cambridge University Press.

Bogdanor, V. and Skidelsky, R. (eds) 1970. *The Age of Affluence 1951–1964*. London: Macmillan.

Booker, C. 1970. *The Neophiliacs: A Study of the Revolution in English Life in the Fifties and Sixties*. London: Fontana.

Brown, G. 1972. *In My Way*. Harmondsworth: Penguin.

Butler, D. and King, A. 1965. *The British General Election of 1964*. London: Macmillan.

Butler, D. and Pinto-Duschinsky, M. 1971. *The British General Election of 1970*. London: Macmillan.

Butler, D. and Rose, R. 1960. *The British General Election of 1959*. London: Macmillan.

Chalmers, M. 1985. *Paying For Defence: Military Spending and British Decline*. London: Pluto.

Chapman, B. 1963. *British Government Observed*. London: George Allen & Unwin.

Churchill, R. 1964. *The Fight for the Tory Leadership: A Contemporary Chronicle*. London: Heinemann.

Coates, K. and Silburn, R. 1970. *Poverty: the Forgotten Englishmen*. Harmondsworth: Penguin.

Cronin, J. E. 1984. *Labour and Society in Britain 1918–1979*. London: Batsford.

Crosland, A. 1956. *The Future of Socialism*. London: Cape.

Crosland, A. 1974. *Socialism Now and Other Essays*. London: Cape.

Crosland, S. 1982. *Tony Crosland*. London: Cape.

Davenport, N. 1964. *The Split Society*. London: Gollancz.

Foot, P. 1965. *Immigration and Race in British Politics*. Harmondsworth: Penguin.

Foot, P. 1968. *The Politics of Harold Wilson*. Harmondsworth: Penguin.

Gamble, A. 1974. *The Conservative Nation*. London: Routledge & Kegan Paul.

Gamble, A. 1985. *Britain in Decline: Economic Policy, Political Strategy and the British State*. London: Macmillan.

Glynn, A. and Harrison, J. 1980. *The British Economic Disaster*. London: Pluto.

Glynn, A. and Sutcliffe, B. 1972. *Workers, British Capitalism and the Profits Squeeze*. Harmondsworth: Penguin.

Hall, S. 1988. *The Hard Road to Renewal: Thatcherism and the Crisis of the Left*. London: Verso.

Hall, S. *et al.* 1978. *Policing the Crisis: Mugging, the State, Law and Order*. London: Hutchinson.

Halsey, A. H. 1972. *Trends in British Society Since 1900: A Guide to the Changing Social Structure of Britain.* London: Macmillan.

Hartley, A. 1963. *A State of England.* London: Hutchinson.

Hill, A. and Whichelow, A. 1964. *What's Wrong with Parliament?* Harmondsworth: Penguin.

Hutchinson, G. 1980. *The Last Edwardian at No. 10: An Impression of Harold Macmillan.* London: Quartet.

Ingham, G. 1984. *Capitalism Divided? The City and Industry in British Social Development.* London: Macmillan.

Jenkins, P. 1970. *The Battle of Downing Street.* London: Charles Knight.

Jenkins, R. 1980. *Tony Benn: A Political Biography.* London: Writers & Readers.

Johnson, R. 1976. 'Barrington Moore, Perry Anderson and English social development'. *Working Papers in Cultural Studies,* 9.

Kincaid, J. C. 1973. *Poverty and Equality in Britain.* Harmondsworth: Penguin.

Koestler, A. 1963. *Suicide of a Nation? An Enquiry into the State of Britain Today.* London: Hutchinson.

Laing, S. 1986. *Representations of Working Class Life: 1957–1964.* London: Macmillan.

Leavis, F. R. 1968 *A Selection from* Scrutiny, Volume 1. Cambridge: Cambridge University Press.

Leys, C. 1986. *Politics in Britain: An Introduction.* London: Verso.

Mander, J. 1963. *Great Britain or Little England?* Harmondsworth: Penguin.

Middlemas, K. 1990. *Power, Competition and the State.* Vol. 2 *Threats to the Postwar Settlement: Britain 1961–74.* London: Macmillan.

Minkin, L. 1978. *The Labour Party Conference.* London: Allen Lane.

Nelson, E. 1989. *The British Counter-Culture 1966–73: A Study of the Underground Press.* London: Macmillan.

Nield, K. 1980. 'A symptomatic dispute? Notes on the relation between Marxian theory and historical practice in Britain'. *Social Research,* 47.

Nuttall, J. 1968. *Bomb Culture.* London: MacGibbon & Kee.

Overbeek, H. 1990. *Global Capitalism and National Decline: The Thatcher Decade in Perspective.* London: Unwin Hyman.

Oxford University Socialist Discussion Group 1989. *Out of Apathy: Voices of the New Left Thirty Years On.* London: Verso.

Parkin, F. 1908. *Middle-Class Radicalism. The Social Bases of the British Campaign for Nuclear Disarmament.* Manchester: Manchester University Press.

Pollard, S. 1984. *The Wasting of the British Economy,* 2nd edn. London: Croom Helm.

Potter, D. 1967. 'The gaudy roundabout'. *New Society,* 21 Sept.

Saville, J. 1988. *The Labour Movement in Britain: A Commentary.* London: Faber & Faber.

Sedgwick, P. 1964. 'The two New Lefts'. *International Socialism,* 17, Summer.

Shanks, M. 1961. *The Stagnant Society: A Warning.* London: Penguin.

Shonfield, A. 1958. *British Economic Policy Since the War.* London: Penguin.

Sillitoe, A. 1958. *Saturday Night and Sunday Morning.* New edn, 1985. London: Grafton.

Sked, A. and Cook, C. 1984. *Post-war Britain: A Political History*. London: Penguin.

Socialist Union 1956. *Twentieth Century Socialism*. London: Penguin.

Strachey, J. 1956 *Contemporary Capitalism*. London: Gollancz.

Thompson, E. P. 1978. *The Poverty of Theory and Other Essays*. London: Merlin.

Thompson, E. P. 1980. *Writing by Candlelight*. London: Merlin.

Titmuss, R. M. 1958. *Essays on 'The Welfare State'*. London: Unwin.

Titmuss, R. M. 1962. *Income Distribution and Social Change: A Study in Criticism*. London: Unwin.

Tracey, M. and Morrison, D. 1979. *Whitehouse*. London: Macmillan.

Wainwright, H. 1987. *Labour: A Tale of Two Parties*. London: Hogarth Press.

Walker, M. 1978. *Daily Sketches: A Cartoon History of British Twentieth-Century Politics*. London: Paladin.

Wapshott, N. and Brock, G. 1983. *Thatcher*. London: Macdonald.

Westergaard, J. 1965. 'The withering away of class: a contemporary myth'. In Anderson, P. and Blackburn, R. (eds). *Towards Socialism*. London: Fontana.

Widgery, D. 1976. *The Left in Britain, 1956–68*. Harmondsworth: Penguin.

Williams, R. (ed.) 1968. *May Day Manifesto 1968*. Harmondsworth: Penguin.

Williams, R. 1979. *Politics and Letters: Interviews with* New Left Review. London: Verso.

Wilson, H. 1964. *The New Britain: Labour's Plan*. Harmondsworth: Penguin.

Wybrow, R. J. 1989. *Britain Speaks Out, 1937–87. A Social History As Seen Through the Gallup Data*. London: Macmillan.

Young, W. 1963. *The Profumo Affair: Aspects of Conservatism*. Harmondsworth: Penguin.

FURTHER READING

Of the general histories of the period, the most useful introductory surveys are probably Sked and Cook (1984) and Leys (1986). There is no adequate analysis of the crisis of the Conservative Party in the early 1960s, but Gamble (1974) is a useful starting place. For general perspectives on the labour movement in these years see Cronin (1984) and Saville (1988). Foot (1968) gives a thorough and sharply critical account of Harold Wilson and his government. The economic difficulties of Britain since the 1950s have generated a huge and diverse literature – see, for instance, Glynn and Sutcliffe (1972), Bacon and Eltis (1976), Glynn and Harrison (1980), Pollard (1984), Gamble (1985), Overbeek (1990). To investigate further the New Left see Widgery (1976), Williams (1979), Anderson (1980) and Oxford University Socialist Discussion Group (1989). Nelson (1989) provides a valuable introduction to the counter-culture, and Nuttall (1968) is still worth reading. For a sometimes insightful conservative perspective see Booker (1970). On the reconstitution of hegemony in the 1970s, of central importance are Thompson (1980) and Hall (1988).

Chapter 3

The new radicalism: the politics of culture in Britain, America and France, 1956–73

Alf Louvre

INTRODUCTION

This essay offers two narratives. One concerns the dramatic political and social conflicts in America and western Europe during the 1960s. These conflicts are dealt with in roughly chronological sequence, early sections in the essay referring to events in the late 1950s, late sections of the essay to the late 1960s and beyond. Inevitably, the historical and geographical range of the narrative makes for drastic elision. This is a matter of choice as well as necessity, for extensive detail about events is omitted so that room can be made for another kind of narrative. The second narrative concerns how these events were perceived and interpreted, and the theories of social development, political association and personal and cultural style that came in their wake, and that sometimes created currents of their own.

This second (and here more important) narrative speaks of ideologies. Initially, it describes the dominant ideas in western European and American political debate in the late 1950s. Extended attention is then given to the radical challenges to these ideas in the mid and late 1960s, a time when, significantly, traditional Marxist ideas were increasingly discredited by events in eastern Europe. New kinds of radical synthesis were offered, emphasizing, among other things, the political significance of matters previously thought peripheral to the cause. The nuances of everyday style, lifestyle, language and taste were no longer to be seen merely as private or individual quirks, but as symptomatic, as telling indices of more general values and allegiances. The second narrative thus tells of how culture and subjectivity were politicized.

Sustained textual scrutiny features prominently in this essay, its premise being that to define ideologies and assess their appeal it is necessary to examine their formal articulation in some detail. Understanding their premises and their implications means looking carefully at the style and form of their exposition, not merely at summary slogans. If the first narrative, of events, is sparse and elided, the narrative of ideologies is from time to time closely focused and expansively detailed.

In the movement from global sketch to detailed textual snapshot, and from Britain to America to France, little attempt is made to give empirical or institutional evidence about the influence of chosen texts in their domestic cultures or, indeed, abroad. To do this would mean another kind of essay, one that would consider such themes as: the sociology of higher education (at a time of rapid and problematic expansion causing considerable 'customer' dissatisfaction); the reaction against national political parties (including, and especially, the parties of the left); the consequent appetite for other analyses, other theories (often, of course, in translation); the expansion of radical publishing in terms of both established companies (like Penguin) and journals (like *New Left Review*) and alternative and often ephemeral publications such as *Oz* and *International Times*. As these latter titles suggest, the cross-fertilization of ideas and movements, the international circulation of radical social analyses and political strategies, rested, above all, on a sense of the transnational nature of the economic and political powers to be confronted. And on the perception that resistance to this power entailed a new but common struggle. In any one location – Paris, London, Berkeley (or, for that matter, Prague or Tokyo) – radical groups could learn from the analyses and the examples of others; not least, because the television that carried such immediate images of the international *cause célèbre*, Vietnam, had dramatic footage, too, of how people elsewhere protested its obscenities.

This is not, however, to suggest or assent to a facile globalism; indeed, one function of the analyses that follow is to make clear the particularity of ideologies, their determination not just by a given international conjuncture but by their own national traditions and situations. The coincidence of ideologies from different nations is usually only partial (even at a time of self-consciously internationalist movements) and native; in Gramsci's term, 'organic' features cannot be ignored.

CONSENSUS ASSUMED

As these objectives are also gradually fulfilled, and society becomes more social-democratic with the passing of the old collective grievances and injustices (and perhaps as automation carries us towards the 30- or even 20-hour week), we shall turn our attention increasingly to other, in the long run, more important spheres – of personal freedom, happiness and cultural endeavour: the cultivation of leisure, beauty, grace, gaiety, excitement, and of all the proper pursuits, whether elevated, vulgar, or eccentric, which contribute to the varied fabric of a full private and family life . . .

We need not only higher exports and old-age pensions, but more open-air cafes, brighter and gayer streets at night, later closing-hours for public houses, more local repertory theatres, better and more hospitable hoteliers and restaurateurs, brighter and cleaner eating-houses, more riverside cafes, more pleasure-gardens on the Battersea model, more murals and pictures in public places, better designs for furniture and pottery and women's clothes, statues in the centre of new housing estates, better-designed street lamps and telephone kiosks, and so on ad infinitum . . .

Today we are all incipient bureaucrats and practical administrators. We have all, so to speak, been trained at the L. S. E., and are familiar with Blue Books and White Papers, and know our way around Whitehall. We realise that we must guard against romantic or Utopian notions: that hard work and research are virtues: that we must do nothing foolish or impulsive: and that Fabian pamphlets must be diligently studied. We know these things too well. Posthumously, the Webbs have won their battle, and converted a generation to their standards. Now the time has come for a reaction: for a greater emphasis on private life, on freedom and dissent, on culture, beauty, leisure, and even frivolity. Total abstinence and a good filing system are not now the right sign-posts to the socialist Utopia: or at least, if they are, some of us will fall by the wayside.

(Crosland 1956: 520–4)

In a conference, 'Re-reading the Sixties',[1] Paul Foot quoted this passage from Crosland's *The Future of Socialism* in sarcastically dismissive fashion: Crosland's naivety in painting so rosy a future (among other things he rejected the possibility of British

Conservatives ever dismantling the postwar welfare state) was compounded by the narrowness of his social experience. A social-democratic utopia with more hospitable hoteliers and more riverside cafes revealed the social isolation of Labour's leaders, their distance from ordinary people's experience.

It is of course impossible to read Crosland's book without becoming conscious of profound ironies. Indeed, in the period between the end of the conference and the present, in those revolutionary months that so clearly separate the 1980s from the 1990s, new and more complex ironies have been created. Those who in the late 1980s pointed to the catastrophic errors in Crosland's prognoses must in the early 1990s at least admit the perspicacity of his critique of Soviet and eastern European communism. In the face of the dramatic transformations of meaning that new contexts create, aiming for a balanced or objective reading of *The Future of Socialism* is clearly idealist; but even before the recent cataclysms, a dismissive attitude to Crosland was, I think, mistaken. For if, on the one hand, he articulated every major assumption of an emergent (transatlantic) progressivism, he also extended the agenda of political discussion and analysis in ways that were to be taken up – and profoundly reworked – in the late 1960s. For all its faults, his book is proof that the politics of culture and the politics of the subject did not simply arrive new-born with the counter-culture.

The Future of Socialism, given its title and its moment (after nearly a decade of Conservative rule) was surprisingly optimistic. Its answer to the poser that had been recurrently put before the Labour party – What is to be done in the face of Conservative dominance? – was to suggest an updating of the socialist agenda in Britain. This needed to take account of the conditions and aspirations evident in the mid-twentieth century, rather than to remain rooted in the assumptions that were current at its emergence and that were affirmed by the deprivation of the 1920s and 1930s. Crosland argued that the reflexes of the old socialism were increasingly defunct because the practices of classic capitalism no longer obtained. The unrelenting class struggle between autonomous capitalist owners and their alienated wage-slaves was no longer relevant, however strong its hold on the theory and practice of socialist politics. In their stead, Crosland recommended a politics capable of exploiting the new opportunities born of prosperity, but in ways that led to public rather than merely personal benefit. He argued the need for a new set of values; the 'cultivation of leisure, beauty, grace, gaiety, excitement' was to be a matter both for individuals, too long accustomed to self denial, and for government, which should attend to civic aesthetics, to planning and to cultural investment as well as to industrial relations and production figures.

In common with other prophets of the social democratic consensus or, to give it its American inflection, the end of ideology (the title of Daniel Bell's book – Bell 1960), Crosland's analysis of contemporary trends rested on several interlocking premises. The first of these was the assumption of a new economic era, an era of plenty rather than scarcity. 'We stand in Britain on the threshold of mass abundance' (Crosland 1956: 515) was Crosland's claim. He contrasted the new era with the deprivations of the interwar years and the austerity of the Second World War and its aftermath. Underlying that contrast was a contrast between the socio-economic system of nineteenth-century capitalism and the relations of production evident by the 1950s. In Crosland's view, the emerging system had been so transformed by the new role of the state in economic planning, by the relatively limited power of owners and particular shareholders, by the leftward movement of the political consensus and by the consequent relaxation of class tensions, that he could say (quoting the title of the book's second chapter), 'to the question "Is this still capitalism?" I would answer "No" ' (75).

At about the same time the argument was put somewhat more modestly by Daniel Bell (Bell 1960), who spoke in terms of a mature and efficient American capitalism capable of creating mass abundance (in fact rather than in prospect). Like Crosland, he contrasted the social democratic evolution of western societies with the decline of the socialist ideal in the Soviet bloc. For both, traditional socialist alternatives to life in the west had been discredited for, in the words of *The Future of Socialism*:

> If we persist in defining capitalism in terms of private ownership and socialism in terms of collectivism, then as socialists we must say that we should prefer, or that the mass of workers would prefer or that we should regard it as more just and moral to live in Socialist Russia than in Britain, Sweden or even the United States. Which only shows how completely these definitions have cut adrift from what people had in mind when they originally used the words.
>
> (Crosland 1956: 75)

Assumptions about the end of red-in-tooth-and-claw capitalism and the end of ideology gave rise to a belief in social engineering. With ideological conflict now marginal, the key discussions would concern means, not ends – how best, cumulatively, gradually, to legislate the new society into being. Despite his apparently Dickensian antipathy to bureaucracy – 'today we are all incipient bureaucrats . . . familiar with Blue Books and White Papers' (524) – Crosland in fact had immense confidence in the achievements of governmental intervention in the recent past (as in his assessment of the welfare state) and he recognized the need for broadening the field of policymaking in the future. Indeed, in the paragraph following the phrase just quoted, he wrote: 'In the field of cultural values what is mainly, indeed desperately, needed is determined government planning' (524). His thoughts about the directions this planning should take were fuelled by quoting sociological surveys by experts in the United States and Sweden, whose work he tended to regard as of scientific force. They were seen to produce the unjaundiced data that increasingly powerful central government, extending its legislative reach, could turn to for objective guidance. The potential new areas of concern listed in the conclusion of *The Future of Socialism* – from town planning to arts funding, from repealing laws on abortion and censorship to fostering equal rights for women – promised, in fact, not the end of Fabian pamphlets but their proliferation on new topics. Even if, in the long run, repealing existing statutes meant a hands-off libertarianism, in the short and medium term such goals entailed a widening of the political agenda and an extension of administrative intervention.

Socialists and legislators of the future would turn their attention to the 'spheres of personal freedom, happiness and cultural endeavour', to 'the cultivation of leisure, beauty, grace' (520). In a society of abundance the personal would be politicized, in the sense of being planned, fostered, facilitated by enlightened administrators. Crosland's formulation brings to mind several antecedents; most obviously (a tradition Crosland acknowledges) it reminds us of William Morris's utopian speculations, which also confronted the problem of what to do after the end of scarcity. There were also echoes of that reforming patrician mid-Victorian liberalism that in its own day argued the case for a mature capitalism capable of extending its benefits to all, and willing to take up social, civic and aesthetic responsibilities rather than consign everything to the whim of market forces. And, of course, there was a running debate with the strain of what Crosland rejects as reductive Marxism, long influential in earlier Labour politics. In one sense, Crosland's attempt to change the political agenda for socialists, to turn attention to these 'other spheres', meant a new emphasis on social and cultural matters previously written off a 'superstructural' by those who insisted the economy came first – and last. (In this respect, if in few others, Crosland's politics can be related to Thompson's history and Hoggart's cultural studies.) And yet the insistent premise that underlined the changed agenda – the assumption of eventual mass abundance – ironically confirmed the determining force of the economic, assigning it a structural primacy as the source, the real foundation of social transformation. Finally, Crosland's conceptualization of the relations between public and private, work and leisure, duty and freedom, his claim that the time had arrived 'for a greater emphasis on private life' (524) recalled a contemporaneous sociological analysis that supplied the personal dimension to the claims about 'the end of ideology'. 'Affluent workers' were indeed found to put a greater emphasis on private life, on the Saturday night and Sunday morning of individual consumption rather than the principled day-to-day pursuit of the class struggle. Just as social and cultural shifts come in the wake of economic change, so, at the personal level, leisure, pleasure and the private life occupy the space after work. The personal was politicized in Crosland, but in a positivist fashion that in fact confirmed its separation from the world of production. The end of ideology was also the end of anxiety. In turning to the private life (even if one facilitated by better public provisions), we would turn away from necessities, confident that they would be taken care of.

The appeal and the influence of Crosland's book clearly owed much to its capacity to speak to everybody, to allow sympathetic identification by readers from a wide political spectrum. Claiming to reflect a growing social consensus, it actively promoted an intellectual one. This should not be taken, however, to indicate banal risklessness, for the positivism of Crosland's cultural politics did challenge powerful and deeply-rooted assumptions about culture among British intellectuals. To speak of the cultivation of leisure, beauty and grace in the context of a programme of legislation was to depart from that line (joining Arnold to Leavis) that saw 'cultivation' as naturally self-propagating, too subtle and profound for political tinkering. To conceptualize cultural life in terms of social as well as narrowly aesthetic pursuits (as cafes and fashion styles as well as concerts and novels) and to speculate on cultural opportunities for the masses was to break with the elitism of liberal theory. And optimistically to see new opportunities for culture as the product of industrial progress and the movement towards abundance was to contest a profound strain of anti-industrialism and anti-modernism among Leavisites and left-Leavisites. For them, culture was dependent (in another kind of organicism) on the traditional but ever-threatened local community.

This belief in the benefits of industrial and economic progress (among them an expanded cultural and personal realm) was, however, soon to be contested by those for whom abundance was a more immediate prospect.

CONSENSUS QUESTIONED

Some would have us believe that Americans feel contentment amidst prosperity – but might it not be better called a glaze above deeply-felt anxieties about their role in the new world? And if these anxieties produce a developed indifference to human affairs, do they not as well produce a yearning to believe that there *is* an alternative to the present, that something *can* be done to change circumstances in the school, the workplaces, the bureaucracies, the government? It is to this latter yearning, at once the spark and engine of change, that we direct our current appeal. The search for truly democratic alternatives to the present, and a commitment to social experimentation with them, is a worthy and fulfilling human enterprise, one which moves us and, we hope, others today. On such a basis do we offer this document of our convictions and our analysis: as an effort in understanding and changing the conditions of humanity in the late twentieth century, an effort rooted in the ancient, still unfulfilled conception of man attaining determining influence over his circumstances of life . . . .

Almost no students value activity as citizens. Passive in public, they are hardly more idealistic in arranging their private lives: Gallup concludes they will settle for 'low success, and won't risk high failure.' There is not much willingness to take risks (not even in business), no setting of dangerous goals, no real conception of personal identity except one manufactured in the image of others, no real urge for personal fulfilment except to be almost as successful as the very successful people. Attention is being paid to social status (the quality of shirt collars, meeting people, getting wives or husbands, making solid contacts for later on); much, too, is paid to academic status (grades, honors, the med. school rat race). But neglected generally is real intellectual status, the personal cultivation of the mind.

(SDS, *Port Huron Statement*, quoted in Franklin 1971: 22–34[2])

The *Port Huron Statement* – the first manifesto of American Students for a Democratic Society – was published in 1962. At that time, according to Bruce Franklin, SDS was 'highly idealistic, vaguely socialist, fairly affluent' (Franklin 1971: 22). This judgement might alert us to the fact that, beneath the evident differences in style and ethos suggesting the emergence of a distinctive new critique, there are surprising continuities with social democratic progressivism.

Bell's *The End of Ideology* (1960) had claimed that 'the end of ideology is not – should not be – the end of utopia as well. . . . There is now, more than ever, some need for utopia, in the sense that men need as they have always needed, some vision of their potential' (Bell 1960: 405). In 1962, students in SDS saw little signs of such vision in their own society. The very imprecision of their idealism early in the manifesto conveyed the frustration and the anomie they complained of. They spoke abstractly and abstractedly of 'a yearning to believe there is an alternative to the present, that something can be done to change circumstances' (Franklin 1971: 24). Their account of the downside of prosperity, the pressures towards social and intellectual conformity and the complacent narrowing of horizons, was reminiscent of Marcuse's notion of American society made one-dimensional. Their plea was, above all else, for a clearing of a critical space, for the consideration of alternatives, to break 'the national quietude . . . [where] elites . . . resolve complex and specialized problems of modern, industrial society' (25). Social engineering and the careful instrumental outlook, the *Port Huron Statement* suggested, took their toll in terms of personal identity and personal fulfilment. Personal cultivation of the mind was offered as a preferable goal to conventional material rewards.

The terms in which this plea was made and the languages it employed were significantly varied. On the one hand there was the suggestion that given 'contentment and prosperity' and a 'developed indifference to human affairs' (24), and given the muting effects of consensus and the dearth of dramatic just causes, political proclivities would surface not in open public controversy but in personal style and lifestyle, in dress, in social habits and personal ambitions.

Amid the quietism of political consensus, culture (in this broad sense) was foregrounded, would become the field of difference. Latent here, but soon to become a staple of counter-cultural politics, was the complementary assumption, that as well as public advocacy, changing style and lifestyle, reaching for 'authentic' personal identity, was essential to the radical project. As yet, in its opening psychologistic lament and in its diagnosis of politics through personal style, the *Port Huron Statement* echoed a well-established American existentialism, the Maileresque, on-the-road angst of rebels without a cause.

But there was, too, the elevated language of an older tradition, the abstract universals of the enlightenment tradition; not the quotidien world of taste and manners, but humanity's heroic struggle for perfection. This kind of (sometimes Paineite) language was a consequence of the global focus the *Statement* initially adopted: 'Two thirds of mankind suffers undernourishment, our own upper classes revel amidst superfluous abundance' (23). Solving the problems of 'development' and 'underdevelopment' and defusing the global threat posed by the bomb . . . the international dimension allowed for a utopian speculation and language that domestic political discourse, muffled by plenitude, excluded.

Given this mixture of traditions and languages, the use of 'cultivation' here was particularly ambivalent. We were told that attention to social and academic status in contemporary America precluded 'real intellectual status, the personal cultivation of the mind' (24). Was the emphasis on the (existential) 'personal', on what was to be seen as the liberating feeding of the head with strange, exotic and often Oriental treasures (such as those described in *The Making of the Counter-culture*)? Or was it on intellectual cultivation in the conventional sense, an engagement with 'great works'?

Reading the *Port Huron Statement* retrospectively, it is tempting to underline incipient counter-cultural values (anti-materialism, nonconformity, a stress on personal growth subjectively measured, and so on), but that is to neglect what is equally prominent – the sense of moral earnestness and personal responsibility that characterized the early American (and British) New Left.

Significantly, after its speculative opening, the *Statement* was marked by its attention to the conventional categories of modern political discourse. It covered the policy spectrum (as Crosland had), taking up foreign policy (attitudes to independence struggles), the economy (relations between the public and private sectors) and the problems of the city: 'The model city must be projected – more community decision-making and participation, true integration of classes, races, vocations – provision for beauty, access to nature and the benefits of the central city as well' (32). It was not just the range but the details of the analysis that recalled Crosland. Like him, its authors argued against what they believed to be outmoded political precepts (for them anti-communism); they called for a necessary mixture of state and private controls in a mixed economy and for national programmes to address social and cultural issues too long left on the periphery (including what we quaintly call 'town planning'). Like him, they also celebrated the achievements of the welfare state, urging American developments along the same lines to deal with the problems of health and poverty. And like him, too, they were ambivalent about bureaucracy – against the faceless social engineers, but urging the extension of legislation into new areas (through health and anti-poverty programmes).

To say these things in America was, of course, to go against the grain. These students went east, or leftward, to the ground they shared with Crosland (who went west). Despite the correspondences, their opposite trajectories served to produce strange ironies. Whilst he called for a new attention to the private life, they bemoaned 'American . . . withdrawal from public life' (25). The *Port Huron Statement* was a utopian manifesto that ended with a call for precisely the Fabian pamphleteering virtues Crosland hoped were redundant:

A New Left must transform modern complexity into issues that can be understood and felt close-up by every human being. It must give form to the feelings of helplessness and indifference so that people may see the political, social and economic sources of their private troubles and organize to change society. In a time of supposed prosperity, moral complacency and political manipu lation, a New Left cannot rely only on aching stomachs to be the engine of social reform. The case for change, for alternatives that will involve uncomfortable personal efforts, must be urged as never before.

(Franklin 1971: 33)

This insisted on the connection, not the separation, of public and private, on the social determinations of personal life. It called for social analysis to be scaled down and humanized so that 'private troubles' could be seen in context. These determinations were harder to demonstrate in a prosperous (or allegedly prosperous) society than in one where deprivations were immediate, felt in the belly. Issues had to be clarified to people mystified by 'modern complexity' and unaware of larger causes. Argument, demonstration, moral suasion were the means by which reform would be achieved. And the changes would mean 'uncomfortable personal efforts'; loosing conformist shackles, personally participating in the democratic process, takes its toll on quietist pleasures. For all its qualifications, this conclusion assumed, like Bell and Crosland, a stable and uncontroversial consensus society, but one in which perceived affluence stifled complaint. Crosland's future had arrived, but with a cloying wealth. The task of the New Left was to shake the complacency.

Four or five years on, however, this assumption was impossible to sustain in America; the social determinations of the personal were all too dramatically obvious, resistance and complaint ubiquitous.

CONSENSUS IN COLLAPSE

Our single objective in South Vietnam has been and remains to help that country ensure self-determination and become capable of maintaining security and ensuring its own future. At the same time, we seek methodically to terminate American combat involvement in Indo-China. . . .

The first phase consists of turning over to South Vietnam the ground combat responsibility against VC-NVA forces. As I have said many times before, we expect to complete Phase 1 by this summer, although American ground combat forces will remain in a security role to protect U.S. forces as Phase 2 progresses.

The second phase consists of developing within South Vietnam the air, naval, artillery, logistics and other support capabilities necessary to maintain effective independent security. Phase 2 has been in process concurrently with Phase 1, but will take longer to complete.

(Melvin Laird, *Defence Report to Congress*, 29 March 1971, quoted in Rosenberger and Tobin 1971/2: 24, 616)

People are always asking us, 'What's your program?' I hand them a Mets scorecard. Or I tell them to check the yellow pages. 'Our program's there'. *Fuck programs!* The goal of revolution is to

abolish programs and turn spectators into actors. It's a do-it-yourself revolution, and we'll work out the future as we go.
Castro says: 'The goal of the Cuban revolution is to turn *every* individual into a legislator'.
Representative democracy is the enemy. The goal is each-man-his-own-revolution. . . .
Turn every event into historic and mythic significance. Make yourself a symbol.
The revolution is a battle between symbols. Fuck, what's Vietnam anyway? The United States doesn't give a shit about that little piece of real estate. Vietnam is a symbol. The Viet Kong are in San Diego.

(Rubin 1970: 125–8)

For radical student movements in London, Paris and Tokyo as well as Berkeley, Kent State and Washington, Vietnam was indeed a symbol – of American corruption, interventionism and neo-imperialism – a symbol so potent as to inspire bloody demonstrations around the globe. The domestic impact of Vietnam on American attitudes and American prestige was no less profound. If the era to the early 1960s saw the 'end of ideology', then the Vietnam years were the age of ideology, when the grand consensus and the assumptions underlying it were destroyed. Economic, social, political and moral conflicts resurfaced so dramatically that the notion of frictionless social progress under beneficent capitalism simply appeared absurd. At all these levels, the consensus was broken – replaced by a strident self-interested factionalism so ubiquitous that public discourse itself splintered.

Crosland, Bell and the writers of the *Port Huron Statement* assumed a common discourse, a shared language of political analysis through which commentators across the spectrum could make clear their positions. The idea of a consensus assumed and implied as much. Contrast this with the evident partisanship of the two extracts above. Laird's Pentagonese is characterized by Latinate abstraction ('methodically to terminate'), by a monotonously cumulative syntax favouring adjectival piles ('air, naval, artillery, logistics and other support capabilities'), by the alphabet soup of expert abbreviations (NC-NVA) and by a would-be objectivism, albeit comically self-subverting (distinct 'phases' of the policy are yet simultaneous). The consequence of these features is a depersonalized, scientistic discourse repressing the specificities of time, place and reason that conventional clause structures promote, and evacuating the moral and human implications from the processes it seeks so functionally to describe. Rubin's Yippie speech sees the return of the repressed, a discourse personalized by intonation (by its use of italics), by informality, by spontaneous conversational switches, by mimicry (echoes of Lyndon Baines Johnson, the foul-mouthed Texan president, in the notion of Vietnam as real estate – or at least of Mailer's LBJ) and by its frequent use of profanities. The tense, tight, small-print linearity of Pentagonese is subverted by Rubin's typographical liberation. The variety in size and style of print (including irregular hand-scrawled headlines) suggests not just the timbre of a voice but an alert, responsive (not to say speeding), rather than a programmed, consciousness. There is a variety of visual as well as verbal stimuli (cartoons, photographs, portraits) to provide for the more active engagement of the reader's senses. In the symbolic politics of contestation, where radical parody sought to undermine the repressive spectacle of conventional politics (in the Yippies' case by electing a pig as the presidential candidate at their Chicago convention), the medium was the message. The particular content of programmes – or 'phases' – was less significant than their technocratic logic, a logic that induced passivity among adherents and hence endorsed the political hierarchy. Laird's speech is closed and monologic; Rubin's open, loose and dialogic. Pentagonese pretends to and increasingly fakes a technocratic consensus; the Yippies' language expects and provokes dissent.

The monologue was at an end, too, in the economic arena. For two decades there had been unparalleled corporate expansion, the extremely profitable export of American capital into territories that were exploited for their resources and their labour power, and the continuing growth of world markets for home-produced goods. Radical critics argued that American prosperity in the 1950s was buttressed by foreign investment and domestic defence spending, but in a period of expansion different economic sectors (including those outside the boom areas) could peacefully coexist. But the spiralling costs of the Vietnam war, the increasing preponderance of defence expenditure and the damage to American prestige caused by the war (which took its toll in the loss of potential markets) led to increasing disagreement between different economic interests in the US. On the one hand the representatives of Wall Street (finance and investment capital and many multinational corporations) began to see the war as against their long-term interests (and the traditional aims of American foreign policy). American diplomatic and economic influence worldwide was being threatened because of the stigma created by its involvement. The increasingly fervid anti-communist rhetoric and the dramatic actions America took against Vietnam, including bombing cities and mining ports, hardened Russian and Chinese attitudes and meant that potential new markets in these and other eastern European countries were more likely to fall to competitors such as Germany and Japan. On the other hand, the 'military-industrial complex' – those companies involved in war production, either directly contracted to government or in related research and development fields – continued to profit from the continuation of the war.

According to Defence Department estimates, the conduct of the Vietnam war had added $112 billion to its regular budget by June 1974, and in the financial year 1969 alone cost $21.5 billion. Between 1960 and 1971 government debt rose from $336 to $557 billion. The massive American expenditure on the war upset the South Vietnamese economy and thereafter helped produce unprecedented inflation in the US itself. In a famously dyspeptic essay, 'The Democratic distemper', Samuel P. Huntington pointed to the double-bind the American government, faced with these deficits, found itself in (the language is suitably Lairdian): 'At the same time as the expansion of governmental activity creates problems of financial solvency for the government, the decline in governmental authority reduces still further the ability of government to deal effectively with these problems' (Huntington 1975: 103–4).

In domestic political terms, the cost of the war was severe. Soaring inflation led to the postponement of social welfare programmes instituted by Johnson – programmes that would at least have taken some steps in the direction pointed by the *Port Huron Statement*. Those most directly affected – racial minorities living in the ghettoes of major cities – were all too well aware of bleak and profound ironies. First, that the cost of prosecuting the war (by an army in which their own men were over-represented) was responsible for the abandonment of social programmes. Second, that the war was being fought against an under-developed non-white country, the sufferings of whose citizens were all too reminiscent of their own. The consequence was a growing radicalism, the increasing visibility of exclusivist ethnic politics (with such groups as the Black Panthers and the Young Lions) and popular manifestos making common cause between oppressed sections of American society and the North

Vietnamese. The war was brought home, too, during riots in such cities as Chicago and Detroit, where the massed presence of police and national guardsmen made clear the mechanics of armed suppression, the heavy hand of the violent state.

The collapse of consensus went along with the weakening of hegemonic control, the increasing need for partisan political intervention. Press reactions to his domestic and international policies led Richard Nixon to place overt controls on media coverage. Academic resistance to the war programme brought fevered attacks from Spiro Agnew on the 'effete intellectual snobs' of the east coast university establishment. There were instances of police and FBI infiltration into radical political, educational and media groups. In support of Agnew and Nixon, in reaction to east coast liberals and ethnic and student radicals, pro-war minorities took to the streets (most famously in the 'hard hat' marches of construction workers in New York). Indeed, a regional fractionalism surfaced in the major parties, with Californian extremists and southern populists threatening both Republican and Democrat orthodoxies.

And there were, of course, those infamous moments of naked state violence, inflicted upon peaceful marchers and demonstrators. These participants in symbolic counter-politics thus exposed the reality of state repression, though the power of their exposé was proportional to their powerlessness before its assaults. At Chicago, before Mayor Daley's police; at the Pentagon, before army regiments; and most pitifully at Kent State, under the guns of the national guard, protestors paid a savage price.

And a public one, for all to see on prime-time television. The ubiquity of TV cameras, there at moments of domestic crisis and at the monotonously routine moments of suffering in Vietnam, intensified the growing visibility of political and military conflict. They brought the war and the protests to the living room, and to the consciousness and the conscience of the American public. The dramatic immediacy of the images (however much repetition eventually may have dulled their impact) served personally to implicate the viewers, especially those who might expect themselves or their sons soon to be drafted.

Underlying the burgeoning economic and social conflicts, this is to say, there was, for these and many other people, a personal, moral conflict focused on an unavoidable decision – draft or resistance. The insistent formulation of this conflict in starkly ethical terms (and not just by prospective draftees) owed much to dominant

American philosophies of individualism and individual responsibility, now turned, not for the first time, against the interests of the state. Television images of napalm victims, agent-orange deforestation, 'pacified' villages, and of the immensely sophisticated technologies responsible for them, increasingly created an intense and direct rather than abstract and rhetorical sense of what it meant to be an American in the endless days of the war.

By the late 1960s all the assumptions of social democratic progressivism, so powerful a decade earlier, were laid bare. The sense of sustainable abundance was laid to rest by the economic consequences of the war. The belief in social engineering, in a gradualist, problem-solving approach to social inequalities was revealed as inadequate before the obdurate and worsening realities of ghetto life. Technocratic expertise produced, not a massive reduction in labour and an increase in private freedoms, but, among other diversions, a high-tech, remote-controlled weaponry, the risklessness of whose use only deepened its depravity. National pride, whether in the strident form of the early Cold War period or in the more relaxed vein of the era of plenty, now nosedived, America and its complicit allies (Britain as ever in the van) stigmatized by its engagement. Bell and Crosland assumed a mature capitalism (whether they dared speak its name or not), capable of delivering to all. Now, in addition to the stringencies of domestic inflation, American capital faced growing competition from Europe and the east. The growth of political and social conflict, the visibility of the war and the implication of much of the population in its pursuit now meant not, as the authors of the *Port Huron Statement* had feared, a 'withdrawal from public life' (Franklin 1971: 25) but, increasingly, willingly or not, an inevitable engagement. Even that fraction of the American counter-culture who opted, not for contestation, but for the creation of an alternative lifestyle, were involved in something other than private retreat. For, finally, such were the pressures during the end of consensus that the personal and the private became inescapably politicized by social and economic necessity, rather than being supplementary to it.

The American radicalism thus produced was, however, highly volatile. Its agents were disaffected with the state (and the state's violence) and with the assumptions of progressivism (abundance, social engineering and technological advance). Their interest in the situationist politics of symbolic assertion (reliant on individual imagination as much as collective discipline) left them coolly disposed towards established Marxist and communist positions in eastern and western Europe. And events in Czechoslovakia, Hungary and Paris during 1968 guaranteed that the ethos of Marxist-Leninism and the commissarial sense of the 'brickwork logic of the next step' (Mailer 1969: 85) would be rejected. An emerging transatlantic (and trans-European) conjunction in the late 1960s took the place of the transatlantic conjunction of the late 1950s.

Perceiving the simultaneous failure of capitalist and communist regimes, radicals east and west attempted a new politics. They noted parallels between American and Soviet interventions abroad, the imperialistic invasion of client or satellite state, and the complicity of erstwhile progressive forces in the repressive actions of the state (exemplified by the French Communist Party, the British Labour Party and the American Democratic Party, as well as more predictably by eastern European parties). They saw, too, the conflict between the interests of the state and those of the citizen (evidenced by the common spectacle of internal violence) and the obdurate self-promotion of the political machines (run by an international gerontocracy). The betrayal of ideals on both sides of the Cold War divide meant that for radicals on either side there could be no easy endorsement of the other. The culture of politics – in general and in its subtlest reaches – was now in question.

C'EST POUR TOI QUE TU FAIS LA REVOLUTION

We can get some idea of the form that the movement of the future must take. Every action committee, no less than every mass movement which seeks to improve the lives of all men, must resolve:

1. to respect and guarantee the plurality and diversity of political currents within the revolutionary mainstream. It must accordingly grant minority groups the right of independent action – only if the plurality of ideas is allowed *to express itself in social practice* does this idea have any real meaning;

2. to ensure that all delegates are accountable to, and subject to immediate recall by, those who have elected them, and to oppose the introduction of specialists and specialization at every step by widening the skill and knowledge of all;

3. to ensure a continuous exchange of ideas, and to oppose any control of information and knowledge;

4. to struggle against the formation of any kind of hierarchy;

5. to abolish all artificial distinctions within labour, in particular between manual and intellectual work, and discrimination on grounds of sex;

6. to ensure that all factories and businesses are run by those who work in them;

7. to rid ourselves, in practice, of the Judaeo-Christian ethic, with its call for renunciation and sacrifice. There is only one reason for being a revolutionary – because it is the best way to live.

Reaction, which is bound to become more and more violent as the revolutionary movement increases its impact on society, forces us to look to our defences. But our main task is to keep on challenging the traditional bureaucratic structures both in the government and also in the working-class movements.

How can anyone represent anyone else? All we can do is to involve them. We can try to get a few movements going, inject politics into all the structures of society, into the Youth Clubs, Youth Hostels, the YMCA and the Saturday Night dance, get out on to the streets, out on to all the streets of all the towns. To bring real politics into everyday life is to get rid of the politicians.

(Cohn-Bendit 1969: 254–5)

The last chapter of Cohn-Bendit's book is called *C'est pour toi que tu fais la révolution*, which, like Rubin's *Do it!*, makes it clear that revolutionary activity is not to be seen as in the service of future material gain or egalitarianism-to-come, but as an immediate, qualitative transformation; being a revolutionary is the 'best way to live' (255).

In response to the diseased culture of conventional politics, there is the demand for a politicized culture, the realization that our most intimate, erstwhile private and personal activities carry profound political meanings and must be transformed. The political and the personal are seen as indivisible, and revolution therefore must be also personal liberation. For Cohn-Bendit an alternative culture of politics must promote modes of expression and organization that allow the self free rein. 'Renunciation', 'sacrifice' – and the self-sacrifice that acknowledges leaders, experts and authorities (the willing self-subordination to the cause) – was no longer enough. Anti-bureaucratic, anti-centralist, in favour of participative rather than representative democracy, Cohn-Bendit's manifesto sought to create the conditions in which the self could be remade and a new ethic emerge.

These emphases are also apparent (albeit inflected according to different national traditions and preoccupations) in a wide range of other manifestos from the late 1960s: in the pamphlets of the Berkeley Free Speech movement; in the writings of the British New Left; and recurrently in the critiques made of various eastern European states.

Obsolete Communism (Cohn-Bendit 1969) investigated the history of collusion between the French government and Communist Party leaders in the handling of industrial conflicts, culminating in their mutual efforts to defuse the events of May 1968. The Party bureaucracy was seen as 'very much as in the capitalist system, it has a hierarchical structure in which the top becomes increasingly remote from the bottom' (70). In America, even in the late 1960s, such critiques took on a more individualist and humanist gloss, condemning the dehumanizing effects of, say, the educational buraucracy in the name of traditional liberal ideals. With education industrialized, the campus had become a 'knowledge factory'; 'as a human being seeking to enrich himself, the student has no place in the multiversity. Instead he becomes a mercenary, paid off in grades, status and degrees' (Franklin 1971: 37).

In Czechoslovakia the radicals pointed to the more or less indistinguishable bureaucracies of state and party. The Stalinist machinery controlling economy, culture and education was seen as inert, repressive and a drag on material and intellectual development, the more resented because of growing material deprivations. Whether inflected in moral, political or economic terms, the critique of centralization was likewise recurrent. In the US (one thinks of Chomsky's work) the relations between centre and periphery were sometimes seen in international terms; the capacity of expert researchers and technicians at the centre dispassionately to develop the technology of destruction (and the language of alibi) for use in the distant periphery of Vietnam signalled their dehumanization. In France, Cohn-Bendit pointed to the phenomenon of political leadership among communists by those above and beyond, by a centralized collection of experts physically and experientially removed from the industrial situations they sought to influence. He advocated, instead, 'leader-free' local initiatives and the power of factory soviets, resisting the status divisions that inevitably produce an active centre and compliant margins. Those challenging the economic system in Czechoslovakia similarly urged a balance between centralized socialist planning and market demands (in relation to which local initiatives should be encouraged, not stifled). Personal effort was also to be fostered by the use of differentials as reward and incentive for individuals. Centralization, it was argued, had produced a rigid, formalistic and empty egalitarianism.

To reject bureaucracy and centralization was also to reject the fixed hierarchical demarcations so deeply established in political life: between (party) leader, activist, member, supporter and citizen; between national and local, executive and operative; between politics, as formalized enquiry, debate and decision, and everyday life. The established mechanics of political representation were necessarily a third common target. As Cohn-Bendit's bald assertion made clear, 'how can anyone represent anyone else?' (Cohn-Bendit 1969 255); challenging the conventional demarcations entailed both a liberation and the assumption of new responsibilities.

The hypocrisy of Sunday-suited, allegedly representative democracy was laid bare by acts of symbolic and sometimes literal 'contestation'. Dramatic radical scenarios (the Yippies' election of the pig, the 'levitation' of the Pentagon, the use of the Paris Odeon as 'parliament') aimed, through parodic debunking, to reveal the rituals of role and status that oiled political machines everywhere. Representative democracy, exemplified at its apogee by the 1968 Democratic Convention, was as a result seen as a bread-and-circus spectacular of leader and led. At the point when contestation became literal and violent conflict, symbolically repressive spectaculars gave way to the practical spectacle of repression, by democracy's finest (the national guard, the CRS, the Metropolitan police).

Challenging established and distancing modes of political representation meant, most dramatically, taking to the streets. But it also involved the attempt to evolve day-to-day organizations capable of sustaining the movement: 'To bring real politics into everyday life is to get rid of the politicans' (Cohn-Bendit 1969: 255). The attack on politics as a career (for those delegated to advance our values and ideals) produced new imperatives. Ending the false segregation of politics meant an end to the hitherto safely 'unpolitical'. How we behaved at work, at home, in relationships and 'at leisure' was to be a matter for self-conscious scrutiny. New insights could not be passed over for action to 'officials' or 'representatives' (for 'how can anyone represent anyone else?'). According to this ethic, we were obliged to represent ourselves and, finally, re-present ourself, aware of the implications of the most quotidien habits, instincts and reflexes. The subject, who in the cheerful social democratic and progressivist orthodoxy could simply be him or herself in the demarcated realms of 'leisure, beauty, grace, gaiety and excitement', was thereby politicized not just as member of party, union or movement but even, and perhaps especially, in the places once thought of as 'private' – in jobs and in gender, in sexuality and in taste, in the whole lived culture.

Culture was now the site not of contentment but of conflict. And made so not simply by acts of radical will but, according to the most influential public philosopher of the era, because the state had already insinuated itself in the allegedly 'private' reaches of our activity. Marcuse's project, fusing Freud and Marx, had been to lay bare the mechanics of oppression/repression, to show that the forces of social containment operated not simply in terms of class and ideological rule, but psychologically by structuring the personality of the oppressed, by repression surplus to the social norm. According to such studies as *One-Dimensional Man* (1964) and *Essay on Liberation* (published the year after the May 1968 events, and dedicated to the student revolutionaries), the psychic reflexes of capitalism had been so thoroughly introjected by the working class as to produce a condition of voluntary servitude. The peculiar (and obscene) traits of the dominant ethos – aggressive, competitive, sexist, racist and acquisitive – had assumed a natural status, were seen as simply 'human'. A society dominated by necessity and conformity pictured itself ideologically as free, individualist and expressive. (It was in this context that Marcuse spoke, instancing the Playboy syndrome, of repressive desublimation.) The vast majority of the American and the western population had been accommodated in the capitalist system, not simply materially, but culturally, psychically. According to Marcuse, there remained as the source of revolutionary hope those minorities for whom the orthodox vision of wealth and freedom remained a sick joke (among them blacks and, increasingly, students). If at the time of *One-Dimensional Man* the prospect for change seemed bleak, then *Essay on Liberation* was written in part to celebrate a potential transformation, one anticipated by the upheavals we have been describing.

Marcuse produced a diabolic inversion of social democratic progressivism. In contrast to affirmative commentators like Bell and Crosland, he pointed to the Faustian price to be paid for acquisitive materialism – both in terms of an unknowing conformism at the level of the individual, and of destructive greed globally (western economies perverted the potential of new productive techniques in service to their own short-term enrichment). And in place of the progressivist belief in sustainable, benificent abundance under 'mature' capitalism, Marcuse offered the prospect of technological apocalypse. Contradictions between new technologies of production (which made possible global abundance) and regressive relations of production (structured in subordination to profit), had grown more and more profound. Crisis was at hand; the era would either see the final victory of capitalist domination, reaching into every aspect of our behaviour, or a breakthrough, the alternative use of economic capacities and the development of a genuinely human culture. Once again, and this implication was a constant feature of the various phases of the movement we have described, the final outcome would be a consequence not of irreversible currents (whether ameliorative, as in Bell or Crosland, or degenerative, as in the bleaker versions of Marxism) but of actions taken and commitments made in struggle. The marriage of Marx and Freud allowed a much more complex account of ideological domination than classic Marxism. (Indeed in other hands, such as Althusser's, it was soon to produce a much more profoundly deterministic account.) But in Marcuse it was also used to promote innovative imperatives for any coming revolution; the sense that truly to confront and overthrow capitalist domination in all its aspects involved addressing the ethics of the interior and subjective life and the discovery of a new psyche.

In positing a subject who had been ideologically and psychologically invaded by the ethos of corporate capitalism (or for that matter, the Stalinist state), radical theorists of the 1960s assumed the possibility of an essential self, a clean free agent, who could be, the powers of domination once removed, the basis of a transformed society. Marcuse spoke indeed of 'the biological foundation for socialism', the innately humane personality that capitalism repressed (1972: 17). The years since that era have witnessed two major shifts. The first, increasingly prominent up to the mid-1980s, saw that analysis as hopelessly idealistic. The insistent implication of structuralist, Althusserian, poststructuralist and Lacanian readings was that it was not merely the 'corrupt' society that pervaded and defined the self, but any and all societies; that the subject was determined by psychological, linguistic and cultural practices that were inescapably part of any social fabric. The subject could not stand pure outside these practices because it only existed through them. The splintering of social analysis into a number of specialist and relatively self-contained discourses – linguistics, psychoanalysis, semiology, literary criticism and so on – despite the partial fusions and cross-references, was an implicit and often explicit critique of the holism, the organicism, the overly synthesizing approach of earlier figures.

In what might be seen as a strange irony, given the starting point of this account, the social engineering so central in earlier social democratic thinking came, by the mid-1970s, to be replaced by an intellectual engineering, likewise dedicatedly specialist. The initial attempt, evident in Crosland's own writing, to separate out different strands of the social totality – economic, social, educational and so on – in order to dispute what he regarded as a simplistic sense of some overarching determination (the reductive Marxism of the 1930s) found an echo in the work of theorists in the 1970s. In their tirades against a singular determination there emerged a number of others (chiefly psychological and linguistic) that, whilst narrower in range, yet exercised a profound, indeed inescapable, influence, creating the subject behind the back of the subject. In contrast to both these periods, the politics of the subject in the late 1960s was exceptional because of the lateral connections it made between different institutional sites (family, education, work, politics, leisure), and because it sought terms to analyse a culture in its entirety, a culture that was taken as an index of the socio-economic system. The New Left's advocacy of a genuinely 'common culture' was underpinned by a belief that concepts adequate to speak of existing culture as an entity were available (be they drawn from the fusion of Marx and Freud, from Marxist humanism or from the historical readings of such as E. P. Thompson and Raymond Williams).

We are perhaps in the early phases of a second shift, in reaction to what increasingly appear the atomistic and, in effect, quietist tendencies of the first. This phase is marked by the return to prominence of theories emphasizing human agency, the capacity for struggle and change (whatever the determinations). In the area of linguistics, for example, the resolutely anti-synchronic views of Volosinov/Bakhtin have assumed a new centrality, just as there seems in other fields (soon to be conjoined?) a re-awakening interest in synthesizing theorists (Jameson and Eagleton, say, in literary and cultural studies). This accelerating counter-current to the dominant theoretical ethos since the 1960s clearly owes much, too, to a political map now in such rapid transformation that theories so intricately accounting for ideological subordination seem suddenly irrelevant. There is apocalypse now, brought about not by the wind from the east but, it seems, by the wind from the west. Whether developments in eastern Europe will continue to confirm progressivist assumptions about western superiority or whether, as in the dreams of the 1960s, new democratic models east and west will be produced, yet remains to be seen.

CONCLUSION

Mainly through a series of textual 'snapshots', this essay has tried to trace the development of a distinctive political ethos during the 1960s, one giving prominence to the politics of culture and the culture of politics, to the nature of our personal and collective implication in established systems and in what might replace them. Moving more or less chronologically from one manifesto to another, it has foregrounded statements from very different cultures and situations, statements whose targets have been, variously, the American corporate system, the war in Vietnam, the French Communist Party and so on. The implication of this study is that, taken in conjunction, these manifestos demonstrate the development of a common set of radical attitudes and goals that had an international currency by the late 1960s.

The essay's shifts of focus (for example, from English centrist socialism, to the American SDS, to Rubin's Yippies, to French student revolutionaries) make two assumptions. First, that a given manifesto is aware of and responsive to its own native radical traditions; that, for instance, Rubin and his colleagues (often through their own earlier involvement) had close knowledge of the politics of the SDS, just as Cohn-Bendit's allies had of the French Communist Party. These linear connections have not been spelled out, except as the selected extracts themselves include such references. Second, the shifts of focus assume the manifestos' makers knew of each other's politics, were responding not just to native traditions but to recent and contemporary radical initiatives across the Atlantic and the Channel. Proving the 'influence' of one grouping on another or of one figure on another through biographical or autobiographical reference, or through tracing the circulation of texts (and translations) or through sustained comparison of contemporaneous manifestos, involves a different kind of study, a descriptive and empirical history.

Here the intention has been to offer readers, who now inhabit a very different political universe, a sense of the texture, the development and the major interconnections of a set of innovative political concepts, commonly held but variously inflected in the radical movements of the 1960s.

NOTES

1 The conference 'Re-reading the Sixties' was held at Roehampton Institute, London, November 1988.
2 Franklin's book is an excellent anthology of radical pamphlets and manifestos covering civil rights, Vietnam, black liberation and women's liberation.

BIBLIOGRAPHY

Bell, Daniel 1960. *The End of Ideology*. New York: Free Press.
Blackburn, R. (ed.) 1972. *Ideology in the Social Sciences*. London: Fontana.
Cleaver, Eldridge 1969. *Soul On Ice*. London: Cape.
Cohn-Bendit, Daniel 1969. *Obsolete Communism: A Left Wing Alternative*. Harmondsworth: Penguin.
Cranston, M. (ed.) 1970. *The New Left: Six Critical Essays*. London: The Bodley Head.
Crosland, Antony 1956. *The Future of Socialism*. London: Cape.
Franklin, Bruce 1971. *From the Movement Toward Revolution*. New York: Van Nostrand Reinhold.
Huntington, Samuel P. 1975. 'The Democratic distemper'. In Huntington, S. P., Crozier, M. J. and Watanuki, J. 1975. *The Crisis of Democracy: Report on the Governability of Democracies to the Trilateral Commission*. New York: New York University Press.
Jackson, George 1971. *Soledad Brother*. Harmondsworth: Penguin.
Mailer, Norman 1968. *The Armies of the Night*. London: Weidenfeld & Nicolson.
Marcuse, Herbert 1968. *One-Dimensional Man*. London: Sphere.
Marcuse, Herbert 1972. *Essay on Liberation*. Harmondsworth: Penguin.
Morgan, Robin (ed.) 1970. *Sisterhood Is Powerful*. New York: Random House.
Pateman, Trevor (ed.) 1972. *Counter-Course: A Handbook for Course Criticism*. Harmondsworth: Penguin.
Reich, Charles 1971. *The Greening of America*. Harmondsworth: Penguin.
Roszak, Theodore 1970. *The Making of a Counter-Culture*. London: Faber & Faber.
Rubin, Jerry 1970. *Do It!: Scenarios from the Revolution*. London: Cape.
Teodori, Massimo 1970. *The New Left: A Documentary History*. London: Cape.
Williams, Raymond 1968. *May Day Manifesto*. Harmondsworth: Penguin.

FURTHER READING

As well as Franklin (1971), Marcuse (1972) and Cohn-Bendit (1969), first-hand accounts describing and often exemplifying aspects of the new radicalism can be found in Raymond Williams' *May Day Manifesto* (1968) and in contemporaneous issues of *New Left Review* (each addressing political and cultural theory); in Robin Blackburn (ed.) *Ideology in the Social Sciences* (1972) and Trevor Pateman (ed.) *Counter-Course: A Handbook for Course Criticism* (1972) (both collections expose the assumptions of established intellectual disciplines and suggest alternatives); in Robin Morgan (ed.) (1970) *Sisterhood Is Powerful* ('An anthology of writings from the Women's Liberation movement'); and in George Jackson's autobiographical *Soledad Brother* (1970) and Eldridge Cleaver's *Soul On Ice* (1969) (exemplifying different responses to black separatism).

Several general accounts of the New Left were written during this period, among them M. Cranston (ed.) *The New Left: Six Critical Essays* (1970) and Massimo Teodori *The New Left: A Documentary History* (1970). C. Reich's *The Greening of America* (1971), and T. Roszak's *The Making of a Counter-Culture* (1970) were impressionistic (and sometimes indulgent) accounts written very close to the events they interpret.

It is, I think, significant that several of these texts were published simultaneously in different countries (such as *Essay on Liberation*), or translated very soon after their original publication (such as *Obsolete Communism*, brought out in England as a Penguin Special).

Chapter 4

The politics of culture: institutional change

Stuart Laing

INTRODUCTION

The term 'culture' can be used in many senses. In one of its selective meanings 'culture' refers to principles of discrimination and evaluation within the arts – and their practical outcomes (these valued institutions, that list of 'serious' works with clear artistic merit). In a more inclusive and descriptive meaning, 'culture' may mean 'all the "signifying practices" – from language through the arts and philosophy to journalism, fashion and advertising' of a given society (Williams 1981: 13).

The 1960s' cultural institutions are considered here in relation to both senses of the word. During the 1950s cultural standards had been maintained by a hierarchical educational system (with universities, public schools and grammar schools at the pinnacle), key quasi-state institutions (including the BBC and the still new Arts Council) and a network of commercial institutions, including 'quality' newspapers, journals, magazines, publishing houses and theatres. The provision and reproduction of culture in its broader sense was also maintained by a mixture of market forces and state regulated institutions. Thus by 1960 a potential conflict, between 'education' (an expanding and still confident operation, inculcating the values of citizenship and a broad humanism, as well as the skills and disciplines needed for employment) and the 'mass media', especially in its commercial form (educating the consumer, training for leisure and orchestrating the political process), had emerged. This was to become a major fault-line within the dominant value-system during the following decade.

As the 1960s unrolled, the practical separation between the kinds of activities denoted by these two meanings of 'culture' became more difficult to preserve, just as the unity of purpose within each set of institutions came under increasing strain, and dissolved into open conflicts by end of the decade. An underlying cause was the fallout from the remarkable economic growth of the late 1950s (as Britain emerged from the last vestiges of austerity and rationing into the consumer boom, the 'never-had-it-so-good' wonderland of affluence), which appeared to be sustained and sustainable even within a new (Wilsonian) and moral (permissive) climate. Full employment was still seen as an attainable and essential goal, and earnings were rising at double the rate of inflation. Certain key consumer durables came to symbolize this new world. By the end of the 1960s refrigerators and washing-machines were in most domestic kitchens, television had become a necessity and telephones were in nearly half of all homes. Most visibly of all, car ownership more than doubled during the decade.

Many of these items bolstered the idea of the home-centred and family-centred society as the means to the good life. Yet other constituents of the postwar boom created countervailing pressures. Those born during the baby-boom of the late 1940s were now becoming teenagers, just at the time when increasing affluence and educational expansion were together creating the conditions for the growth of a separate and distinctive youth culture. The growth of the pop record industry at the start of the decade (with the full introduction of the 45 rpm single and the smaller self-contained record-player) and the slightly later expansion in the teenage fashion market (by 1967 the 15–19 age group accounted for 50 per cent of all clothes bought) were, in commercial terms, the most marked features of this. The leisure and cultural industries saw major new opportunities in this market, as part of the continuing development of an ethic of personal and domestic consumption across the whole society – most notably through the advertising power of the mass media. Both television soap-powder commercials and the message that 'The Revolution's on CBS' may have derived from the same underlying commercial imperatives, but (in a world of increasingly targeted marketing) the sets of social and cultural values that they endorsed were by no means necessarily in harmony.

Economic growth was also the precondition for the expansion in selective cultural provision. The number of book titles increased by 60 per cent between 1959 and 1970, while Arts Council expenditure increased by 60 per cent during the decade. Such growth reflected a new public for the arts. The number of students in higher education more than doubled during the decade, as did the number of school-leavers with arts-based A levels. The overall growth in state education and arts funding created space for increased kinds of explicitly non-commercial cultural and artistic activity, whose practitioners then sought a position outside state control while still claiming the right to public funding – thus apparently taking at their word the conventional platitudes about freedom of thought and the need for no restriction to the artist's imaginative and creative sensibility. While such attempts to break free from state control often entailed an equally vehement opposition to the directions of a new commercial market, at times these two positions could unite in their championing of an 'independent' position free from state regulation (compare the libertarian rhetoric of the pirate radios of the mid-1960s with that of certain alternative theatre groups later in the decade). The dominant cultural bloc frequently sought to deal with such developments by absorbing them within existing institutions, as in the incorporation of the pop radio format within the BBC or the extension of Arts Council patronage into new fields. A broader challenge to all cultural producers, whether state, commercial or alternative, was the ability of the population at large to make their own selection from what was being offered, in ways that did not fit any preconceived pattern. Youth culture throughout the 1960s was a frantic dialectic between the 'consumer' taking what was offered and a more active making and re-making of culture – in the thousands of amateur 'beat' groups, the dress, style and behaviour of the 'mods', and the diverse use of drugs by the different subcultures. Such cultural 'resistance', however, has to be seen as occurring within, and frequently against the grain of, the powerful dominant media, cultural and arts institutions that inevitably set most of the cultural agenda.

THE MASS MEDIA

The 1960s was the first decade when television unequivocally dominated the media stage in Britain. Between 1955 and 1960 the number of people possessing television sets doubled; as the decade began, already 82 per cent of the population had access to a set, the great majority of these being two-channel (by the end of the 1950s all of the major outlying ITV regions had begun to broadcast). During the 1960s this dominance was such as to force a re-definition of the functions of the other media. In a decade of 'cultural expansion' (Williams 1965: 319), radio, cinema and the national press all suffered some diminution of audience directly attributable to television; equally significant was their adaptation to new secondary roles as television came to dominate the provision of evening entertainment and news. Television was now the central medium of the culture. It offered huge audiences for new drama, both serious (David Mercer, Dennis Potter, Loach and Garnett) and popular (*Coronation Street* or *Z Cars*), for 'satire' (*TW3* and its descendants), for news (CND demonstrations, Vietnam, May '68, Ulster) and for quiz shows, *Crossroads* and advertising. Television could reflect, even promote, revolutionary change. In his play *The Party* (1973) Trevor Griffiths showed the television transmissions of the May 1968 events in Paris fuelling the revolutionary debates in London. Perhaps, as a medium of world integration and information exchange, television was even revolutionary in itself – creating Marshall McLuhan's 'global village' (McLuhan 1964) or transmitting live across the world the Beatles singing 'All You Need is Love' in 1967. Equally, to figures as diverse as Sillitoe's working-class hero Arthur Seaton, educationalists of the traditionalist variety and counter-cultural critics of the 'spectacle' of advertising and consumption, television represented all that was complacent, passive and materialistic.

The decade opened with a major educational conference in London in autumn 1960, on 'Popular Culture and Personal Responsibility', at which a major target was commercialism, notably that of independent television. In theory commercial television in Britain was a highly regulated service, reflecting the long public-service tradition of broadcasting, which incorporated the fear of 'Americanization' that had dominated government thinking on British popular culture since 1919. From its inception in 1955 ITV was subject to considerable regulation – of the amount of advertising and non-British programming, of balance within news, of political broadcasting and of overall programming, and of regional provision. During the late 1950s, however, the new companies often appeared to be failing to comply with the requirements for quality and serious programming as, in order to build an audience at speed and cheaply, game shows, quizzes and down-market entertainment seemed to dominate. The report of the Pilkington Committee in 1962 reflected the strong concern of the educational and traditional lobby (with a dash of New Left influence also); as a result the control of the Independent Television Authority (ITA, not to become the IBA until the advent of legal commercial radio in the 1970s) over the ITV companies was strengthened and the third channel was awarded to the BBC (starting broadcasting as BBC2 in 1964). In fact the 1960s saw the BBC setting the pace on television; the decade began with the new director-general, Hugh Carleton-Greene, recruiting a fresh team to beat ITV at their own game by producing popular programmes, but without reducing standards. It was the BBC, rather than ITV, that became associated with the dissident mood of the early 1960s – the sense of a new generation replacing the tired and almost ridiculous figures of old Tory Britain.

By the mid–1960s television had reached virtual saturation point; from 1966 the proportion of the population (93 per cent) who had sets remained the same, as did the overall amount of viewing. There was no pressure from the technological production side of the industry for further expansion since they had major new markets in the conversion of 405-line sets to 625-line sets (necessary to receive BBC2) and the sale of colour sets from 1968. By 1970 over half the population had converted to 625, although only 3 per cent had colour; the average viewers spent 90 minutes every evening in front of the 'box', splitting their time evenly between BBC and ITV (Silvey 1974).

Television's most dramatic effect on another medium was the collapse of the cinema. In 1955 cinema audiences stood at 1,082 million per year, still above prewar levels. By 1960 they had dropped to 600 million, fell to 326 million in 1965 and to under 20 million in 1970. There was a vicious circle of decrease in audience followed by closure of cinemas followed by a further decline in the cinema-going habit; by 1970 the number of cinemas open was less than half those in 1959. Audience composition also changed. While the 'family audience' concept of the 1930s and 1940s was perhaps something of a myth, nevertheless it was the young adult category who now remained as the staple of cinema audiences. For this group the attraction of remaining within the family home in the evening was significantly less than for older or younger people. Cinema's decline as a mass medium lent more credence to those who were seeking to promote the idea, within education or elsewhere, of 'film' as an art form. Television had now replaced cinema as the perceived key corrupter of the social fabric.

At the end of the 1950s the future for radio looked similarly bleak. Daytime listening, although less than in the early 1950s, had stabilized at mid-1950s levels, but evening listening had collapsed to 20 per cent of its 1950 audience. Gathering round the TV set had now replaced gathering round the wireless set as the evening family ritual. In fact, however, the seeds of radio's new and central cultural role in mid-1960s Britain had already been sown. From the late 1950s the recorded popular music industry entered a new phase, with the replacement of the '78' by the more durable '45', the growth of smaller compact record-players replacing the older gramophones, the impact of American rock, blues, country and jazz styles, and the availability of a larger teenage market with more disposable income. Paralleling this from the end of the 1950s, the portable transistor radio began to be marketed in Britain, allowing a broader range of places where radio could be listened to – both within the home (homes increasingly came to have a number of sets, potentially one for each family member) and on the streets, in the parks, on the beach and elsewhere. Also, as car ownership grew from 3.6 million in 1955 to 13 million by 1969, a higher number of cars were fitted with radios, providing a mobile base for radio listening, including the young out and about in the evening.

During the early 1960s the sole alternative to BBC radio was Radio Luxembourg, the only survivor from a number of commercial continental radio stations that in the 1960s had sought British audiences for British advertisers. For both political and commercial reasons the drive to commercial broadcasting in postwar Britain had exclusively concerned television, and no compromise had been reached between the public service and market-driven models of radio. As the pop music industry expanded rapidly in the early 1960s it was television (with a number of key early evening shows) and Radio Luxembourg that were as much involved as daytime radio in marketing the artists and records. The contrast with American Top 40 radio was marked, and it was this format that was used by Radio London, the most successful of the pirate radio stations that broadcast predominantly to south-east England between 1965 and 1967. Pirate radio reflects in a particularly clear form (both in its ideology and in reality) a double challenge to the cultural establishment of the 1960s, locked in an unholy alliance. At root this was a nakedly commercial enterprise funded substantially by American money and supported by advertising, including that for such quintessentially British institutions as Weetabix, the Egg Marketing Board and the National Coal Board (Barnard 1989: 45). It was the epitome of unregulated broadcasting – no balance, no formal public responsibility, no recognition of copyright laws and no cultural standards. Equally it constituted a space where the young could compose their cultural identity (both through the music and through the very act of listening to an unauthorized station). For some, too, pirate radio was a form of local radio; such stations as Radio Essex and Radio Scotland announced a clear regional identity, while Radio Caroline sought direct contact with its audience through the lines of cars on the Essex coast, which in the evening flashed their lights within range of the *Mi Amigo* anchored off Frinton-on-Sea. Further, while a centrally prescribed Top 40 was often the core of the play list, other minority cult programmes (Mike Raven's blues on Radio 390, John Peel's 'Perfumed Garden' on Radio London) were able to flourish on the margins.

Legal restrictions on advertising both goods and services forced virtually all the pirates to cease broadcasting in August 1967. Their existence did, however, accelerate the pace of change in legal British radio in three respects. From September 1967 the BBC split their existing Light Programme into two channels, with a new Radio 1 designed to combine a watered down Top 40 format (and many of the pirate DJs) with some existing BBC programming. Second, from October 1967 the first of the new BBC local radio stations opened, following up ideas proposed in the Pilkington Report but clearly accelerated into actuality by the pirates. Legal commercial radio had to wait until the election of the Heath government of 1970; here the early promotion of radio competition for the BBC provided a particularly clear opportunity to contrast free-market Conservatism with statist Labour, and the first ILR stations opened in 1973.

While radio found a new post-television role, the national press entered a period of considerable uncertainty. The decade began with the closure of that classic middle-market paper, the liberal *News Chronicle* in autumn 1960. Despite still selling over a million copies a day (four times more than *The Times*), its readers were too old and too poor to be of sufficient interest to the advertisers, whose control over the fate of papers had re-asserted itself after nearly two decades in which they had been severely restricted by the effects of newsprint rationing. The growing power of television, both in attracting advertising revenue and in establishing itself as the pre-eminent national news medium, also had its effect during the decade – and a clear pattern of increasing polarization within the newspaper market between the qualities and the tabloids emerged. In 1960 four middle-market 'populars' (the *Daily Express, Daily Mail,*

Daily Herald and the *News Chronicle*) sold a total of over 9 million copies daily – around 60 per cent of the market. By 1971 only the first two of these had survived, selling 5 million – barely one-third of the total sales. As the *Express* began its long slow decline from a dominant position in the mid-1950s (*the* paper of affluence), so the *Daily Mirror* reached new heights (outstripping even its success of the late 1940s), selling over 5 million copies a day in the mid-1960s; it was a paper with no obvious competitor at the lower end of the market, and was revelling in a period of Labour dominance. Quality paper sales also improved, from under 12 per cent to 16 per cent during the decade, benefiting from the growth in the educated middle class.

The paper that tells the story of the decade is the *Daily Herald*. During the 1930s this TUC-backed paper had momentarily led national circulation, but by the late 1950s its circulation had fallen, its readership had aged and was too heavily represented in social classes D and E to attract advertisers. In 1961 it was bought by IPC as part of a wider purchase of the Odhams Group. A condition of the sale was that they guaranteed to maintain the paper for at least seven years. Initial attempts to improve sales failed, and in 1964 an entire re-launch was planned under a new title, *The Sun* – a middle-market broadsheet paper aimed at the new young left-of-centre generation. The moment of launch seemed timely, only weeks before Wilson's election victory in October 1964. However the fate of the IPC *Sun* paralleled that of the Wilsonian social-democratic consensus of the mid-1960s, although its failure came a year earlier and was more spectacular. By 1969 sales had fallen below 1 million, and a commercial solution had to be found. A further re-launch as a downmarket tabloid was ruled out since IPC would have been foolish to launch a competitor to their own *Daily Mirror*; equally it would be expensive and risking an industrial dispute to go for closure. The cheapest option was to sell – to a relative newcomer to the British newspaper industry, who had just bought the *News of the World*, Rupert Murdoch. This was, of course, to inaugurate a rather different kind of cultural revolution to that for which the 1960s is usually famed, and one that presaged the sharper political and cultural divisions to come in the 1970s and 1980s.

MAINTAINING CULTURAL STANDARDS

The continuing presence of a commercial mass media was only one of a number of threats that defenders of traditional cultural standards had to contend with during the 1960s. In Britain such standards are typically maintained as much by informal assumptions as by formal codifications. Nevertheless, during the 1960s a number of key sites of cultural reference can be identified as instrumental in the setting of artistic norms and standards and, equally important, as possessing the power, influence and material resources to make their judgements operative. Writing at the end of the decade, the 'underground' poet and impresario Mike Horovitz was still protesting that 'as long as the weekend reviews, Arts Council/ BBC/Printing House Square and university conspiracies are looked up to as the acme of good taste and reputations, poetry and the arts are lost to the mercies of state-political control' (Horowitz 1970: 8). Horovitz here links commercial organizations (*The Times*, other journals) with a number of quasi-state organizations (universities, BBC, the Arts Council) as a single cultural power-bloc. Such a view has a good deal of plausibility. Certainly the same kinds of people, and often the very same people, occupied key positions in all of them – and there were clear overlaps of intention between the cultural discriminations of the publicly funded bodies and the identification of a distinctive quality readership by up-market newspapers and 'serious' literary publishers. In the 1960s such institutions increasingly found their assumptions and practices coming under challenge from both the commercial imperatives of a rapidly expanding and competitive cultural market and the call for a wholesale re-definition of cultural values by alternative, avant-garde and explicitly political groups. By focusing especially on two major institutions, one publicly funded (the Arts Council) and one a commercial company (Penguin Books), the range of responses of such bodies to these pressures and new opportunities can be well illustrated.

Like a number of representative postwar institutions, the Arts Council had its origins in measures taken as an emergency response to wartime conditions, when its immediate predecessor CEMA (Council for the Encouragement of Music and the Arts) had been set up to preserve artistic standards, to provide 'opportunities for hearing good music and the enjoyment of the arts generally' and to encourage 'music-making and play-acting by the people themselves'

(White 1975: 25). From the beginning, however, the Arts Council was lukewarm about any commitment to the 'amateur' and, even, to any significant amount of regional cultural activity, and by the mid-1950s it had developed a very clear policy of 'few, but roses'. As William Emrys Williams, the secretary-general from 1951 to 1963, put it in 1958, the Council's duty was to 'maintain a limited number of what may be called the national institutions of the arts . . . where exemplary standards can be pursued' (Williams, 1958: 5). In the 1950s the main job of the Arts Council was the sustaining of the major national (i.e. London) musical institutions; in 1959–60 Covent Garden and Sadler's Wells together received 55 per cent of all Arts Council funding (music as a whole received 75 per cent). Meanwhile all the regional offices had been closed (the last in 1956) and the total drama budget (at £112,000) was only 9 per cent of the whole, and less than a quarter that of Covent Garden alone.

The early 1960s saw the beginnings of a change. During the 1950s the total Arts Council funding had remained virtually static, averaging only 5 per cent increases between 1952 and 1960 (when it stood at £1.2 million); between 1960 and 1964 it more than doubled, although still within a policy framework of mainly funding the major national institutions, to which had now been added the Royal Shakespeare Company, following the opening of its London base at the Aldwych in 1960, and the National Theatre, which first opened at the Old Vic in 1963. The four institutions in 1964–5 shared 53 per cent of the total budget, now £3.2 million, with the drama proportion having risen to 20 per cent. There then followed a period of rapid growth and, of equal importance, of more varied policy and practice. Following the Labour election victory in October 1964, Harold Wilson appointed Jenny Lee as the first ever Minister for the Arts, and within a few months of taking office a White Paper, *A Policy for the Arts*, announced a transfer of responsibility of Arts funding from the Treasury to the Department of Education and Science. This was to inaugurate a significant expansion of the Arts Council's remit, which now came to include all literature (rather than just poetry), an attempt to assist in 'housing the arts' (123 schemes were aided by 1971, including 36 theatres), a re-commitment to regional policy (funding for regional arts associations, RAAs, rose from £33,000 in 1985 to nearly £250,000 in 1970) and the inclusion of new art forms as eligible for support (jazz was funded for the first time in 1967).

The scale of the overall increase in the Arts Council budget during this period ensured that the basic policy of underwriting the prestigious national institutions could still be sustained. The grant nearly trebled between 1965 and 1971 (to £9.3 million), far outstripping the growing problem of inflation (annual rates still below 6 per cent), and from the mid-1960s a new set of expectations about the Arts Council's role began to emerge. As the Council's annual report put it in 1965–6, there was the sense of 'a transition from the poor-law technique of limiting our assistance to a bare subsistence level, with stringent means tests, towards a system of planned subsidies for improvement and growth' (Hewison 1986: 80).

Such a possibility brought problems as well as opportunities for artists. There was now much more to gain or lose in being deemed 'worthy of support on grounds of artistic merit' than previously; equally, the question of what kind of responsibility was incumbent upon artists funded in this way had become more pressing. Were they responsible to the government, the public (however conceived), the cultural inspectors of the Arts Council (who might well be determining whether funding was renewed) or their own individual consciences and sensibilities? At the same time the wider cultural climate of the mid-1960s, with its fast commercial expansion in youth, popular and pop cultures, was producing new and sometimes unrecognizable forms of artistic activity that the Arts Council had to try and fit into its existing categories, and that certainly did not fit into that traditional category of 'amateur' dramatics and music-making against which the Arts Council was still setting its face. In 1972 Lord Goodman, chairman of the Arts Council since 1965, told his fellow lords, 'I speak for the Arts; I do not speak for amateur theatricals' (Hutchinson 1982: 50).

In the late 1960s the Arts Council attempted to come to terms with these 'new activities', as part of its wider attempt to set the cultural agenda. In 1968, in parallel with its working party on the obscenity laws (which reported in 1969 that the relevant Acts should be repealed), a sub-committee under the Tory 'wet' Sir Edward Boyle was set up to advise the Council how to handle these 'new activities' (particularly problematic were mixed-media events, performance art and anything else that did not have a clearly defined artistic product that fell within the terms of an existing specialist panel). In the Council's 1968–9 report, Goodman noted that 'We have endeavoured to throw a bridge across to what we loosely describe as the 'new activities', needless to say of the

young . . . . We have tried to remain contemporary and "with it" '
(Arts Council 1969: 6). A lengthy metaphor about small barques,
hurricanes and navigational skill then followed, which embodied
the style of patronizing good humour with which he clearly felt the
Council should deal with the subject. An equally revealing comment
is the Arts Council assistant secretary's memory that 'one wondered
whether the Crazy Gang had broken into the committee room at
105 Piccadilly' (White 1975: 255).

   In the event, as a result of Boyle's report, a New Activities
Committee was set up for 1969–70, with a budget of £15,000; among
activities supported in that year were the music of Cornelius
Cardew, the performance art of Bruce Lacey and the theatre of
Inter-Action, the People Show, Portable Theatre and the Pip Simmons Theatre Group. Goodman's urbane tone of toleration was
maintained in the 1969–70 Report, where he mildly rebuked the
press's response to the New Activities Committee: 'Why, I was
asked, have you subsidised a collection of weirdly attired, hirsute
bohemians . . . . Why are you stirring up anarchy in St. Ives and
communism in Cullompton?' (Arts Council 1970: 6). However,
within the Council itself there was more substantive disquiet. The
New Activities Committee failed to agree on the contents of its own
report in 1970, with the chairman and vice-chairman submitting a
minority report much less enthusiastic than the Committee's request
for a strengthened New Activities and Multi-Media Committee with
a £100,000 budget. In July 1970 an internal Arts Council document
(co-drafted by Nigel Abercrombie, a former secretary-general, now
the chief regional adviser) supported the minority report, arguing
that the 'new activities' had been shown to be not 'of a sufficiently high standard, sufficiently national in concept and sufficiently responsibly envisaged in a professional sense both as to . . .
administration and . . . execution' to deserve support. Instead the
'problem' should be re-defined as a 'mainly regional one', where
local government and RAAs would judge the 'likely benefit to the
artistic life of the community' of activities that 'may be essentially
non-cultural in content and largely amateur in execution' (Hutchison 1982: 110). This return to a traditional way of declaring certain
activities 'not art' (or even 'culture') prefigured one of the major
cultural battlegrounds of the 1970s – the issue of who should fund
'community arts'. Meanwhile the Arts Council replaced the New
Activities Committee with an Experimental Projects Committee,
responding to Abercrombie's plea that, otherwise, 'genuine new

activities of the more orthodox and professional variety may unfairly come to be tarred with the same anti-cultural brush' (Hutchinson: 110); this committee lasted only until 1973. Other initiatives of the late 1960s were, however, more successful. Much new theatre was taken on by the drama panel, and the extent (and political implications) of fringe theatre funding was a recurrent feature of 1970s debates on public support for the arts. Literature funding, including bursaries to individual writers and a systematic attempt to influence the development of fiction writing and publishing, was another 1960s innovation that developed more substantially in the first half of the following decade.

Despite this entry of literature into the Arts Council's remit in the mid-1960s, its funding for this source remained very small (only around 1 per cent of the total budget). It was generally assumed that books and the habit of reading could be best funded by other means. There was, for example, a major expansion in local government spending on public libraries during the 1960s. Expenditure doubled between 1960 and 1968, and book issues rose from 397 million in 1959 to over 600 million by 1970. This was a case both of expansion and of a switch from commercial to public funding (both Smith's and Boots's lending libraries closed during the decade). Equally, however, it was a period of fast growth in the individual purchase of books. More titles were available. In 1955 just under 20,000 titles were published in Britain; by 1960 this had grown to nearly 24,000, and by 1970 to 33,000. Most notable was the expansion in paperback publishing. Between 1960 and 1970 the number of paperback titles in print rose from 6,000 to 37,000. Among paperback publishers Penguin remained dominant, still taking one-third of all paperback sales in the late 1960s, despite increasing competition from Pan (their oldest postwar rival) and newer brands such as Corgi and Panther (Laing 1983). The progress of Penguin during the decade constitutes a microcosm of some of the issues facing many publishers in trying to deal with (and perhaps influence) a fast changing cultural scene.

In 1960 Penguin was celebrating its silver jubilee. Founded in 1935, its reputation and success had been built in the 1940s on the basis of providing books ('at a price of ten cigarettes') of cultural quality that were popular and accessible. In 1960 Compton Mackenzie saluted the 'silver jubilee of Penguin Books as the silver jubilee of Penguin University' (*Penguin's Progress* 1960: 17). To mark both its own birthday and to commemorate the 30th anniversary of

D. H. Lawrence's death, Penguin proposed to publish a 'Lawrence Million' (100,000 copies of 10 Lawrence texts), including the previously banned *Lady Chatterley's Lover* (the new 1959 Obscenity Act, which allowed defence against obscenity by showing the book had literary merit, giving some confidence that it would now prove legal to do so). The notorious 'Trial of Lady Chatterley' in autumn 1960 was in fact the trial of Penguin Books, and the galaxy of churchmen, academics, public figures and famous authors whose appearance secured the not-guilty verdict placed Penguin Books at the centre of a distinct liberalization of public taste within an emergent dominant consensus. It is significant that one of the defence witnesses at the trial was Sir William Emrys Williams, who was not only secretary-general of the Arts Council but also a director of Penguin Books (for whom he acted as an editorial adviser). Williams had little difficulty in attesting to the novel's clear artistic merit. The acquittal also proved commercially successful. Within six weeks Penguin had sold 2 million copies (followed by a further 1.3 million in 1961). At a stroke, Penguin entered the new decade combining cultural centrality, commercial success and an aura of liberal permissiveness (with undertones of political radicalism). Throughout the 1960s it was the strain of trying to hold these three positions simultaneously that marked Penguin's development.

Another major initiative of the early 1960s was the Penguin Modern Poets series. Launched in 1962, it published an average of two volumes a year through the decade, selling overall about half a million copies by 1969. Each volume contained selections from three poets of the 1960s and defined itself as 'an attempt to introduce contemporary poetry to the general reader'. While most poets were British, the fourth volume (in 1963) featured the work of Corso, Ferlinghetti and Ginsberg, in a public recognition of the seriousness and significance of the poetry of contemporary American 'beat' culture. Even less obviously canonical were the 'Liverpool poets', Patten, McGough and Henri, in Modern Poets No. 10 in 1967 (subtitled *The Mersey Sound*). This volume featured a variation on the normal predominantly black cover – a mixture of red and black, containing silhouettes of Liverpool landmarks and a black-and-white photo of a pop fan. Cover design became an important signal of cultural adaptation by Penguin during the decade. Allen Lane, the firm's founder, had traditionally defined the nature of Penguin through its plain and straightforward covers. Such a style, appropriate for the austerity of the 1940s and early 1950s, was already under strain by the end of that decade. In May 1960 Tony Godwin, a successful London bookseller from Better Books, was brought in as an editorial adviser and he soon became chief editor; among other innovations in 1963 he recruited Alan Aldridge to become head of the Penguin fiction art department. Aldridge introduced new forms of cover design from art nouveau and pop art, and a philosophy that implied a need to shock or at least to engage curiosity, with developments in Penguin cover styles that matched those in high-street fashion and pop LP sleeves.

Penguin non-fiction also became re-energized, with the revival of Penguin Specials, its 'What's Wrong with Britain' series (in the run-up to the 1964 election) and the formation of what became a radical Penguin Education section in 1966. Together these initiatives reflected a return to the more sustained engagement with contemporary social issues that had characterized prewar and wartime Penguins. In particular, Penguin became the publishers of new kinds of contemporary cultural analysis, with paperback versions of Hoggart's *The Uses of Literacy* (1958), Williams's *Culture and Society* (1961) and *The Long Revolution* (1965), and commissioned original texts – Williams's *Communications* (1962) and the more Leavisite compilation *Discrimination and Popular Culture* (1964), edited by *Scrutiny* veteran Denys Thompson. It was also Penguin Books that provided funds to assist in the setting up of Richard Hoggart and Stuart Hall's Centre for Contemporary Cultural Studies at Birmingham University from 1964.

It was this relatively serious side of the new cultural climate that particularly appealed to Allen Lane. During the mid-1960s he became increasingly concerned that Godwin's marketing policy (whatever its commercial success) might be dissipating the traditional unitary Penguin identity. Some cover designs had upset authors, and in the case of one book, Sine's *Massacre* (comprising satirical cartoons of a violent, religiously offensive and scatological kind), Allen Lane himself took offence and personally organized the burning of all the copies (see Morpurgo 1979: 346). In mid-1967 Godwin left and the cover designs became rather more muted, at least for a time. Lane had, however, less reservation about more explicitly political radicalism. Penguin remained a major publisher of the British New Left through the late 1960s. *The May Day Manifesto 1968* (edited by Raymond Williams), offering the Left alternative programme to that of the Wilson government, the proceedings of the Dialectics of Liberation conference (including speeches from

Marcuse and Stokely Carmichael), edited by Cockburn and Blackburn as *Student Power* (1969), Horovitz's anthology of underground
poetry *Children of Albion* (1969) – all these key texts of the would-
be British Revolution were published by Penguin, as had been those
of one of the few home-grown British gurus, R. D. Laing, *The Divided
Self, Sanity, Madness and the Family* and *The Politics of Experience*.

The late 1960s were, however, to be Penguin's final (as well as
perhaps its finest) hour as an independent company reflecting British progressive culture back to itself. After the purge of Godwin
and his associates in 1967, Lane himself had begun to look for
suitable partners for the company, and on his death in 1970 Penguin
was quickly merged with the publishing giant Pearson Longman.
By 1972, in a new political moment, the link between Penguin and
the Arts Council had been re-established when Patrick Gibson,
chairman of Pearson Longman, replaced Lord Goodman as chairman of the Arts Council in a move that must only have served to
confirm Mike Horovitz's perception of a cultural world run by a
self-perpetuating elite.

RE-MAKING CULTURAL INSTITUTIONS: THE NEW
AND THE ALTERNATIVE

While some new cultural content might be accepted by established
institutions (the Wednesday Play on BBC, *Marat-Sade* at the Royal
Shakespeare Company, the new poetry in Penguin), equally there
were many pressing reasons for setting up entirely new structures of
production and distribution. Such a step could be an indispensable
means of breaking into an otherwise closed commercial market or
a necessary political act in the spreading of the arts to a much
wider audience. It might be part of the attempt to create a whole
new alternative culture or simply the only way of creating the
required physical and material conditions for some new multi-media
or performance art project. Such reasons are not mutually exclusive;
many new enterprises combined two or more such motives, and
frequently discovered that their rationales had changed in mid-
stream. Two further general factors should be noted that influenced
the kinds of new and alternative institutions that arose. Issues of
scale (and initial economic outlay) within the different cultural
forms were crucial. It is relatively easy to start a small poetry
magazine of limited circulation (and of irregular appearance);
indeed, while these especially flourished in the 1960s, they have

also been one of the basic modes for the distribution of poetry throughout the twentieth century. Labour costs are small, investment minimal (depending on whether printing is contracted out) and contributors' costs usually negligible. Larger scale literary magazines are more difficult, and independent fiction publishing (in the sense of authors setting up a company to publish their own work) more difficult still. Theatre can be even more expensive, although late-1960s re-definitions of what constituted theatre and of where plays might be presented (streets, factories, pubs), together with the effects of Arts Council support, allowed a fast growth of new forms of theatre group. The mass media tend to be most expensive of all, both in production and distribution; there was no way into television, although a little independent film-making, pirate radio (piggy-backing illegally on existing distribution systems) and, most significantly, the underground press showed there were possibilities of setting up some alternative networks.

A second consideration is the degree of receptiveness to new cultural ventures created by the general economic, cultural and political environment. The first postwar decade had proved most unreceptive to radical, left-wing cultural activity. The thriving Left culture of the 1930s (in film, theatre, poetry and magazines) had been absorbed into the more general anti-fascist war effort and, in the period of the Cold War, had never re-emerged as a separate entity. From the late 1950s, however, two parallel (and apparently contradictory) trends encouraged new kinds of cultural adventure. On the one hand the speed-up in the consumer society (with the end of rationing, rise in real incomes and the price reductions in many consumer durables) opened up new possibilities in the retailing of all kinds of leisure and luxury goods. Equally the post-1956 realignments on the British Left (with the recognition that a Gaitskellite Labour Party and a Stalinist Communist Party were not the only alternatives) liberated thinking about what cultural politics might mean.

Examples of the first kind of development were successful new enterprises in fashion and furnishings. Mary Quant's Bazaar boutique opened in King's Road Chelsea as early as 1955, but it was not until the early 1960s that she made an extensive impact; the new informal retailing style made it 'a sort of permanently running cocktail party' (Harris *et al.* 1986: 55). John Stephen's first shop in Carnaby Street opened in 1959 and the cult shop of the late 1960s, Biba, in 1964 (the same year as Terence Conran's first Habitat shop). Spreading these fashions and designs nationally was greatly assisted by a related development within the quality national press, the rise of the colour supplement (initiated by the *Sunday Times* in 1962, and followed by the *Daily Telegraph* in 1964 and the *Observer* in 1965). While at first the frenzied activity, 'revolutionary' styles and emphasis on youth could be seen as part of a generalized 'anti-establishment' mood, by the end of the decade some were identifying these developments as part of the problem rather than the solution. On May Day 1971 Biba was bombed by the situationist-inspired Angry Brigade, in whose analysis the shop was part of the capitalist 'spectacle' needing to be demystified.

Among those on the Left in the early 1960s, there was no clear agreement as to how a new cultural politics should develop. The most self-conscious and publicized initiative was Arnold Wesker's Centre 42 which attempted to use the trade union movement as a base to bring art and culture to working people. Founded in 1960, its most active year was 1962 when it held six festivals (each a week long) in provincial cities and parts of London. The mixed programme reflected the varying intentions of those involved. Local artists' work, folksongs and jazz, and a production of *Hamlet* were all included, in a way that reopened issues from the mid-1940s about whether to present the best art to the people or, alternatively, to attempt the creation and support of a genuinely popular culture (as opposed to that supplied by the media). It was the lack of finance as much as disagreements over policy that resulted in a long slow decline, and the projected move to a permanent home in the Roundhouse in Chalk Farm in north London was never fully achieved.

More successful was a different route forward from the late 1950s, which grew out of the new cultural constituency created by CND. On the CND Easter marches (from 1958), music (mainly folk or jazz), poetry and, especially, the experience of living a different kind of life as part of a large collective of like-minded people were laying the basis for much of the counter-cultural practice of the late 1960s. Similar kinds of events were the growing number of jazz festivals, such as that at Beaulieu in 1960, where poets Mike Horovitz and Pete Brown met and decided to turn Horovitz's recently launched poetry magazine *New Departures* into a live 'circus'; by 1969 Horovitz was claiming '1,500 shows – involving spoken poetry with jazz, plays, mime, new music, electronics, speeches, film, light/sound projections, sculpture, dance' (Horovitz 1969: 321). It was also in these jazz festivals of the early 1960s (particularly the National Jazz and Blues Festival, held at Richmond) that the many open-air live concerts and big pop festivals of the late 1960s had their roots.

This emphasis on the live event, the cultural process ('performance', 'happening') rather than the fixed product was a central feature of much would-be revolutionary culture of the decade – which explains both why many existing cultural institutions simply could not accommodate new work and also why live theatre, although not in the traditional 'proscenium arch' sense, became the paradigmatic form of the counter-culture. Adrian Henri claims to have organized the first 'happenings' in England in Liverpool in 1962, while in the following year John Calder (publisher of key avant-garde figures, Henry Miller, Robbe-Grillet and Beckett) organized his second successive writers' conference at the Edinburgh Festival (that of 1962 had first brought William Burroughs to the attention of the British literary world), which this time incorporated its own 'happening' (a naked girl being transported in a wheelbarrow to the sound of bagpipes). An informal network of institutions and organizations now began to form to promote a range of new ideas and practices. The influence and example of America was central (this was one of the issues dividing more traditional New Left approaches from the evolving 'underground'); an American ex-airforceman, Jim Haynes, opened his innovative paperback bookshop in Edinburgh in 1959, followed by the Traverse Theatre Club in 1962. In 1965 he moved it to London and then opened the first Arts Lab in 1967. The poet Allen Ginsberg had always been an exemplary figure for Horovitz, and he figured centrally in the Poetry International event at the Albert Hall in June 1965, where the emphasis on poetry as performance and the role of the audience as vocal participants replaced more conventional ideas of poetry as safe words on a page that would hold still to be repeatedly scrutinized.

During the second half of the decade a whole range of live events was organized that proved increasingly difficult to categorize. The People Show, a group founded in 1966, combined 'techniques from music hall, happening, straight drama, cabaret, funhouse and children's party' (Nuttall 1968: 210); an early performance was a mixture of living sculpture and speech in the basement of Better Books in the Charing Cross Road. Better Books was another of the London venues where traditionally separate kinds of cultural activity were now mixed; in early 1965 its basement had staged the 'sTigma' environmental exhibition, the title of which referred to Alex Trocchi's abortive 'sigma' project. Trocchi, a Scot whose allegiances were to the American 'beat' generation, had chaired Calder's first Edinburgh conference, and in 1964 began circulating a number of pamphlets that attempted to outline the philosophy and plan of action for the coming cultural revolution. According to Trocchi, it was necessary to 'seize the grids of expression and the powerhouses of the mind' (Hewison 1986: 108), an interesting, but presumably unconscious, riposte to the secretary-general of the Arts Council's view in 1962 that 'If the power-houses [i.e. the great national artistic institutions] were to fail there would be a black-out of the living arts in Britain' (Hutchison 1982: 60). In Trocchi's view, such a 'black-out' would be replaced by a 'cultural jam session: out of this will evolve the prototype of our *spontaneous university*' (Hewison 1986: 109).

By invoking the idea of the university, Trocchi at once cited both the actual and potential material base of the new culture (students not only at university, but at teacher training colleges, art schools and technical colleges) and also one of the major institutional sites at which cultural conflict would be fought out. Starting additional poetry magazines and theatre groups, alternative bookshops or new galleries posed no serious threat to established institutions, providing they did not undermine their viability or authority; the same was true of such alternative educational operations as the Notting Hill London Free School or the London Anti-University of 1967–8 (set up following the Dialectics of Liberation conference at the Roundhouse in July 1967). Alternative universities could never hope to match the massively-funded core institutions of the nation's scholastic culture. It was necessarily within the universities and among the formally constituted student body that some of the fiercest cultural battles of the decade were fought; it would be difficult, and unproductive, here to try and separate the political and the cultural. Protests about Vietnam and *apartheid* took place alongside the living out of new lifestyles and the beginnings of challenges to forms of examination and to curriculum content. At the national level the Vietnam Solidarity Committee and the Radical Students Alliance (formed in 1966 and 1967 respectively) provided new focal points, while local disputes at LSE, Essex, Hull, Hornsey and Guildford Schools of Art and many other institutions flared up from 1967 onwards. There was no single set of demands or goals involved, but this only seemed to confirm Herbert Marcuse's analysis of the similar American situation as 'sexual, moral, intellectual and political rebellion all in one . . . in them perhaps a new type of consciousness is appearing, a new type of person with another instinct for reality, life and happiness' (Marcuse 1969: 372). Juliet Mitchell provided a rather more specific diagnosis of the cause of student unrest, pointing to the rapid expansion of numbers and the changed situation affecting students in arts subjects especially:

> Gradually, since the war, but far more acutely during the sixties, the position of students in the Arts subjects has been shifting out of its ivory tower possibilities . . . . The university has become the training ground for the agents of the consumer society . . . . University courses cling vainly to an appropriate tradition against whose conservative content students protest, while courses introduced to fit organically into their future jobs reveal a banality that condemns both themselves and those jobs. It is the Arts students who are the vanguard and mainstay of the Student Movement.
>
> (Mitchell 1971: 25)

It was certainly students, ex-students and aspiring students who provided the core of readership for the underground press that flourished at the end of the decade. As with radical cultural movements as a whole in the 1960s, there was a division within the alternative press between those publications that saw their task as political education and those that wished to preach (and exemplify in their very form and language) a new way of life. The very early *New Left Review* (1960–1) attempted to bridge the gap between these two positions with a popular magazine format; by 1962, however, a palace revolution had transformed it into a more heavyweight and self-consciously theoretical and international journal. *Peace News* (the CND newspaper) more successfully bridged the gap between the early 1960s New Left and the 'underground'. As the moment of mass support for CND began to pass and as many of its adherents began the transition into more extreme positions (either with regard to Vietnam or in terms of cultural politics), so *Peace News* reported on American campus riots, campaigns to legalize marijuana, the views of R. D. Laing and the Albert Hall Poetry Festival. The first editor of *It* (also known as the *International Times*), the most successful underground paper of the late 1960s, was Tom McGrath, a former *Peace News* journalist, while a forerunner of *It*, the *Longhair*

Times, was sold on the 1966 CND Easter march. *It* was launched in October 1966, with an 'All-Night Rave' at the Roundhouse (as an example of how far things had changed since Centre 42, the Roundhouse became a regular venue for counter-cultural events in 1967–8). *It* appeared fortnightly, with a format and contents designed to contrast strongly with both the establishment press and the traditional left-wing alternatives. At its peak, in 1969, it was selling around 40,000 copies, mainly in London.

Oz was also clearly a London-based magazine – a monthly launched in January 1967, and loosely based on the Australian *Oz* originally edited by Richard Neville in 1963. This had been an amalgam of *Private Eye* (itself launched in 1961 as part of the 'satire boom' of early 1960s Britain) and New York's *Village Voice;* the new *Oz* was much closer to *It* in its celebration of newer counter-cultural values (especially in the area of sexual freedom, which frequently turned out to mean freedom for men at the expense of women). *Oz* had higher quality production than *It* and, especially through the graphic work of Martin Sharp, set the visual styles for others to follow; it also achieved sales of 40,000 at its peak.

As the decade drew to a close the number of alternative papers grew, and the market became increasingly volatile. The (politically) revolutionary *Black Dwarf* was launched in June 1968, while the almost self-parodic *Gandalf's Garden* only briefly flourished in 1969. *Time Out* began on a very small scale in August 1968, but had grown to a circulation of over 40,000 by mid-1973, by which time such titles as *Red Mole, Idiot International, Seven Days, Ink* and *Frendz* had all come and gone. Both *It* and *Oz* (following legal battles and numerous fluctuations of fortune) effectively closed that year also, leaving only *Time Out* and the newly launched *Spare Rib* as significant survivors into the quite different cultural terrain of the mid-1970s.

CONCLUSION

As in all cultural struggles there are no final victories or defeats. While many (perhaps most) of the particular publications, theatre groups, bookshops and other institutions (or 'non-institutions' as Jim Haynes described the Arts Lab in 1969, shortly before its closure) failed to survive the chill economic winds and harsher political climate of the early 1970s, there were distinct legacies that did flourish. The women's liberation movement in Britain (and the major advances in the 1970s in the understanding of what constituted sexual politics) grew out of both the example of, and profound disillusionment with, the political and cultural alternatives developed in the late 1960s. The active fringe theatre culture and the struggles over the nature and funding of community arts made the 1970s a continuing battleground for issues of what kinds of cultural policy the state should finance. Even in the apparently closed world of broadcasting it was the late 1960s and early 1970s that saw the beginnings of the agitation for a more open system (which led, after many more twists and turns, ultimately to the formation of Channel Four). In all these fields the experiences of the 1960s taught those who followed that no cultural revolution that did not concern itself as much with transforming the institutions of production and distribution as with the character of the cultural message in itself would be worthy of the name. During the decade that followed it became increasingly clear that this was a lesson that in Britain had been learned as fully by the new political Right as by the post-1960s Left.

BIBLIOGRAPHY

Arts Council 1969. *Annual Report 1968–9*. London: Arts Council.
Arts Council 1970. *Annual Report 1969–70*. London: Arts Council.
Barnard, S. 1989. *On the Radio*. Milton Keynes: Open University Press.
Cockburn, A. and Blackburn, R. (eds) 1969. *Student Power*. Harmondsworth: Penguin.
Fifty Penguin Years 1985. Harmondsworth: Penguin.
Fountain, N. 1988. *Underground*. London: Routledge.
Harris, J., Hyde, S. and Smith, G. 1986. *1966 and All That*. London: Trefoil.
Hewison, R. 1986. *Too Much: Art and Society in the Sixties 1960–75*. London: Methuen.
Hoggart, R. 1958. *The Uses of Literacy*. Harmondsworth: Penguin.
Horovitz, M. (ed.) 1969. *Children of Albion*. Harmondsworth: Penguin.
Horovitz, M. 1970. *Resurgence* vol. 2 no. 12 /*New Departures* 5/Joint Issue.
Hutchison, R. 1982. *The Politics of the Arts Council*. London: Sinclair Browne.
Laing, R. D. 1964. *The Divided Self*. Harmondsworth: Penguin.
Laing, R. D. 1967. *The Politics of Experience*. Harmondsworth: Penguin.
Laing, R. D. and Esterson, A. 1970. *Sanity, Madness and the Family*. Harmondsworth: Penguin.
Laing, S. 1983. 'The production of literature'. In Sinfield, A. (ed.) *Society and Literature 1945–70*. London: Methuen.
Marcuse, H. 1969. 'On Revolution'. In Cockburn, A. and Blackburn, R. (eds), *Student Power*. Harmondsworth: Penguin.
McLuhan, M. 1964. *Understanding Media*. London: Routledge & Kegan Paul.
Mitchell, J. 1971. *Woman's Estate*. Harmondsworth: Penguin.

Morpurgo, J. 1979. *Allen Lane: King Penguin*. London: Hutchinson.
Nuttall, J. 1968. *Bomb Culture*. London: MacGibbon & Kee.
Penguins Progress 1935–60. 1960. Harmondsworth: Penguin.
Silvey, R. 1974. *Who's Listening?* London: Allen & Unwin.
Thompson, D. (ed.) 1964. *Discrimination and Popular Culture*. Harmondsworth: Penguin.
Tunstall, J. 1983. *The Media in Britain*. London: Constable.
White, E. W. 1975. *The Arts Council of Great Britain*. London: Davis-Poynter.
Williams, R. 1961. *Culture and Society 1780–1950*. Harmondsworth: Penguin.
Williams, R. 1962. *Communications*. Harmondsworth: Penguin.
Williams, R. 1965. *The Long Revolution*. Harmondsworth: Penguin.
Williams, R. (ed.) 1968. *May Day Manifesto 1968*. Harmondsworth: Penguin.
Williams, R. 1981. *Culture*. Glasgow: Fontana.
Williams, W. E. 1958. *The Arts and Public Patronage*. London: Arts Council.

FURTHER READING

The best starting point is Hewison's (1986) account of art and its social contexts. For the mass media this needs to be supplemented by Tunstall (1983), while Laing (1983) attempts a more analytical account of literary production and institutions since 1945. The language and data in the Arts Council's annual reports are a good indicator of how much changed during the decade, while Hutchison (1982) provides a concise introduction to many of the underlying issues. Morpurgo (1979) supplies the best general account of Penguin Books, and should be supplemented by *Fifty Penguin Years* (1985), which contains excellent material for considering design changes. A number of issues concerning broader changes in design and general consumption are raised in Harris *et al.* (1986). For alternative institutions see Fountain (1988) on the underground press, Nuttall (1968) on the general context, and Cockburn and Blackburn (1969) on challenges within higher education. Mitchell (1971) presents an early analysis of how the women's movement emerged out of the confusions of the late 1960s.

Chapter 5

From equality to liberation: contextualizing the emergence of the Women's Liberation Movement

Jane Lewis

INTRODUCTION

The Women's Liberation Movement seemed to erupt at the end of the 1960s and to bear little resemblance to previous 'waves' of publicly visible feminist activity. The media image of the movement was dominated by the 'bra-burning' – more correctly bra-dumping – that took place at the Miss America pageant in 1968. (A similar protest against the Miss World competition took place in this country in 1970.) The rhetoric of liberation, which demanded the end to women's oppression by men, was very different from that of equality used by earlier feminists, who petitioned both to join men's world of work and public office and to achieve greater recognition for what was accepted as women's work of housekeeping and child-rearing. The energy and anger of the Women's Liberation Movement made it a force to be reckoned with while also putting it beyond the pale of respectable pressure group action.

In large measure because the Women's Liberation Movement appeared so different from the feminisms that had gone before and because it comprised young women, it has been explained in terms of a reaction to the cult of femininity that was so strong in the 1950s and for most of the 1960s (Coote and Campbell 1982). But it will be argued that this is to miss some important links with the shifts in thinking that also informed the social legislation of the 1960s. The dominant reading of women's liberation is of an explosive movement challenging patriarchal authority and erupting out of nowhere. Indeed, we have very little firm idea as to where it did come from or who participated in it. While it was very different from earlier feminisms, it was nevertheless an outgrowth of, as much as a reaction against, particular intellectual, cultural and social currents. This essay suggests that in retrospect it is possible to see that the importance attached by the Women's Liberation Movement to personal life had much in common with those promoting social reform during the 1960s, who had no desire to challenge the gender order. In addition, it will be suggested that while the WLM did give rise (in the 1970s) to a much more sophisticated analysis of the relationship between the structures framing women's lives (identified by Mitchell in 1966 as sexuality, reproduction, production and socialization) that enabled it to break free of the more traditional feminist preoccupation with gaining equal treatment for like individuals, it failed to resolve the central dilemma of whether claims should be based on equality (in the sense of sameness) or difference. Finally, its commitment to generalizing from individual experience made it vulnerable in other fundamental respects.

1960s EQUAL RIGHTS FEMINISM

In 1968 the Six Point Group, a feminist organization set up during the interwar years, published a book to promote equality for women in order to mark the 50th anniversary of votes for women and to try and deter teenage girls from both early marriage and dead-end jobs. In it Nancy Seear, who had published a number of studies of women's position in industry, rehearsed the statistics of women's inferior position in the workplace and urged women to apply for higher level jobs. But she also made a point of saying that 'it would be hard to find anywhere the kind of feminist who argued that careers should be pursued at whatever cost to family life' (Hallinan 1968: 50). Such traditional feminism pursued a running battle (in which it was very much the loser) with the women's magazines, which continued to deliver a similar message – centred on catching a man – throughout the 1950s and 1960s. The readership for such magazines did not begin significantly to decline until the late 1960s.

Nineteenth-century feminists had pursued equal rights in the public sphere. Sometimes they refused the idea of sexual difference and emphasized women's common humanity and a faith in reason; sometimes they used the commonly accepted idea of 'natural' sexual difference (grounded in biological difference) to support their arguments. Millicent Garrett Fawcett, for example, suggested that women needed the vote as mothers in order the better to protect their homes. During the interwar years, organized feminism shifted the focus of its attention to women's position in the private sphere of the family, campaigning both for access to birth control and for family allowances, initially conceived of as including a payment for housework as well as for children. Before World War II, few feminists questioned the idea that women had to choose between a family and a career. While the War legitimized the idea of the 'working mother', the wartime conditions of female employment were held to be abnormal by a majority of women as well as men, and after the conflict was over the day nurseries closed that had made such extensive labour market participation by married women possible. It was Alva Myrdal and Viola Klein's book *Women's Two Roles* (1956) that was the first to suggest, extremely cautiously, that women might be able to be both paid workers and mothers, albeit sequentially, becoming first workers, then wives and mothers, and finally re-entering the labour market to become workers again. Their book was nevertheless considerably more radical than other feminist contributions of the 1950s. Judith Hubback (1957: 155), for example, granted college-educated wives the right to a life of their own only if 'the husband, the children and the home are not neglected' and as long as they had their husbands' full support and approval. Similarly, a Conference on the Feminine Point of View held in 1952, in which prominent interwar feminists such as Eva Hubback and Mary Stocks participated, announced that it fully acknowledged sexual difference; women were more compassionate than men, had more intuitive sympathy and a greater commitment to selfless personal service. Furthermore, girls were advised to expect their careers to be seriously interrupted by childbearing and should 'give this time joyfully not grudgingly' (Campbell 1952: 40).

In the context of the 1950s, Myrdal and Klein's ideas were courageous. Functionalist sociologists were lauding the male bread-winner family model, in which husbands and wives 'specialized' in terms of their roles, husbands becoming economic providers and wives carers and domestic labourers (Parsons and Bales 1955). Child psychologists followed the work of John Bowlby (1951) in associating delinquent behaviour in later life with 'maternal depri-vation', and policymakers such as William Beveridge expressed concern about the falling birth rate and the need to 'rebuild the family' as a crucial part of postwar reconstruction. Given this con-text, Myrdal and Klein developed their argument in favour of a 'bimodal' career pattern for women by stressing the needs of nation rather than of individual women. Agreeing that the nation needed the services of full-time mothers, they also argued – during a period of labour market shortfall – that it was extremely wasteful not to welcome women (especially educated middle-class women) back into the labour force. In fact, the 1951 figures on adult women's employment in the UK showed the first hint of the kind of two-phase career model advocated by Myrdal and Klein. After a sharp drop in the economic activity rate in the 24–34 age group, there was a very slight increase for married women aged 35–44. By 1961 this trend had emerged clearly, and by 1971 older wives were more likely to be working than younger ones. A book like *Women's Two Roles* helped to legitimize this trend; in the early 1970s it was still selling a steady 1,500 copies a year.

Like the Women's Liberation Movement, Myrdal and Klein focused on the relationship between family life and paid work, but there was a world of difference between their optimistic belief that women could combine home and work and the feminist analysis of the mid-1970s that the burden of the 'double day' underpinned the subordinate position of women in society. Myrdal and Klein were anxious not to adopt a notion of equality for women based on the idea that women were the same as men, and yet they also had reservations about making claims on the basis of difference. Such a tension has always been central within feminism (Scott 1988), although it became submerged for a while in the confident universalization of the female experience propounded by the Women's Liberation Movement. Myrdal and Klein opted to ground their claims for women's right to combine paid work and motherhood in an argument that emphasized the contribution women might make to economic progress, rather than in women's demands on the basis of an analysis of their position in society. This was in part a tactical decision, but it meant that Myrdal and Klein settled for a limited extension of women's participation in paid employment on what essentially remained men's terms, rather than calling for the radical restructuring of both paid and unpaid work.

By the early 1960s the climate of opinion was in many respects less hostile than that in which Myrdal and Klein had prepared *Women's Two Roles*, and yet there were signs – in terms of early marriage and childbearing, and high sales for women's magazines – that the 'culture of femininity' had an even stronger hold on the hearts and minds of young women. The bulk of British feminists writing during the 1960s continued in the mould set by Myrdal and Klein. As fears of population decline dwindled rapidly in the wake of the postwar baby boom, and as the shortage of teachers and nurses and other (traditionally female) service workers became more acute with the expansion of the postwar welfare state, so both the number of contributions calling for more effort to be devoted to persuading women to combine family and employment grew and their tone became bolder. By the end of the decade, many were drawing attention to discrimination on the basis of sex (something Myrdal and Klein had played down), calling for state intervention to secure equal opportunities, on the model of the Commission for Racial Equality, set up in 1965, and in imitation of the Equal Employment Opportunities Commission in the USA. But the nature of the arguments used showed little development from those used by Myrdal and Klein.

Those seeking to promote the possibility of married women combining motherhood and paid work in the early 1960s were able to write considerably less cautiously than Myrdal and Klein. In 1958 Richard Titmuss's 1952 Fawcett Society Lecture on the position of women was republished; this drew fresh attention to the difference between the options of the working-class mother of the 1890s, who would expect to spend about 15 years in a state of pregnancy or nursing, and her equivalent in the 1950s, who spent only four years of her life in such a state. This allowed writers to point out that after childbearing and early childrearing half women's total life expectancy lay before them, and to use this fact to push additionally for their re-entry to the labour market. Le Gros Clark (1962) also reiterated that earlier marriage, earlier childbirth and smaller families made it possible for married women to engage in paid employment, while labour market demand made it desirable. The problem was that the kind of thinking that pushed young women into marriage and motherhood early, thus providing them with the space for pursuing their careers later, also worked against the kind of planning that was needed if this was to be accomplished successfully.

An increasing number of female social scientists, most of whom shared a generalized commitment to improving the position of women, took up the study of what were perceived as the 'problems' posed by married women's paid employment in the late 1950s and early 1960s. Viola Klein went on to carry out two more surveys, in which she found that the 1951 Census had seriously underestimated the amount of married women's part-time work; in her representative sample of 1,068 women, 50 per cent worked part time. *Women's*

Two Roles had not been keen on the idea of part-time work, believing that it would prove disadvantageous to employers. But in practice virtually all the increase in married women's work during the 1960s and 1970s came from the expansion of this form of employment. Part-time work proved a cheaper and more flexible option for employers than Myrdal and Klein had envisaged, and in Britain, where childcare facilities were exceptionally limited, it proved the only feasible option for most married women. Researchers at the LSE carried out two influential surveys of women's work, at Peak Freans and amongst wives in Bermondsey during the mid and late 1950s (Jephcott *et al.* 1962), that also stressed the significance of married women's part-time employment and furthermore concluded (using school progress reports and records from the juvenile courts) that there was no evidence that any harm resulted to the women's children. This conclusion received important confirmation from an authoritative study by Yudkin and Holme, published in 1963, entitled *Working Mothers and their Children*, which reviewed both the British and American evidence concerning the dangers of women's work to children's welfare, most of it casting considerable doubt on Bowlby's conclusion that separation of a child from its mother resulted in 'delinquent character development and persistent misbehaviour'. Yudkin and Holme concluded (123) that while it was probably better for children under three to be with their mothers, 'in favourable circumstances' (which meant a stable mother substitute) many children could do without their mother's constant presence after the age of three.

The work of female social scientists, following that of Myrdal and Klein, relied on the marshalling of aggregate data much in the manner of a government report, and was designed to present a rational case for the consumption of policymakers. Unlike either early twentieth-century women social investigators or later activists within the Women's Liberation Movement, this research did not include interviews with working women or seek to investigate their perceptions. In addition, the data collected in the course of the surveys tended to be interpreted conservatively. For example, to Klein, young women's expressed lack of interest in returning to work indicated their overwhelming prior commitment to home and family. She recorded that there was no trace of any feminist pursuit of equality in her sample, only a growing sense that it might be lazy to stay at home and that there might be an obligation to engage in paid employment. Much of this may have been correct, but the last part of the analysis in particular represented a rather convenient realization of Myrdal and Klein's earlier prescriptions. These studies shared the faith in both the power of social scientific data to persuade and rational planning that characterized policymaking more generally under the Labour government of the 1960s.

By the mid-1960s the battle to legitimize a married woman working either full time after her children had finished school, or part time from an earlier stage in the child's development, was largely won. Women's labour market participation was accepted to be crucial for economic growth and social progress. Political parties were beginning to use the kind of social research carried out by Klein and Jephcott to produce catalogues of economic needs and female wastage. But advocates of married women's work still walked a tightrope. As Nancy Seear indicated in 1964, no (established) feminist would dream of asking women to put a career before marriage and family; but on the other hand most feminist observers viewed with alarm the falling age of marriage and childbearing (the average age of marriage fell to 22 for women during the 1960s, and three out of five births occurred to women under 25). This made it easier for employers and many parents to regard the further education or training of young women as a 'waste'. While women working outside the home had been a theme 'marginally present' in the popular women's magazines of the 1950s, it was entirely absent during the 1960s (Ferguson 1983: 55). A number of studies of the mid-1960s therefore began to address the issue of equal opportunities in schools. At the LSE, Nancy Seear (1964) investigated the lack of girls taking science subjects at O level, acknowledging their 'realistic' worry as to whether part-time work would be available after marriage in occupations such as engineering. The NCCL (1965) both deplored the fact that women remained unequal and seemed apparently indifferent to it, and exposed the huge differential in expenditure in science teaching per head between boys and girls (to the latter's detriment) that was sanctioned by the Ministry of Education.

Outside the world of social research and pamphlet literature, among some male commentators on women's position, there were the beginnings of suggestions that all was not necessarily well with young wives and mothers in the home, something that feminist social researchers of the 1950s and early 1960s did not dare to suggest. Doubts of this kind did not enter the women's magazines until the 1970s, with the beginnings of the use of the reader survey.

But in his controversial series of Reith lectures of 1962, G. M. Carstairs, a professor of psychological medicine, made reference to the incidence of mental illness among young married women who stayed at home with children. This had first been recognized in the late 1930s by Stephen Taylor, a doctor and politician, who had labelled the condition of many women living isolated lives on the new housing estates as one of 'suburban neurosis'. His solution was to recommend that they consider having another baby, rather than saving for another consumer durable. In 1963 the issue emerged again in the form of Betty Friedan's 'problem that has no name' – the description she accorded the loss of identity suffered by wives and mothers. While no writer working in the tradition established by Myrdal and Klein cited Friedan's work, Carstair's observation was picked up towards the end of the decade (Gavron 1966) and used as additional support for the idea that female talent was being allowed to go to waste. In 1967 a woman journalist, Elizabeth Gundrey, published a book about women who began a conversation with the sentence 'I'm so lucky to be happily married, but . . .' (Gundrey 1967: 11). The Women's Liberation Movement was to articulate women's loss of identity in wife and motherhood in such a way that other women were immediately able to recognize and empathize with it, but this was not part of the aims of the 1960s feminist social research literature, which was anxious to highlight women's competencies and under-used capacity rather than their problems.

The Labour and Conservative parties were agreed by the end of the decade that married women's work was crucial for economic development. In 1966 the Fabian Society estimated that Britain would need 400,000 more workers by 1970 to achieve a 25 per cent growth in output, and married women were the only substantial labour 'reserve' left (Young Fabian Society 1966). By 1968 the chorus of concern had become sufficiently widespread for the issue of possible sexual discrimination and its remedy to be introduced. Myrdal and Klein's original analysis had been anxious to avoid any suggestion of conflict between men and women. The emphasis was placed not on discriminatory practices, but rather on the advantages to be reaped from drawing on the unused pool of female skills. However, in 1968 Margarita Rendel, in a pamphlet prepared for the Fabian Society, stated as her main concern 'forms of discrimination in work, pay, education and training' (Rendel 1968: 1) and advocated the setting up of an Equal Opportunities Commission.

The Conservative Party brought out their pamphlet 'Fair Shares for the Fair Sex' in 1969, which also acknowledged discrimination against women but put its faith in work to change attitudes rather than in recourse to the law (see also Cooper and Howe 1969). The National Labour Women's Advisory Committee (1968) was alone in suggesting that not all discrimination against women was negative and that women needed a measure of 'protection' in the form of protective legislation at work and within the family (for example, in the form of alimony payments on divorce). This raised, albeit in what appeared as a rather reactionary form, the crucial question of the nature of the relationship between women's position in the family and their position in paid employment. Like Myrdal and Klein, the political parties focused firmly on conditions in the workplace and what could be done to accommodate women's 'dual role'. Little was said about the gendered division of labour in the home.

Myrdal and Klein had condemned the way in which housework, 'like no other work', lent itself to the dissipation of time and energy, and cited studies that suggested that married women who went out to work managed to reduce their housework by 10 hours a week if they were childless, and 30 hours if they had children. Elizabeth Gundrey (1967) gave practical advice as to how this might be achieved, calling for the 'rationalisation' of housework in a manner not dissimilar to the early twentieth-century teachers of the new subject of 'domestic science'. No social researcher or pamphlet writer on the position of women in the 1960s suggested that the work of the private sphere should be shared equally between husbands and wives. This meant in the end acknowledging that any married woman taking on paid work outside the home would inevitably shoulder a double burden. Certainly many writers suggested that women be praised rather than criticized for their double contribution, while at the same time playing down the burden imposed by housework.

Those arguing for women's right to combine marriage and motherhood with paid employment were anxious to avoid any notion of conflict. Married women workers were rather 'working wonders' with energy to spare (see, for example, Williams 1969). The case for greater participation by adult women in the workforce was made primarily on the grounds of national economic need; while there was also concern to promote greater choice for women, there was little by way of any gender-based analysis. The latter would have involved confronting the privileges exercised by husbands and by male workers. Myrdal and Klein were at pains to stress that, given the sexual segregation of the workforce, male workers need not fear female competition, and, given their accept-ance of the domestic division of labour, they were also prepared to acknowledge that husbands might feel that wives were doing too much and counsel against taking on a paid job. The logic of Myrdal and Klein's position meant that women had to be the ones to change; they had to be prepared to plan for an interrupted work career. Later contributors were more willing to acknowledge the existence of discrimination, or at least 'prejudice', on the part of men as employers, if not as husbands, and in 1968 Barbara Castle took the step of piloting through an Equal Pay Act (that became effective in 1975). But at least equal weight was given (for example, by the National Labour Women's Advisory Committee) to women themselves contributing to changing male attitudes by applying for higher grade and better paid jobs. The solutions to women's inferior position in society were always the same and reflected the limited nature of the analysis: more educational opportunity, in science and in higher education (the latter was substantially aided by the Rob-bins Report on higher education, PP Cmnd 2154, 1963, which both recognized gender inequality in education and recommended a major expansion of the university sector); more training and re-training for women re-entering the workforce; and a more flexible set of attitudes on the part of men as employers, for example regarding the provision of part-time work.

PERMISSIVENESS

The Women's Liberation Movement made the private rather than the public sphere the centre of its analysis. Three of the four struc-tures identified by Juliet Mitchell in her early (1966) exposition of women's position related to their role within the family, and these had not been touched by the more traditional 'women's equality' literature. Furthermore, Mitchell observed that 'it is difficult not to conclude that the major structure which is at present in rapid evolution is sexuality' (32). In part this observation derived from a recognition of new possibilities for sexual activity with the use of the pill. Surveys of sexual behaviour continued to reveal a large measure of traditionalism and conservatism among the population at large; for example, Geoffrey Gorer's survey of 949 men and 1,037 women's views on sex and marriage published in 1971 found that one-quarter of the men and two-thirds of the married women claimed to have been virgins when they married, and that a further 20 per cent of the men and 25 per cent of the women had had sex only with their spouse before marriage. Similarly, while Michael Schofield's (1965) sample of 1,873 15–19-year-olds revealed a considerable amount of 'heavy petting' (experienced by over one-third of the boys and under one-third of the girls), most boys expected to marry a girl if she became pregnant. However, it is possible that the attitudes and behaviour of the relatively small college-educated group, which was in turn extremely active within the WLM, was changing more rapidly than the population in general. In part Mitchell's observation must also have related to the profound shifts in moral beliefs that formed the backdrop to the wide range of 'permissive' legislation passed during the 1960s, of which the Divorce Reform Act and the Abortion Act had the most immediate effects for women.

The opening up of sexual morality as a subject of public debate had begun in earnest during the interwar years, when many of the manual writers still popular in the 1960s had first begun to rethink questions concerning sex and marriage in response to the challenges thrown down by 'sexual radicals', such as Bertrand Russell (1929), who questioned the need to regulate sexual relationships that did not involve children. In reply, moderate churchmen openly distanced themselves from the old church teaching that sex was sinful and that, while it was 'better to marry than to burn', the married state was necessarily second best to celibacy. They began to redefine the nature and purpose of sex such that it became both positive and capable only of its highest expression in marriage. For example, the Reverend Herbert Gray (1923), a Presbyterian minister and founder of the marriage guidance movement, argued that sex was God-given and should therefore be regarded as something beautiful, to be studied and 'rightly understood', rather than as something sinful. Following the sexual psychologists, Gray argued that, correctly handled, sexual passion provided the driving force for life. It was crucial that sexual expression be the fruit of body, mind and spirit, and it was this that distinguished love from lust. Love in turn was properly unselfish and permanent. Thus Gray arrived at the purpose of sex as an expression of married love. Gray joined forces with Maude Royden, a leading feminist and lay preacher, to stress additionally the importance of mutual sexual satisfaction in marriage, something that also characterized the writings of sexologists such as Marie Stopes, whose pioneering book *Married Love* (1918) had more to say on this issue than on birth control. But having defined sex as the expression of love, there was no logical reason why unselfish love, uniting body, mind and spirit, could not be found outside the institution of marriage. Nor could the possibility of divorce in the case of an impossibly loveless marriage be logically denied. In his influential work of moral philosophy, published in 1935, John MacMurray argued that sex was the expression of personality and could not be regulated by social institutions. Sexual morality had to come from within and could not be externally imposed. The recognition that marriage alone would not necessarily secure a moral sexual relationship – an idea that was firmly suppressed during the interwar period and in the years following the War – became much more of an issue in the literature of the late 1950s and 1960s.

After World War II considerable effort was devoted by churchmen, medical doctors and politicians to the task of 'rebuilding the family' and of securing the public institution of marriage. Politicians expressed concern about the rise in the divorce rate during the mid and late 1940s and were prepared to give a substantial grant to the marriage guidance movement in the hope of promoting reconciliation between husbands and wives. The Royal Commission on Marriage and Divorce, which reported in 1956, opposed any relaxation in the divorce laws and justified its views on the grounds that 'it is obvious that life-long marriage is the basis of a secure family life, and that to ensure their well-being children must have that background. We have therefore had in mind throughout our inquiry the importance of seeking ways and means of strengthening the resolution of husbands and wives to realise the ideal of a partnership for life' (PP Cmd 9678, para 37). The Commission viewed with great suspicion both the effects of women's 'emancipation', suggesting that some women did not realize that 'new rights do not release them from the obligations arising out of marriage' (para 45), and modern psychology, which in their view emphasized self-expression rather than self-discipline and over-emphasized the importance of sex in marriage.

The Commission was not alone in stressing women's responsibilities for family life. The emphasis on female failings was common to many other analyses of social problems centring on the family during the 1950s and early 1960s. Juvenile delinquency was linked by child psychologists and magistrates to married women's work, while child neglect became interpreted as a sign of maternal inadequacy. As Linda Gordon (1988) has recently observed, even marital violence became a sign of wifely dysfunction. The focus on women's need to adjust to their proper tasks of wife and motherhood was all pervasive. In the burgeoning field of marital counselling, ideas about the normality of traditional gender roles informed practice. Counsellors were told that it was crucial that wives accept their femininity and not feel resentment about their domestic responsibilities, while husbands' expectations would be affected by the extent to which their mothers had adjusted to the role of wife and mother (Wallis 1963). The emphasis was, above all, on the need for wives to adjust to what were considered to be their traditional responsibilities in order for marital stability to be secured.

And yet, by the late 1950s, fundamental tensions were emerging between the desire to prop up the public institutions of marriage and family life and the increasing importance attached to their private, relational aspects. In marital counselling, for example, while traditional ideas about the roles of husbands and wives informed practice, the method used changed from one of overt guidance to non-directive counselling, in which the aim was to increase the client's ability to recognize and solve his or her own problems. The outcome of such counselling could just as easily be agreement to divorce as reconciliation. Even in the case of a public sex scandal such as the Profumo affair in 1963, the political outcry centred on Profumo's lie to the House of Commons rather than on the details of the sexual affair itself (Wayland Young 1963). Increasingly, the trend among writers about marriage and the family was to focus on the analysis of personal life, to the exclusion of the external world. This in turn provided the space (whether this was the intention or not) for rethinking the ordering of personal relationships in their own terms, without the constraint of societal sanctions. Kenneth Walker and Peter Fletcher (1955), who had begun in the late 1930s to develop the idea of 'spiritual reconstruction' through the development of the personality in marriage, encouraged their readers to escape from a world saturated with utilitarianism into the higher life of personal relationships. They contended that neuroses were the result of a particular form of ignorance of personal life and that what personal life had to offer was above all love. A couple's love life should be understood, they argued, as 'discourse', or a form of conversation. This was not dissimilar from the much more famous analysis of Berger and

Kellner (1964) that talked about each partner writing and rewriting
the marital script. Like Walker and Fletcher, Berger and Kellner
wrote of such 'scripts' as if they were composed in isolation from
the world outside (Morgan 1985). The emphasis on love as the true
moral cement of relationships, rather than legal ties, meant that by
the early 1960s the argument that sex should be regulated from
within rather than from without was more broadly accepted. Theo-
logians began to express honest doubt as to what constituted 'good'
and 'bad' marriages and to acknowledge that while the cessation
of love was hard to verify, it was none the less the fundamental
ground for divorce (Bailey 1957).

Writers of sex manuals went somewhat further and began openly
to question the link between sex and marriage. When Eustace
Chesser questioned the value of pre-marital chastity in 1959, the
outcry was enormous. Chesser asked bluntly why there was a premium on marital virginity and whether a girl could remain a virgin
and yet lose chastity – a reference to 'heavy petting', which absorbed
American and to a lesser extent British writers on sex in the 1950s
(Weeks 1981). Chesser was not advocating promiscuous sexual
relationships among the young, nor extra-marital sex, but his matter-of-fact presentation of his position without any real attempt at
a moral defence caused grave concern. Published under the auspices
of the BMA, his book was withdrawn from sale and Chesser
resigned from the BMA. But the issue would not go away. The
reaction to the third of G. M. Carstairs's Reith lectures in 1962,
which also asked whether chastity was the supreme moral virtue,
provoked a similar fuss. In Carstairs's view, 'Our young people are
rapidly turning our own society into one in which sexual experience,
with precautions against conception, is being accepted as a sensible
preliminary to marriage, making marriage itself more mutually
considerate and satisfying' (51).

The degree of the shift in the debate over sexual morality that
had taken place since the late 1950s was signalled by the change
in the views of churchmen. In 1963 a group of Quakers published
a defence of homosexuality, using as their definition of sexual morality the idea that it could only come from within and could only be
based on the avoidance of exploitation of another human being.
Such a morality would, they argued, prove 'deeper' and more
'creative' and would release warmth and generosity into the world:
'The life of society desperately needs this warmth of contact and
intimacy . . . the emphasis on morality has so often gone with a

cold and inhibitive attitude' (Heron 1963: 100). With the benefit of hindsight it may be argued – in the manner of Germaine Greer (1985) – that such ideals failed, first, to perceive how a commitment to self-generated morality could feed into, rather than replace, the kind of emotional and material selfishness that was being condemned; and, second, to underestimate the power relations in society, particularly between the sexes, that would exert pressure on women especially to conform to the new morality, without any resort to more direct forms of exploitation. But the writing in the essay was powerful in its commitment, openness and invitation to a brighter world. Three years later, a group of Church of England clergymen came to similarly liberal conclusions about reform of the divorce law. The Bishop of Woolwich (Robinson 1963) had already publicly advocated a position on marriage and divorce 'based on love', whereby nothing could be labelled as 'wrong' – not divorce, not pre-marital sex – unless it lacked love. He also favoured making abortion a matter of a woman's individual choice. In 1966 the Archbishop of Canterbury's group on divorce law reform also stressed the link between sex and love and advocated that 'irretrievable breakdown' be made the only ground for divorce. Further negotiations with the Law Commission resulted in the passing of a no-fault Divorce Act in 1969, something that caused a leading legal expert on divorce to bemoan the fact that public morality was determined in the end more by the thinking of professors of sociology than by bishops (Latey 1970: 168).

In fact it was not the intention of politicians to give encouragement to more permissive behaviour. The 1969 Act was justified in terms of bringing to an end so-called 'empty-shell' marriages and permitting remarriage. Similarly politicians did not envisage the steep rise in the abortion rate after 1967. The roots of the moral and social reforms passed by Parliament during the 1960s may, for the most part, be traced much further back. The Divorce Law Reform Association dated from 1906 and the Abortion Law Reform Association had been active since the 1930s. But the intentions behind legislation say little about how it is received. While it was not the aim of politicians to move dramatically away from public regulation and towards individual consent, the idea that morality should come from within and should be based on love became, in the context of the 1960s youth culture, 'all you need is love', where love meant not so much unselfish love, uniting body, mind and spirit, as a more adventurous and experimental and, some have suggested, self-indulgent and highly stylized approach to personal relationships. When Drusilla Beyfus (1968) looked for couples to illustrate the English marriage of the 1960s, she deliberately sought diversity and began with the case of the cohabiting (upper-class) Alexander and (working-class) Rosie, who celebrated their LSD and freelove lifestyle.

THE WOMEN'S LIBERATION MOVEMENT

The WLM focused primarily on the private sphere and on women's sexuality and experience of marriage and family life. It paid relatively little attention to the kind of equality campaigns that preoccupied women such as Viola Klein or Nancy Seear, although some of the first women's liberation groups began as equal pay groups. Nor did it attach first priority to legal reform, although feminists became very concerned to defend the 1967 Abortion Act. When the WLM expressed concern about issues around paid employment it was more likely to take the form of campaigns supporting working-class women than tracts to deplore the wastage of professional women's talents. The successful 1968 Ford women's strike for equal grading was an important source of inspiration and the WLM offered support to the nightcleaners in the fight for unionization during 1970 and 1971. In its early stages, the WLM concentrated most on exploring women's feelings about their position, raising the individual woman's awareness of her situation, and insisting on individual choice. Suzanne Gail offered an early and revealing picture of wife and motherhood in Ronald Fraser's collection of personal accounts of work, published in 1968. Her strong feelings about her loss of identity and about the meaninglessness of housework routines was to be reiterated by many early participants in women's liberation. While the WLM also began to offer structural explanations of women's subordination, the root of popular feminist understanding lay in the interrogation of personal life, just as those promoting social reform during the 1960s were concerned with the personal foundations of morality.

The women who discovered feminism via women's liberation were in the main young. While reflecting on the absence of women in the public domain of the New Left during the 1960s, Sheila Benson (1989) commented that her generation of female socialist activists did not register either sexual discrimination or that women had not acheived equality with men in the postwar welfare state. In all probability a significant proportion of the women becoming feminists at the end of the 1960s were registering the discrepancy between the rosy world of equal expectations engendered by the college education that so many more women obtained during the late 1960s, and the reality of early marriage and children that followed. A majority would not have read Simone de Beauvoir's *The Second Sex* (1956), Betty Friedan's *The Feminine Mystique* (1963) or Juliet Mitchell's pathbreaking analysis of women's position in *New Left Review* (1966). That reading was done after consciousness had been raised about some aspect of a woman's personal situation; why, for example, she felt trapped or angry as a wife and mother. Raised consciousness depended on discussing experiences and generalizing from them. In this way 'the personal became political'. Even after joining the Women's Liberation Movement, these young women did not read the work of the established spokeswomen.

The WLM was diffuse. The activists who captured newspaper headlines were probably for the most part college-educated women who had also become involved in the student politics of the late 1960s. This connection has been traced in some detail for the USA, where the origins of the WLM have been closely connected to the activities of Students for a Democratic Society and the frustration of the women concerned at being confined to the traditional tea-making role. In this country the first women's liberation conference, held in Oxford in 1970, included many women active in socialist politics, but the strength of the WLM proved to be the way in which its main organizing structure – the consciousness raising group – could be and was used by women from all social classes and in very different circumstances. The nature of the consciousness raising varied considerably, depending on the composition of the group. But the numbers of women involved, and in which parts of the country, remains unexplored. Certainly the consciousness raising group built as much on women's traditional cultural forms – get-togethers over tea and coffee – as it did on 1960s socialist politics.

The activists and theorists of women's liberation were probably more radical than many of the consciousness raising groups that met. Socialist feminism was a stronger part of the WLM in this country than in the United States, and considerable theoretical effort was devoted to reconciling Marxism and feminism, an alliance that Heidi Hartman was later to refer to as an essentially 'unhappy marriage' (Hartman 1981). The emphasis on the analysis of personal experience, beginning with personal relationships and women's oppression within the family, was very much linked to the wider assault on authority being mounted by the student movement. Male authority and male power in the family and in the wider society were the targets. Young women wanted to attack the institution of the family as much as men, but the language of personal choice that they used was not dissimilar to that of the liberal reformers, who hoped in contrast to revitalize marriage and family life. However, women were at one and the same time in the position of attacking not just societal norms and values but, at the more personal level, the norms and values of the men in the student movement. These men might have been prepared to support abortion reform; but they generally believed that women's liberation would follow the socialist revolution and this must therefore take priority; and they also failed to understand that something like sexual liberation would have profoundly different meanings for men and women.

The early WLM in a very real sense set out consciously to 'discover' women; retrieving women's past and the beginnings of women's history was very much part of this feminism (Rowbotham 1989). The aim was not so much separatism (from men) – that came later – but celebration of a kind not unknown to earlier generations of feminist activists, especially the suffragettes. Personal freedom and self-expression were the most consistent themes of the movement. While the importance of social reform as a means to changing crucial structures of oppression was recognized and embodied in the central claim to more collective provision of childcare, somehow the temper of the movement was better captured in some of the campaigning slogans it developed (mainly in the 1970s), such as 'Y be a wife', and in the radical literature that circulated. Many influential articles were imported from the USA, such as Anne Koedt's 'The myth of the vaginal orgasm' (1970), but much was homegrown and published in new journals like *Shrew*. Attacking taboos, asserting the validity of female experience and demanding greater female autonomy were central concerns. The WLM was not interested in confining its claims to equality with men because it attacked male norms, structures and authority. But nor did it think through the basis of its claims, which were to some extent based on a claim to equal freedom and to some extent were grounded in a celebration of female difference. These two strands were to separate further during the 1970s and 1980s.

CONCLUSION

Traditional feminists had placed their faith either in an attempt to secure equal treatment by legislative means, such as the 1968 Equal Pay Act (implemented in 1975), that relied on comparing like individuals rather than addressing the structures in which they were located, or in an effort to find some way of fitting wives and mothers into essentially male employment structures on terms that were inevitably adverse. Those who were suspicious of equal treatment on men's terms were forced back on arguments that depended on an appeal to sexual difference. For example, Shirley Summerskill and the Married Women's Association opposed the fact that the 1969 Divorce Act permitted a spouse to divorce after five years separation irrespective of the other spouse's wishes, because they felt this would operate to the detriment of blameless wives and mothers who, it was argued, required protection. Activists in the WLM highlighted women's subordination to men, especially within the family, and called for a wide variety of changes, including social reform, such as more childcare, freedom of sexual expression and control over sexuality. The early WLM was more interested in exposing and attacking the institutional forms of men's power and authority, including male ideas about female sexuality, than it was in thinking about the kind of equality it wanted to see and the nature of change required to achieve it. In addition, the WLM remained vulnerable to problems arising from generalization on the basis of individual experience. It tended confidently to include all women in its analysis, when differences on the basis of social class, race and age were often overwhelming. Only recently has feminism begun to realize the necessity both of refusing the dichotomy between equality and difference, and of pursuing a strategy that pays more attention to differences and diversity in the female condition.

BIBLIOGRAPHY

Archbishop of Canterbury's Group on Divorce 1966. *Putting Asunder*. London: SPCK.
Bailey, Derrick Sherwin 1957. 'Marriage and the family: some theological

considerations'. In C. H. Rolph (ed.) *The Human Sum* London: Heinemann.

de Beauvoir, Simone 1964. *The Second Sex*. New York: Bantam.

Benson, Sheila 1989. 'Experiences in the London New Left'. In Oxford University Socialist Discussion Group, *Out of Apathy*. London: Verso.

Berger, P. L. and Kellner, H. 1964. 'Marriage and the construction of reality'. *Diogenes* 46, summer, 1–23.

Beyfus, Drusilla 1968. *The English Marriage: What It Is Like to be Married Today*. London: Weidenfeld & Nicolson.

Bowlby, J. 1951. *Maternal Care and Mental Health*. Geneva: WHO.

Campbell, Olwen W. 1952. *Report of a Conference on the Feminine Point of View*. London: Williams & Norgate.

Carstairs, G. M. 1962. *This Island Now*. London: Hogarth Press.

Chesser, E. 1960. *Is Chastity Outmoded?* London: Heinemann.

Clark, F. Le Gros 1962. *Women, Work and Age*. London: Nuffield Trust.

Cooper, Beryl and Howe, Geoffrey 1969. *Opportunity for Women*, Conservative Political Centre pamphlet no. 435. London: Conservative Party.

Coote, Anna and Campbell, Beatrice 1982. *Sweet Freedom: The Struggle for Women's Liberation*. London: Picador.

Ferguson, M. 1983. *Forever Feminine: Women's Magazines and the Cult of Femininity*. London: Heinemann.

Friedan, Betty 1963. *The Feminine Mystique*. London: Gollancz.

Gail, Suzanne 1968. 'The housewife'. In Fraser, Ronald (ed.) *Work*. Harmondsworth: Penguin.

Gavron, Hannah 1966. *The Captive Wife*. London: Routledge & Kegan Paul.

Gordon, Linda 1988. *Heroes of their Own Lives*. New York: Viking.

Gorer, G. 1971. *Sex and Marriage in England Today*. London: Nelson.

Gray, Herbert 1923. *Men, Women and God*. London: Student Christian Movement.

Greer, G. 1985. *Sex and Destiny: The Politics of Human Fertility*. London: Picador.

Gundrey, Elizabeth 1967. *Jobs for Mothers*. London: Zenith.

Hallinan, Hazel Hunkins 1968. *In Her Own Right*. London: Harrap.

Hartman, H. 1981. 'The unhappy marriage of Marxism and feminism: towards a more progressive union.' In L. Sargent, *Women and Revolution: The Unhappy Marriage of Marxism and Feminism* London: Pluto.

Heron, A. (ed.) 1963. *An Essay by a Group of Friends: Towards a Quaker View of Sex*. London: Friends Home Service Committee.

Hubback, Judith 1957. *Wives Who Went to College*. London: Heinemann.

Jephcott, Pearl *et al.* 1962. *Married Women Working*. London: Allen & Unwin.

Klein, Viola 1965. *Britain's Married Women Workers*. London: Routledge & Kegan Paul.

Koedt, A. 1970. 'The myth of the vaginal orgasm'. In L. B. Tanner, *Voices from Women's Liberation*. Chicago: Signet.

Latey, W. 1970. *The Tide of Divorce*. London: Longman.

MacMurray, John 1935. *Reason and Emotion*. London: Faber & Faber.

Mitchell, Juliet 1966. 'Women: the longest revolution'. *New Left Review*, 40. Nov./Dec.

Morgan, D. H. J. 1985. *The Family, Politics and Social Theory*. London: Routledge & Kegan Paul.

Myrdal, Alva and Klein, Viola 1956. *Women's Two Roles*. London: Routledge & Kegan Paul.

National Labour Women's Advisory Committee 1968. *Discrimination Against Women*. London: Labour Women's Conference.

NCCL 1965. *Women*. London: NCCL.

Parsons, T. and Bales, Robert F. 1955. *Family Socialization and Interaction Process*. Glencoe, Illinois: Free Press.

PP (1956) Cmd 9678. *Report of the Royal Commission on Marriage and Divorce*. London: HMSO.

PP (1963) Cmnd 2154. *Report of the Committee appointed by the Prime Minister on Higher Education*. London: HMSO.

Rendel, M. 1968. *Equality for Women*, Fabian Research Series no. 268. London: Fabian Society.

Robinson, John A. T. 1963. *Honest to God*. London: SCM Press.

Rowbotham, Sheila 1989. *The Past is Before Us: Feminism in Action since the 1960s*. London: Pandora.

Russell, Bertrand 1929. *Marriage and Morals*. London: Unwin Paperbacks.

Schofield, M. 1965. *The Sexual Behaviour of Young People*. Harmondsworth: Penguin.

Scott, Joan 1988. *Gender and the Politics of History*. New York: Columbia University Press.

Seear, Nancy *et al.* 1964. *A Career for Women in Industry*. London: Oliver Boyd.

Stopes, Marie 1918. *Married Love*. New York: Critic and Guide Company.

Taylor, Stephen 1938. 'The suburban neurosis'. *Lancet* 1: 759.

Titmuss, R. M. 1958. 'The position of women'. In R. M. Titmuss, *Essays on 'The Welfare State'*. London: Allen & Unwin.

Walker, K. and Fletcher, P. 1955. *Sex and Society: A Psychological Study of Sexual Behaviour in a Competitive Culture*. London: Frederick Muller.

Wallis, John 1963. *Thinking About Marriage*. Harmondsworth: Penguin.

Wayland Young 1963. *The Profumo Affair: Aspects of Conservatism*. Harmondsworth: Penguin.

Weeks, J. 1981. *Sex, Politics and Society*. London: Longman.

Williams, Pat 1969. *Working Wonders: The Success Story of Wives Engaged in Professional Work Part-Time*. London: Hodder & Stoughton.

Young Fabian Society 1966. *Woman-Power*. Young Fabian Pamphlet no. 11. London: Fabian Society.

Yudkin, S. and Holme A. 1963. *Working Mothers and their Children*. London: Michael Joseph.

FURTHER READING

Ferguson (1983) provides a good guide to the 'cult of femininity' literature, especially women's magazines, that formed the backdrop to both equal rights feminism and the emergence of the women's liberation movement. On equal rights feminism, Hallinan (1968) provides an account of its aims, but Myrdal and Klein (1956) provide the classic description of the period. On the women's liberation movement, Rowbotham (1989) and Coote and Campbell (1982) are guides. Weeks (1981) gives the crucial broader background on the politics of sex and sexuality.

Chapter 6

A critical stage: drama in the 1960s

Martin Priestman

INTRODUCTION: SOME STORYLINES

The question 'Was there a cultural revolution in British theatre in
the 1960s?' would seem to demand an overwhelming 'Yes'. Not
only did the theatre itself change beyond recognition, but it focused
the many changes taking place in the surrounding society more
sharply than any other then-established art-form. Behind this bald
fact, however, there lurk many possible interpretations of the exact
significance of the developments involved; interpretations both
affecting and affected by our understanding of the present. In this
chapter I shall consider some of the ways in which the stage focused
the age, and the changes in such matters as the audience, funding
and censorship laws that enabled it to do so. But I shall also be
considering some of the means by which our present array of readings has been mediated to us. It will therefore be useful to have an
initial shuffle through some of the various 'stories' told about drama
in the 1960s.

The most broadly accepted story, some of whose details I shall
be filling out later in this chapter, can be briefly sketched as
follows. In the late 1950s a conservative and complacent middle-
class theatre (routinely caricatured in terms of French windows and
tennis parties) was displaced by a three-pronged attack headed by
John Osborne's *Look Back in Anger* (May 1956), a visit by Bertolt
Brecht's Berliner Ensemble (August 1956), and the slightly earlier
first English staging of Samuel Beckett's *Waiting for Godot* (August
1955). Thereafter the theatre that mattered remained split into the
same three camps: 'angry' – young, rebellious, working-class or
lower-middle-class characters finding their voices in naturalistic
contexts; Brechtian – non-naturalistic, using caricature, back-pro-

jections, harsh songs and nothing-up-the-sleeve sets to confront the audience with stark political choices; and Absurd – using underdog characters, austere settings and conversational non sequiturs to exemplify a general 'post-God' human condition. In the early 1960s Arnold Wesker, John Arden and Harold Pinter represented each camp respectively, before handing on their batons to David Mercer, Edward Bond and Tom Stoppard. The advent of the 'fringe' circa 1968 complicates matters slightly for a time, but when the mist clears writers like Barry Keefe and groups like 7:84 and The People Show have picked the same batons up and carried on running with them well into the 1970s.

Another story, from the more committed Left, would discount this picture of unbroken progress, except in the case of Joan Littlewood's socialist/Brechtian Theatre Workshop, which created the model for the post-1968 touring political fringe before settling in the Theatre Royal, Stratford East, in London's East End, as early as 1953. It would also point out how the Workshop's West End successes in plays by Brendan Behan and Shelagh Delaney (1956–8), and above all in the group-devised *Oh What a Lovely War* (1963), drastically rewrote the theatrical agenda in terms not only of the classes deemed presentable but also of possible modes of presentation (including especially the use of popular forms to challenge official political images). It might then go on to show how committed work in the Littlewood tradition, including that of such respectable-theatre renegades as John Arden, Margaretta D'Arcy and John McGrath, has been consistently starved of subsidy.

In another story, perhaps closer to the majority experience of the theatre-going classes, 'angry young men', 'kitchen-sink plays' and 'people living in dustbins' chiefly constituted an unpleasant press rumour and cartoonists' standby. The most bearable pretentious foreign influence was at first (ironically) that of Bertolt Brecht, thought to be behind such solid historical dramas as Terence Ratti-gan's *Ross* and Robert Bolt's *A Man for All Seasons* (both 1960), where the disturbance of the unities by back-projections and over-familiar narrators was actually quite helpful in allowing classical stars like Alec Guinness and Paul Scofield to wrestle tragically with their consciences in full costume (even the 'angry' Osborne allowed Albert Finney to do much the same in *Luther*, 1961). Harsh songs and drab-but-revolving sets also accompanied Lionel Bart's *Oliver* (1960), the one British musical to match Rogers and Hammerstein, while the 'epic' techniques of Peter Shaffer's lavishly costumed *The*

Royal Hunt of the Sun (1964) gave the new National Theatre its first undoubted hit. Later in the decade the National had another huge hit with Tom Stoppard's *Rosencrantz and Guildenstern Are Dead* (1967), which finally managed to make sense of all that Beckettian dustbin business in a reasonably undistressing way, and without all the lower-class violence you used to get in Pinter. By 1970 the trick of tingeing middle-class comedy with Absurdism was being mastered by such rising stars as Simon Gray, Alan Bennett, Michael Frayn and, above all, Alan Ayckbourn, ensuring the resurgence of a West End (i.e. bums-on-seats, paying) sector. In this story, then, the great triumph of 1960s British theatre was its successful absorption and detoxification of various initially threatening outside influences.

One further story needs perhaps only to be mentioned; it is the simple continuation of the still immensely powerful West End empire of H. M. Tennent's 'Binkie' Beaumont, whose leading lights from the 1930s onward had been Somerset Maugham, Noel Coward and Terence Rattigan. Were it not for subsidy, Beaumont would have had the power and probably the will to strangle at birth almost every play so far named, apart from those of Robert Bolt, the acclaimed 'successor to Terence Rattigan' (Huggett 1989: 511). Tennent's 'serious-theatre' empire was in turn only a minor cog in the nationwide machine of interlocking theatrical enterprises known as 'The Group', headed by Prince Littler, whose major source of business was American musicals (see Elsom 1976: 12–16; and Marwick 1982: 84–5).

AUDIENCES, FUNDING AND CENSORSHIP

None of the decade's real changes of direction in writing and presentation would have been possible without the existence of a new and newly responsive kind of audience. Famously, the element that made the difference was the newly 'classless' generation of educated young adults produced by the 1944 Education Act, as part of the socially enlightened 1940s and 1950s legislation that was to prove a somewhat one-off benefit of the class-cohesion of wartime. There really was, however briefly, a significant correlation of experience between this significant new audience fragment and such working- or lower-middle-class writers as Osborne, Wesker, Pinter, Behan and Delaney. Hence Kenneth Tynan's ironic reminder that *Look Back in Anger*'s 'minority' appeal was limited to 'roughly 6,733,000, which is the number of people in this country between the ages of twenty and thirty', but in particular to 'the class of State-aided university students' recently dismissed by Somerset Maugham as 'scum' (see Tynan 1984: 176–8).

At the same time, this question of audiences can be oversimplified. Despite a few shocks, the theatre clearly continued to attract the middle-aged and/or middle-class spectators sometimes claimed to have been routed. John McGrath (1981: 8–9) argues that the new young theatre audience of the 1960s, there in such numbers because of the 1940s baby-boom, was simply seeking the most painless cultural route into the middle class it was anyway being invited into with open arms. In any case, many of the most acclaimed post-1956 dramatists went to public school and/or university (Oxbridge accounting for a high proportion), a very high percentage of a polled Royal Court audience were graduates, and an even higher percentage current undergraduates (see Bigsby 1981: 13–15). This would perhaps mean little in a truly democratic higher education system, but in this country it is arguable that after an initial spurt (the 'boomers' again), the 1944 Education Act did little to alter the overall proportion of working-class students. Against this backdrop, it is perhaps significant that McGrath himself owed his first success, at Oxford, to a review by a fellow-Oxonian (Kenneth Tynan, indeed); and that his two volumes of polemic against élitist theatre started life as Cambridge lectures.

Another key factor making for change was funding. The growth of a subsidized 'public' sector decisively altered the balance of the theatre as a whole. Already during the war, the Council for the Encouragement of Music and the Arts (CEMA) had dispersed a light scatter of subsidy over the worthier end of the market, and semi-accidentally taken on a larger responsibility for the Bristol Old Vic (see Rowell and Jackson 1984: 78–9). Its 1946 replacement by the Arts Council, accompanied by legislation empowering local councils to support theatre from the rates, made possible: the Royal Court Theatre's ground-breaking strategy of encouraging new work, with a 'right to fail', from 1956; the transformation of the Shakespeare Memorial Theatre at Stratford into the Stratford and London based Royal Shakespeare Company, with yet greater powers of patronage for new writing (1961); and the creation of the National Theatre (at the Old Vic from 1963; on the South Bank from 1976), with a similar brief and (ultimately) even greater resources. In the regions the traditional pattern of touring productions before, after or instead of a London run, and the accompanying commercial 'empires' of touring theatres (such as Moss Empires, from which Tennent had initially emerged), began to break down and be replaced by new civic theatres with public money and (often liberating, but sometimes stifling) civic pride behind them; the first of these, the Belgrade, Coventry (1956), was responsible for the premières of Wesker's trilogy and Bond's *Narrow Road to the Deep North*.

With the 1964 Labour victory there was a quantum leap in the philosophy, and ultimately the reality, of state funding for theatre. Jennie Lee, the new Arts Minister, pledged money for a massive building programme that included numerous new regional theatres as well as the National on the South Bank and the RSC's Barbican theatre. The late-1960s explosion of alternative fringe groups was heavily reliant on, and perhaps partly created by, the raised chance of subsidy; at the same time as the state's powers of patronage grew, the paternalistic and undemocratic character of the Arts Council's boards came increasingly under scrutiny. What had earlier been seen as a modest facilitating function was now clearly a steering function, although this only really became evident in the 1970s and 1980s, when the running costs of the new buildings (pre-eminently the South Bank National Theatre, 1976) proved to have been seriously underestimated.

It is possible to overstress the notion of subsidy as 'a victim of its own success', to invidious effect. Despite much valuable research, John Elsom (1976) is in danger of doing this when he divides the decade sharply at 1964, the year of the Labour victory. The period 1956–64 was, apparently, a 'fruitful era' in which subsidy 'rose steadily, under a predominantly Conservative administration' from £820,000 to £3,205,000; while 1964–74 'began very optimistically, and ended in pessimism', as subsidies 'rose dramatically'. The really dramatic rises, however, belong to the inflationary 1970s; Elsom's own figures indicate only a healthy but still fairly steady increase of about £1m a year from 1964 to £9.3m in 1971. But the 1964 dividing line fits snugly with Elsom's later portrait of a drama of 'Many roads, few maps', where such gifted but confused dramatists as Edward Bond, Howard Brenton, David Hare, David Mercer and Tom Stoppard thrash around in a kind of oversubsidized primal soup made up of 'flights of fancy resting securely on Arts Council grants' where 'the right to fail . . . was a privilege that could be too easily invoked' (179). Such direct linkage of specific artistic judgements (the 'maps' may be thought to have emerged by 1976) and the growth of funding can easily suggest a proto-Thatcherite template dating the fall from the Labour years, and ignoring (for instance) the profound cultural changes of 1968 that generated the profusion of fringe activities, whose common denominator was a wholehearted acceptance of the notion and reality of 'poor theatre'.

One of these cultural changes was the abolition of the Lord Chamberlain's draconian and theoretically total powers of theatrical censorship. Since its role as the most mass of media in the Elizabethan period, the English theatre has always been particularly closely monitored by guardians of public morality and political orthodoxy; a situation constitutionalized at one time by a licensed soft-porn duopoly under Charles II and then by the famously corrupt Robert Walpole's 1737 empowerment of the Lord Chamberlain to scrutinize every last comma before performance, in retaliation against the (as it happens Tory) subversion of such riff-raff as Henry Fielding; a piece of legislation that arguably created the English novel. Though sexual content came to be publicly perceived as the chief object of such scrutiny, broader indications of political 'disrespect' and (vitally, for the emergent fringe) the freedom of performers to improvise in immediate response to events, were just as important. While other cultural forms (including, indeed, the Fieldingesque novel) have also had to fight long and hard for their freedoms, and all are still subject to suppression, litigation and quieter pressure from all kinds of directions, none was so directly under the thumb of the ruling establishment in its most traditional garb as was the British theatre from 1737 to 1968.

In fact 'the royal smut-hound' (as Tynan called him) had already lost several teeth during the much-publicized politico-sexual hypocrisies of the 1963 Profumo affair. The quiescence thus induced may well have let through the clear gay allusions of Joe Orton's *Entertaining Mr Sloane* (1964) and the ground-breaking nudity and the equation of political with sexual diversity of Peter Brook's 1964 RSC 'Theatre of Cruelty' season and *Marat/Sade* (featuring Glenda Jackson as, in turn, Christine Keeler, Jackie Kennedy and a flagellant Charlotte Corday). In the latter cases, clearly, the establishment respectability bestowed by large state subsidy was a new and confusing factor; but this did not prevent subsequent assaults on key parts of Edward Bond's *Saved* in 1965 and the whole of his *Early Morning* in 1968. The Royal Court Theatre's courageous determination to go ahead with both Bond productions (using the time-honoured device of the 'club' performance) led to an uproar that led finally to the abolition of the Chamberlain's office.

While this event was generally applauded, there were of course other readings of it; most notably from the anti-'permissive' camp, who saw it as the start of all they most feared. Subtler feminist arguments that the chief liberation gained was that of male directors to get women to take their clothes off were less often heard at the time. I shall discuss later some of the pros and cons of the era as far as the image of women was concerned; but it is useful to remember that circa 1968 men took their clothes off too.

MEDIATION

As I suggested at the beginning, before we can get to it, the 'reality' of 1960s British drama has already been pretty powerfully sifted and/or 'mediated' for us. Clearly, a dramatic production is an 'event', different from a posthumous reading of the text, a film or video, or even later production of the same work. Because of this temporal element, a particular importance attaches to the interpretations of various mediating authorities, of which I shall briefly consider three – reviewers, publishers and academics.

In the short term the most powerful of these is the newspaper reviewer, with his/her famous and much-resented ability (less here than in America) to 'make or break' a show. In the late 1950s and early 1960s a single critic, Kenneth Tynan, can be credited with substantial influence on the pace and direction of change away from the French window and towards political and voice-finding theatre; even his early suspicions of such then-fashionable Absurdists as Beckett, Ionesco and Pinter were to become the orthodoxy of a few years later. With anything less than Tynan's sheer staying power, however, the reviewer's effect on public response is relatively short term, *ad hoc* and non-retrospective.

The publication of play-scripts has much greater retrospective power to re-shape the dramatic past. Like many people's, my own teenage acquaintance with the dramatic upheavals of the time was made much less through the few relatively 'safe' productions I actually attended than through the (somewhat random) Penguin Modern Plays series, and paperback editions of individual plays by Faber and, ever increasingly, Methuen. Such cheap, attractive and prominently marketed editions were, in fact, a new phenomenon of the time; their precursors, the somewhat dour Samuel French 'acting editions', had to be specially sought out or ordered, and may partly account for the oblivion into which pre-1956 drama has subsequently fallen. Publication by Methuen (in particular) virtually guarantees a play-script an afterlife as a literary semi-classic – studied in schools, performed by students, referred to by academics – which may be far more substantial than the impact made by its initial production.

All this lends particular significance to Methuen's attempt to summarize the 1960s and 1970s respectively in a two-volume anthology, *Landmarks of Modern British Drama* (Cornish and Ketels 1985 and 1986), that is certain to be increasingly relied on as a thumbnail guide, both here and abroad (especially in the editors' native America). Most of the seven plays in the 1960s anthology are indisputable classics of the post-1956 'first wave', so that there is some noteworthy filching from 1959 for Arden's *Serjeant Musgrave's Dance* and Wesker's *Roots*, and the years after 1966 are only represented by Peter Barnes's *The Ruling Class* (1969). The 1970s volume, by contrast, consists largely of West-End-style comedy-hits by authors who produced better, though similar, work in the late 1960s, when the two token 'political' writers represented, Howard Brenton and Caryl Churchill, also cut their sharpest teeth. Clearly, history is being rewritten here in a substantial way; the manageable (earnest, largely realistic) post-'Anger' generation, with its big international names, is shoved up a bit in time to account for the 1960s; the even more manageable late-1960s absurd-tinged West-End generation is shoved up even more to redefine the notoriously 'political' 1970s; and the 1968 fringe revolution is effectively removed from the scene altogether.

The issues raised by such publication decisions shade into those raised by the transformation of recent drama into a subject of academic study. Conveniently for our purposes, the first university drama department opened at Bristol in 1960; in his inaugural address its first professor, Glynn Wickham, described the new subject as the 'mirror of moral values in society – of man's interest in himself, of his regard for his neighbour, and of his respect for his gods . . . for it is this balance between the three (or lack of balance) in any society which distinguishes one civilization from another' (Hodgson 1972: 176). Sandwiched with no sense of incongruity between quotes from Robert Bolt, on the inalterability of human evil, and Brecht, on its alterability, this well sums up the kind of eclectic claim for drama studies as a universal social and national panacea easily made in 1960. The lecture was republished in 1972 in a collection of essays with a far less certain feel to it. *The Uses of*

Drama: Acting as a Social and Educational Force, whose editor, the distinguished educationalist John Hodgson, follows a devastating list of 'Why do we need drama anyway?'-type questions with the plaintive plea 'If only we could give ourselves the space to think and re-examine the issues, instead of rushing to take up attitudes' (14). What a somewhat bewildered Hodgson is witnessing is, above all, the decade-long breakdown of a consensus that drama, especially when a bit experimental, is automatically good for you.

The very fact that drama studies started when they did, ready to receive the broader, partially declassed academic intake without the traditional and generational 'layering' of more established subjects, has enabled them to build up certain key tenets and positions with some show of unity over the years since the beginning of the 1960s, even to the point of not being afraid to take up a few 'attitudes' of their own. One such attitude would increasingly be that Wickham's gestural eclecticism, and even Hodgson's pleas for us all to find our own space and relax in our own time, were not quite adequate; and that drama did not just 'mirror' the human condition or (as Wickham and Hodgson both imply elsewhere) facilitate a more efficient interchange between over-inhibited but basically adequate social institutions. Drama also intervened in society, or tried to, and the nature and direction of that intervention was important. The cheerful juxtaposition of such gurus as Artaud, Beckett and Brecht (to name only the most experimental modern masters) thus became increasingly problematic, since the social model implied by each is so different. As to the airy pairing of Brecht with Robert Bolt, still possible in 1960, if drama studies were about anything, they were about becoming a little bit more precise.

In becoming a subject of academic study, the 'essential nature' of 1960s drama has been subject to frequent changes, as the Methuen anthology illustrates. On the one hand the libraries are still dominated by studies such as Martin Esslin's *The Theatre of the Absurd* (1961), John Russell Taylor's *Anger and After* (1962) and *The Second Wave* (1971), and John Elsom's *Post-War British Theatre* (1976), basically registering the great change from what came before, and therefore with an overall tendency to find an exciting unity in the first 'wave', even between writers as diverse as Arden and Pinter, followed by disturbing signs of confusion and fragmentation later on (for instance when a whole generation of writers and performers took a principled step to the left in the later 1960s). On the other hand a more theoretically equipped, broadly left-wing, post-1968 generation of commentators has powerfully retraced the fissures and concerns of 1970s and 1980s drama back into this same period, with such questions as 'Was the Royal Court ever as radical as claimed?', 'Are the shocking metaphors of Artaudian Theatre of Cruelty or the dadaist fringe agencies of political communication or bourgeois mystification?', 'Did the well-subsidized Brecht provide a real model for popular political theatre?' and 'Do venues for working-class theatre already exist, or must they be created?' What is most striking about such academically disciplined debate is that it is led from the front, not by academics but by such ('confused', 'fragmented', etc.) practitioners as Trevor Griffiths, John McGrath and David Edgar.

The symbiosis between academics (usually with some fringe background, if only student) and practitioners (usually with some academic background again, if only student) of course once again bespeaks the importance of the 'scum' floated up by the 1944 Education Act, which eventually led logically to the 1960s expansion of higher education, to whose search for new and popular subjects drama studies was one response. But as academe as a whole has had to move away from Professor Wickham's almost heartrendingly optimistic eclecticism, it has also moved steadily towards the study of cultural signification in specific social contexts, to which drama studies (now proliferated into media studies and cultural studies) pointed the way.

OTHER COUNTRIES AND OTHER ARTS

I would like briefly to consider the relations between British and international theatre, and for this purpose it will be useful to return to the triadic division suggested at the beginning of this chapter – the three tendencies headed by Beckett, Brecht and Osborne.

The first tendency was conveniently labelled by Martin Esslin in 1961 as a Theatre of the Absurd, in which the disruption of naturalistic dramatic conventions gave rise to thoughts about the human condition, particularly a condition in which various older types of religious and philosophical explanation are felt to be lost. The dominance of Beckett, friend and disciple of James Joyce, suggests that Theatre of the Absurd can be seen as a branch of the antipoliticial modernism of the early twentieth century, although in some instances the human condition described clearly merges into more specific oppressions. The two most exportable British dramatists of the 1960s, Harold Pinter and Tom Stoppard, are usually seen as working in the Absurd tradition; in Europe, the two most prominent practitioners have been the Romanian Eugene Ionesco and the Czech Vaclav Havel. Arguably, the whole tradition can be defined in terms of the experience of small but cohesive cultures oppressed by more powerful neighbouring ones, as is suggested by various states of voluntary or involuntary linguistic exile – the Irish Beckett and Romanian Ionesco writing in French, the Czech-born Stoppard and Portuguese-Jewish Pinter in English – with the much-imprisoned internal exile Havel as a kind of symbolic rallying-figure to whom Beckett, Pinter and Stoppard have all at one time or another dedicated work.

Because of the easy route to 'apolitical' self-congratulation offered by this tradition (and followed particularly by Stoppard), it has been largely cold-shouldered by much post-class-of-1968 commentary. It may be time for a reassessment of this position. In particular the two most striking socio-political aspects of (early, pre-middle-class) Pinter – the mandarin contempt for common speech, and the understanding of the powerlessness it expresses – deserve to be re-weighed against each other at greater length than I can manage here; the mixture is in any case a vital starting-point for the work of two writers now seen as far more socially radical, Orton and Bond. (It has also become easy to forget that the early Stoppard was a staunch fringer, whose *After Magritte* was first produced at Inter-Action's Green Banana Restaurant in 1970 alongside Howard Brenton's *The Education of Skinny Spew*.)

Curiously, Esslin's *The Theatre of the Absurd* also finds a certain amount of space for the German Marxist Bertolt Brecht, normally seen as representing the plumb opposite to absurdism. In his early work, Brecht was indeed very happy to subvert conventional expectations of logic and sequence to rather random metaphysical effect; but from about 1930 he specifically harnessed such disruptions of perspective to Marxism in the dramatic practice fairly translated as 'alienation' or 'distancing' (if we remember that the distance being measured is that between accepted social reality and reasonable expectation, rather than between audience and enjoyment). Brecht was in fact marrying together, and moving on from, two strands of German theatre: the subjectivist expressionism that was one branch of a wider European modernism; and a specifically proletarian agit-prop tradition arising from the rapidity (and hence comparative cultural homogeneity) of nineteenth-century German industrialization (see Gray 1976: 3–5) and further boosted by the disillusionment of the ex-cannon-fodder generation that almost created a Marxist Germany in the Spartacist revolt of 1919. Such links between experimentalism, postwar fatigue with imperialistic pretensions and a sense of a real working-class mandate for change gave Brecht's theory and practice a particular relevance for the British theatre of the 1950s and 1960s. Apart, however, from Theatre Workshop and the extraordinary work of John Arden, on the one hand, and such liberal-hero costume dramas as *A Man for All Seasons*, on the other, Brechtianism was more talked about than witnessed in British theatre until 1968, when it became crucial to the political end of the fringe.

The other prong of the revival, in which new kinds of central character 'find their voices' in relatively naturalistic settings, was arguably also the product of a foreign influence – the more diffuse and less pin-downable 'Americanization' of British culture. The domestic dramas of Tennessee Williams and Arthur Miller, frequently staged here since the late 1940s, brought with them not only the theme that 'respect should be paid' to the little man, but also some inklings of the Method acting style appropriate to such themes, in which the simple struggle for articulation could often be far more riveting than this or that twist of the plot. The movie performances of such stars as Marlon Brando and James Dean gave the style much wider currency; while the diffusion of jazz, especially modern jazz, suggested the possibility of other kinds of self-taught, self-made articulation beyond the tainted arena of speech altogether. Hence Osborne's Jimmy Porter expresses his real feelings with his trumpet, the stage directions at least emphasizing the baffled vulnerability that his unstoppable verbal articulacy is supposed to mask, in ways that don't always come over in performance (where the rival tradition of the theatrical loudmouth, such as Noel Coward's self-projection, Gary Essendine, in *Present Laughter*, tends to be all too clear). In *The Entertainer* Archie Rice's inadequate expressive repertoire is more evidently the central point, as is the transcendent importance allotted to jazz in the description of a black blues singer, where Archie briefly finds an authentic voice for his own feelings.

The kinds of voice being found, and the meanings of doing so, however, differed greatly between Britain and America. For Williams and Miller, social class is only of occasional importance in itself; it is for all the self-defining individuals who 'could have been contenders' in a world of theoretically ever-expanding opportunity that the voices are to be found. In Britain, on the other hand, class is always the issue; and the finding of a voice can happen in two ways. In the first, it is primarily the play that discovers a hitherto unexplored working-class constituency, to whose collective voice the theatre audience listens with feelings ranging from shock to 'angry' recognition and solidarity; this can be applied to at least some early work by first-wave writers as apparently diverse as Osborne, Wesker, Arden, Pinter and Bond, before they (almost without exception) 'went middle-class' around the time of play number three. But secondly, a central character may become specifically aware of the limitations of the given class-imposed language, and consciously struggle against it; the classic instance of this is Beatie Bryant in Wesker's *Roots* (1959), who finds her own voice in the act of passing on the ideas of her enlightened but treacherous boyfriend Ronnie to her culturally deprived farmworking family. Ironically, from 1958 to 1963, just as serious drama was exploring such real struggles for articulation, the biggest hit in town was *My Fair Lady*, where the elocutionist Higgins teaches the Cockney Eliza 'how to speak' through an emotional exploitation strikingly similar to that of Ronnie Kahn. As the last great West End stand of 'Binkie' Beaumont, the show brilliantly reasserted the delightfully British cultural supremacy of the upper classes over the workers, through the medium of an American musical.

If we now turn to the end of the 1960s, the balance of international forces looks very different from that obtaining at the beginning, when performances of Pirandello, Sartre and Anouilh were commonplace. Now, despite the elevation to guruhood of such theorists as Jerzy Grotowski, Jan Kott and, above all, Antonin Artaud, the impact of European plays was minimal. The American input, by contrast, rose to a crescendo by the end of the 1960s, though here we have to consider managers and instigators as well as writers: for instance Jim Haynes, who opened the Edinburgh Traverse in 1963 and then the Drury Lane Arts Lab in 1967; and Charles Marowitz, who staged the first credited British 'happening' (at Edinburgh) in 1963, collaborated with Brook on the Artaudian 'Cruelty' season in 1964, directed Orton's *Loot* in 1966, and opened the post-Chamberlain proto-fringe Open Space in 1968. There is no way whatsoever that the British fringe could have got off the ground without the hard work of Haynes or Marowitz, or without the influence of such travelling late-1960s American groups as the Living Theatre or the La Mama Company. Strangely, the fringe activities that best expressed the extraordinary American-led anti-American internationalism of the late 1960s – a mirror-reversal of the complicity of all western governments in America's war with its own demons in Vietnam – also collapsed far more speedily in America itself, with that war's ignominious close, than in Europe, where the fringe's tattered remnants are still on proud annual display at the Mickery Theatre, Amsterdam.

I shall round this section off by looking more closely at the special importance of drama in the 'alternative' British culture of the late 1960s. To conclude my discussion of the international dimension, I need simply say that most of the developments to be described have their American forebears (Allen Ginsberg, John Cage, the Fugs, Living Theatre, Allan Kaprow) who were themselves sometimes popularizing ideas earlier current in the European modernist avant-garde to which Britain is inalienably hostile. In late 1960s 'alternative' culture, then, drama occupied a key place, overlapping with virtually every other form of artistic expression. Poetry turned towards the public reading or, in the case of the 'concrete' Bob Cobbing, full-scale vocal performance. The classical concert hall became a standard site for 'happenings', the American composer John Cage having staged the first of these in 1952 (Hewison 1986: 115). Meanwhile the dominant form of the decade, rock music, attempted to break away from the restrictions of the three-minute love song into narrative, with rock operas like The Who's *Tommy* (1969), while stage performances became increasingly visual. The ethos of the rock tour, with quick set-ups and quick strikes in diverse venues, also largely became that of the new travelling fringe groups; and many of these were rock bands as well as theatre companies (e.g. the Pip Simmons Group). Lastly, the street theatre events, without which no demonstration was complete, were as much a development from 'performance art' as from conventional drama or political vanguardism; most commentators on the fringe discern a clear split between art-college 'dadaists' such as the People Show and clear-political-narrative groups such as 7:84 or the General Will, which in turn overlapped with what might earlier have been seen as the territory of journalism (see Edgar 1988: 163–4).

Why did drama briefly take on this central cultural role? For poetry and the visual arts, clearly, the idea of performance offered a way out of the cultural ghettos of distribution and exhibition that muffled any immediacy of response to the rapidly changing events and atmospheres of the decade. Once it became clear that (in

Brook's phrase) any 'empty space' with an audience in the vicinity was potentially a theatre, it also became clear that this was an effective way for the 'artist' of almost any kind to pick his or her conditions for confronting the public. The large baby-boom generation, with its habit of congregating in large numbers for cultural events such as rock concerts (not too expensive, because of the numbers), and perhaps just as importantly its shared televisual 'global village' cultural awareness, meant that a great deal of good-will and/or common experience (the two prime requisites of any audience, whether it realizes it is one or not) could be assumed. And while much of this new 'performance' ethic actually sprang initially from the abstracter ends of poetry, music, art and even of drama (with Artaud), the increasing politicization of performers and 'constituency' alike in the later 1960s inevitably implied a counter-move from that moment of abstraction back towards narrative and specific content, i.e. towards a 'political drama' with an unprecedented array of sophisticated means at its disposal, and an almost unprecedentedly (though from now on dwindlingly) well prepared audience.

THEMES

Having attempted some necessary contextualization, it will be useful now to focus more closely on some of the recurrent themes of 1960s drama. One of the most important of these themes was that of leadership. The more drama (and perhaps culture, more generally, in the 1960s) became aware of the hopes being pinned on it, the more it agonized over the leader or guru's right to lead or teach. Thus John Osborne's *Luther* (1961), John Arden's *Serjeant Musgrave's Dance* (1959) and Arnold Wesker's *Roots* (1959) and *Chips with Everything* (1962) all centre on characters (Luther, Musgrave, the significantly absent Ronnie Kahn and Pip) who point the way to the promised land for the peasants, the miners, the farmworker's daughter Beatie Bryant or the common troops, while too damaged in themselves to do other than betray their disciples and therefore their own best ideals. But if the burdens of responsibility are great, they are also real and serious, and not to be matched by the representatives of the other, conservative, side, who may be grand but who are also clearly two-dimensional. In a variant of this type, the 'homecoming' play, the alienated intellectual returns to his working-class home amid scenes of mutual incomprehension and deadlock (Sinfield 1989: 266–71).

In the mid-1960s, however, the notion of cultural leadership seems more often to be split between two figures, one representing power and the other aesthetic subversion, but with a great deal of equivocation as to which really represents which: the poet-politician Lindsay and bandit-hero Armstrong in John Arden's *Armstrong's Last Goodnight* (1964); the revolutionary Marat and sexual outcast (but also play-director) de Sade in Peter Brook's 1964 production of Peter Weiss's *Marat/Sade;* the low-born conquistador Pizarro and exotic Inca emperor Atahuallpa in Peter Shaffer's *The Royal Hunt of the Sun* (1964); the dictator Shogo and poet Basho in Edward Bond's *Narrow Road to the Deep North* (1968, but the figures are prefigured by the macho Fred and sensitive Len in *Saved* (1965)). One character is generally of lower class, but also more apparently successful, than the other; and the message of each play is as much about the deep bond between the two characters as about their irreconcilability. To offer a thumbnail interpretation, the working-class dramatist (or his imitator) is now torn between the power that seems to be offered to him (with its uncomfortable connotations of postwar *arriviste* success) and the moral authority represented by his art. Will the former destroy the latter; or is the latter part of a subtle plot to damp the class-energies of the former?

By 1968–9 the whole notion of leadership and cultural authority was being vigorously deconstructed, as an almost random sample of titles suggests: *In His Own Write* (John Lennon/Victor Spinetti: Beatledom); *This Story of Yours* (John Hopkins: the dedicated police-man); *The Hero Rises Up* (Arden and D'Arcy: Nelson); *Hadrian VII* (Peter Luke: the papacy); *The Real Inspector Hound* (Tom Stoppard: fictional dectectives); *Early Morning* (Edward Bond: Queen Victoria); *H* (Charles Wood: the Raj); and *Macrune's Guevara* (John Spurling: Che Guevara). A great many of these confess (through the ironies buried in their titles or otherwise) the authors' own symbiotic involvements with the various hero-worships being questioned. But perhaps the most ironic piece of hero-deconstruction lay in the way in which Joe Orton's most thoroughgoing cultural subversion, *What the Butler Saw* (psychiatry), was accompanied by the literal 'death of the author' at the hands of his jealous male lover, very much in the style of his own work.

With the possible exception of Orton, one kind of cultural authority not very actively questioned in the 1960s was that of patriarchy.

As Michelene Wandor (1987) points out, there is a striking contrast with 1970s theatre in this respect (see especially 157–60). In many of the plays mentioned above, women tend to have highly symbolic functions, either as vessels of the word (Beatie, Annie in *Musgrave*, Charlotte Corday) or as monsters of reaction (especially in Bond and, indeed, Orton). And in the way the decade has come to be written up, the only two women writers to have made much of a mark did so at or before its start. Yet Shelagh Delaney's *A Taste of Honey* (1958) and Ann Jellicoe's *The Knack* (1962) focus the sexual vertigos of the so-called 'angry' generation far more sharply than aggressively male writers like Osborne, since it was young women like Delaney's pregnant unmarried Jo and Jellicoe's variously tempted Nancy who were actually in the firing line of the battle to escape the tyranny of 'home' without replacing it with the new tyrannies of the sexual jungle. Here the 1970s cry that the personal is the political was already being explored. One reason for the relative lack of such work later in the decade (apart from the ingrained sexism of the dramatic establishments, new as well as old) may have been that in the 1960s the prevailing political mode was the historical, an arena where (as Jane Austen remarked) there are virtually 'no women at all'. This in turn was partly to do with a growing boredom with realistic domestic box-sets; the subsidized funding that made the large open stage and the largeish 'ensemble' a realizable dream; and the broader, less definable sense that dramatic reality was 'out there' rather than 'in here'. One of the achievements of the fringe was to adapt such ideas to smaller, studio-sized venues that were also able to house the domestic without the materialistic emphases of the old box-set. The political and the personal had thus already approached each other physically when 1970s feminist writers such as Caryl Churchill and Pam Gems found ways of writing that stressed both equally.

CONCLUSION

It seems sensible to conclude this very general survey with a closer look at how some elements peculiar to the time manifested themselves in a specific play. Edward Bond's *Early Morning* (1968), whose suppression by the Vice Squad after a single club performance finally ensured the abolition of the Lord Chamberlain's office, would be few people's choice as play of the decade, but I can think of none that touch so many 1960s bases so simultaneously.

Briefly, the play concerns an attempted *coup d'état* by Prince Albert and Disraeli against Queen Victoria. One of her sons, Arthur, is sympathetic, but his Siamese twin, George, recently engaged to Florence Nightingale, remains a problem. The *coup* fails, Albert is killed, Victoria rapes Florence, a working-class couple eat a man in a cinema-queue, Gladstone leads a revolution according to union rules, George is killed by Albert's ghost, and Arthur goes mad and in despair tricks most of the population into falling over a cliff. The second part takes place in a heaven where everyone happily eats everyone else, until Arthur disrupts things by staging an anti-cannibalist hunger-strike that attracts strong working-class support until Victoria nails him into a coffin, from which he eventually and mysteriously ascends to a higher plane.

Press cries of 'Lesbian charge in Victoria play' aside, *Early Morning* is clearly an ambitious attempt to combine and comment on the Absurdist, Brechtian and voice-finding strands of 1960s theatre in a single piece. The absurdist strand is evident in the hero Arthur's various attempts at ascetic withdrawal, the 'nothing happens, twice' structure in which the second half repeats the first, and the general deadpan acceptance of incredible postulates, as well as in more specific allusions like Gladstone's lament on time ('Time! Time! . . . the old man leans on 'is 'oe, suddenly 'e looks up, it's winter, and the skull's already on the window-sill' – Bond 1977: 172) that recalls a similar aria by Pozzo in *Waiting for Godot*. While both speeches accompany the savage kicking of an underling, the Brechtian strand in Bond's play adds a dimension of calculated brutality that turns the scene into a political deconstruction of Absurdism itself.

As far as voice-finding goes, this play marks Bond's irrevocable farewell to the working-class realism of *Saved;* a point underlined by a scene where that play's hero, Len (or at least his deliberate namesake), is prosecuted by the Lord Chamberlain for eating a man in a cinema queue. Bond's argument is now that an Establishment unable to see its own responsibility for such everyday horrors as the baby-stoning for which *Saved* was savaged is far more obscene than any new obscenity that can be offered to it. This new, principled, refusal to mine the 'lower depths' for any more instances of shock and horror, except in parody, leads Bond to select as his new hero the symbolic but incidentally high-born Arthur, who strongly echoes the flawed liberal would-be popular leaders of the earlier 1960s. The fact that Arthur is saddled with the dwindling corpse of a reactionary Siamese twin for the first part of the play constitutes its own comment on the mid-1960s historical two-hander; but despite such deconstructive ironies, Bond is not yet prepared to ditch the notion of the hero altogether. While every conceivable Victorian shibboleth is being firmly reduced to Brechtianized rubble, we are still asked to attend to Arthur's semi-incoherent quest for personal authenticity, which finally leads us full circle into a kind of mystical Beckettian abstention that also happens to tally perfectly with the longhaired and bearded Christ-fixation of nascent hippiedom.

The play's closing demand for hippyish renunciation is very much of a piece with the late-1960s' growing perception of Britain as a consumer society, whose every enjoyment is paid for by the exploitation of someone else, somewhere. Bond's ghastly cannibal heaven, where no one feels the pain of being eaten any more, is clearly a parody of this triumphalist affluent society, where the dog-eat-dog ethics of Victorian capitalism are apparently to be re-run forever as a kind of whited, emotionally empty, sepulchre over which Victoria herself is still in undiminished charge. Just as interesting are the ways in which the first half of *Early Morning* reflects on the specific imagery of mid-1960s 'Swinging' London. The play's cod-Victorianism reflects that of a thousand 'I was Kitchener's Valet' clothes-and-souvenir shops, as well as Peter Blake's famous cover for the Beatles' 1967 *Sgt Pepper* LP, where numerous culture-gurus, from the (Victorianized) Beatles backwards, were displayed as if all interchangeable or equally-selectable-from. This Victorian nostalgia was clearly part of a slow-but-terminal cultural ingestion of the collapse of empire, whereby what had once been a powerfully impressed history was now reduced to a simple Monty-Pythonesque choice of costumes.

What was really innovative about *Early Morning* was the way in which it matched such consumptive nostalgias with its own voracious consumption of audience expectations, whereby we move from history to farce to broad symbolism to contemporary satire to a kind of metaphysical grand guignol, so that Arthur's relatively early complaint 'I feel as though I've eaten too much' comes across as being as much a valid comment on the formation of the age as on the content of the specific play.

BIBLIOGRAPHY

Arden, John 1977. *To Present the Pretence: Essays on the Theatre and its Public.* London: Eyre Methuen.

Arden, John and D'Arcy, Margaretta 1988. *Awkward Corners.* London: Methuen.

Bigsby, C. W. E. 1981. 'The language of crisis in British theatre: the drama of cultural pathology'. In Bigsby, C. W. E. (ed.) *Contemporary British Drama.* New York: Holmes & Meier.

Bond, Edward 1977. *Plays: One.* London: Eyre Methuen.

Brook, Peter 1968. *The Empty Space.* London: McGibbon & Kee.

Cornish, Roger, and Ketels, Violet 1985. *Landmarks of Modern British Drama.* Volume 1: *The Plays of the Sixties.* London and New York: Methuen.

Cornish, Roger, and Ketels, Violet 1986. *Landmarks of Modern British Drama.* Volume 2: *The Plays of the Seventies.* London and New York: Methuen.

Edgar, David 1988: *The Second Time as Farce: Reflections on the Drama of Mean Times.* London: Lawrence & Wishart.

Elsom, John 1976. *Post-war British Theatre.* London: Routledge & Kegan Paul.

Esslin, Martin 1961. *The Theatre of the Absurd.* New York: Anchor Books.

Gaskill, William 1988. *A Sense of Direction: Life at the Royal Court.* London: Faber & Faber.

Gray, Ronald 1976. *Brecht the Dramatist.* Cambridge: Cambridge University Press.

Hall, Peter, edited by John Goodwin 1983. *Peter Hall's Diaries.* London: Hamish Hamilton.

Hayman, Ronald 1979. *British Theatre Since 1955: A Reassessment.* Oxford: Oxford University Press.

Hewison, Robert 1986. *Too Much: Art and Society in the Sixties 1960–75.* London: Methuen.

Hodgson, John (ed.) 1972. *The Uses of Drama: Sources Giving a Background to Acting as a Social and Educational Force.* London: Eyre Methuen.

Hugget, Richard 1989. *Binkie Beaumont:* Eminence Grise *of the West End Theatre, 1933–1973.* London: Hodder & Stoughton.

Itzin, Catherine 1980. *Stages in the Revolution: British Political Theatre Since 1968.* London: Eyre Methuen.

McGrath, John 1981: *A Good Night Out: Popular Theatre: Audience, Class and Form.* London: Methuen.

Marwick, Arthur 1982. *British Society Since 1945.* Harmondsworth: Penguin.

Rowell, George and Jackson, Anthony 1984. *The Repertory Movement: A History of Regional Theatre in Britain.* Cambridge: Cambridge University Press.

Sinfield, Alan (ed.) 1983. *Society and Literature 1945–1970.* London: Methuen.

Sinfield, Alan 1989. *Literature, Politics and Culture in Postwar Britain.* Oxford: Basil Blackwell.

Taylor, John Russell 1962. *Anger and After: A Guide to the New British Drama.* London: Methuen.

Taylor, John Russell 1971. *The Second Wave: British Drama for the Seventies.* London: Methuen.

Tynan, Kenneth 1984. *A View of the English Stage, 1944–1965*. London: Methuen.

Wandor, Michelene 1987. *Look Back in Gender: Sexuality and the Family in Post-war British Drama*. London and New York: Methuen.

Wickham, Glynn 1960. 'Drama as a study'. In Hodgson, John (ed.) 1972. *The Uses of Drama: Sources Giving a Background to Acting as a Social and Educational Force*. London: Eyre Methuen.

FURTHER READING

Among numerous much-reprinted classics on post-1956 drama: Taylor (1962, 1971) is solid and was quick off the mark; Elsom (1976) is thought-provoking on links between finance and artistic practice; and Hayman (1979), though textually impressionistic, includes a very useful year-by-year listing of productions. Brook (1968) is the sacred text of the era, and laid down many of the aesthetic, if not social, tenets linking legitimate theatre with the nascent fringe. Gaskill (1988), another seminally important director, gives a fascinatingly downbeat retrospect over the heroic age of the Royal Court. And Hall (1983), while addressing a later period, gives insight into the pre-emptive managerial ability behind the RSC's 1960s dominance of the subsidy market. Rowell and Jackson (1984) are thorough on the regional theatre that this chapter has handled much too briefly. Itzin (1980) is the classic on the political fringe, and Wandor (1987) on changing presentations of gender. To help in distinguishing the wood from the trees, Marwick (1982), Hewison (1986) and Sinfield (1983 and 1989) are among the reassessments of the whole era I have found most illuminating. But the most trenchant and radical commentary on the aspirations and real achievements of the period's drama can be found in the reflections of such practising dramatists as Arden and D'Arcy (1977, 1988), McGrath (1981) and Edgar (1988).

Chapter 7

Inside the liberal heartland: television and the popular imagination in the 1960s

Jeremy Ridgman

INTRODUCTION

The 1960s occupies a distinctive place in the short and tightly compressed history of British television. Sandwiched between the confident assurances of the postwar years, dominated still by the Reithian paternalism of the BBC, and the harsher, more pragmatic and largely economic imperatives of the 1970s, lies an era characterized by experiment, innovation and a particular sort of cultural iconoclasm. New technologies, new practices and institutional structures emerged to provide the basis of the broadcasting that was to prevail for the next quarter of a century – the beginning, as it were, of the modern television period. Key forms and genres established or, at the very least, radically overhauled during this moment – documentary drama, the police series, situation comedy, current affairs journalism – still form the backbone of the broadcaster's schedule in the early 1990s. As the broadcasting industry teeters on the edge of what might be regarded as its post-modern era of deregulated saturation image-bombardment, it is worth attempting to examine more closely the impact of this critical moment.

Competing accounts of the decade have circulated ever since the inevitable reassessments began in the early 1970s. The most prevalent image is of a golden age of broadcasting, tied firmly to the liberal regime of Hugh Carleton-Greene as director general of the BBC, whose appointment from 1960 to 1969 symbolically embraced the decade, and embodied principally in the experimental fields of satire and socially conscious drama. Thus in 1975 that most prolific of television playwrights, Alan Plater, remembered the 'genuine and urgent *search* for new writers' during the early 1960s; 'at a crude level to fill up the schedules, at the proper level stimulated by a real desire to unearth new talent. Television was a real adventure playground' (Gilbert 1975: 12). The breakthroughs in socially conscious drama and anti-establishment satire during the early and middle part of the decade, particularly as exemplified by such emblems of controversy as *That Was The Week That Was* and *The Wednesday Play*, are at the centre of this story of the golden age. A not untypical lament for the passing of that blissful dawn of radical creativity is to be found in David Hare's contribution in 1982 to a volume of essays by television dramatists (Edgar *et al.* 1982), whose very title, *Ah! Mischief*, turns out to be based on a remark by Greene himself: 'I have never seen a man so delighted by a single word. How attractive that spirit is in him, how fine the BBC was when he ran it, how much that sound working principle – "ah, mischief!" – is needed there today' (50). And, in a sobering prognosis for the future of public service broadcasting in the face of a new revolution in the political economy of the medium at the end of the 1980s, Colin MacCabe was to commit himself to the view that, in terms of the early years of the 1960s at least, 'we can indeed talk of a Golden Age of television' (1990: 37).

Commentators from the right, of course, might read the same picture somewhat differently, but more sceptical voices, from both ends of the political spectrum, have warned against too romantic a concentration on the progressive or radical elements in this vast and contradictory field. The small number of programmes associated with the controversy and liberality of the period is relatively small. 'It is easy to exaggerate the revolution that took place under Hugh Greene's stewardship', suggested the critic Milton Shulman in 1973:

> For most viewers the liberating influence of Hugh Greene meant little. They watched the BBC for *Grandstand, The Black and White Minstrel Show, Top of the Pops, Come Dancing, The Billy Cotton Band Show, Dr Finlay's Casebook, Perry Mason, Dr Who, Dick van Dyke, Rolf Harris, Val Doonican,* and they were contented enough.
>
> (Shulman 1973: 94)

A less cynical critic might wish to add to Shulman's list. If the bulk of the BBC's programmes consisted then, as now, of 'undemanding entertainment,' we might also cite *Steptoe and Son, The Likely Lads,* the early *Dad's Army* and, with 14 million viewers within a few weeks of its first episode, the seminal police drama series *Z Cars* – all successful long-running programmes operating within the framework of a schedule of popular entertainment, but which managed to pin down the contradictions of the period and, in particular, the pervasive legacy of the British class system.

Yet we cannot avoid the caveat implied by Shulman's position against the privileging of a particular area of programming, appointed as inherently progressive or socially worthwhile, over what Raymond Williams has called the 'flow' of television as a cultural institution (see Williams 1974: 78–118). One of the central problems with 'golden ageism', however politically well-intentioned, is the set of cultural values implied. The history of television broadcasting contained in such a vision is one centred on the emergence of a newly radical and revitalized BBC, whose energy and inventiveness is forged in response to the competition for audiences presented by the commercial sector from 1955 onwards. The role of ITV is perceived as that of a catalyst, an essential but ultimately expendable ingredient in the vast inspirational experiment. Thus for MacCabe (1990: 38) a programme such as *Z Cars* is 'unthinkable without reference to ITV productions such as *Coronation Street*, and *No Hiding Place*; yet equally unthinkable, it would appear, in such a discourse is any discussion of the cultural significance of those two programmes, which themselves provided important antidotes to the cosy homiletics of earlier BBC serials such as *The Groves* and *Dixon of Dock Green*. Can we talk of the cultural revolution of the Greene regime without taking account also of the early history of the ever adventurous commercial company Granada, who as far back as 1956 had ventured where the BBC had feared to tread by transmitting an unexpurgated version of *Look Back in Anger*? By the early 1960s Granada were pioneering the development of serious political and investigative journalism with *World in Action*, and offering a positive philosophy of regional, counter-metropolitan programming that ranged from local magazine broadcasts and the networking of material as diverse as *Coronation Street* and a season of plays from the Manchester School (see Buscombe 1981) and that fundamentally challenged the middle-class assurances of the postwar consensus.

FRAMING THE DECADE

In so far as the advent of commercial television can be seen as part of a general postwar movement, in which paternalistic Victorian controls were lifted from British society (Marwick 1982: .16), the '1960s' might well be thought of as beginning as far back as

September 1955, with the launch of the first independent companies. If we were looking for an official closing date for the period, we might well choose August 1968 and the launch of the idealistic but ill-fated London Weekend Television, whose dreams of a marriage of commercial viability and intellectual evangelism – under the direction of the former controller of BBC1, Michael Peacock, and the inspirational guidance of the *quondam* scourge of the establishment, David Frost – were to collapse within months amid protests from advertisers, union fears of unemployment and purges by an increasingly interventionist board of directors.

At the more immediately visible level of technological development, the decade is somewhat easier to define. This was manifestly a period of expanding possibilities, the growth in ownership and rental of television sets in itself a key sociological fact that linked the economics of the consumerist boom with the new culture of representation. The evolution during the 1960s of a 'technological civilisation of a sort not previously seen in twentieth century Britain' (Marwick 1982: 114) finds its sharpest focal point in the spread of television, particularly through the pact sealed by commercial television between the consumer market and the powerful new empires of communication, while the first appointment by the end of the decade of academics to the Open University (whose operations were to begin in 1971) marks a fitting recognition of the more ostensibly liberal effects of the communications explosion. In the domestic field of the new technological 'white heat', television glowed ever more powerfully, its spread from 75 per cent to 91 per cent of households between 1961 and 1971 far outstripping the incursion made by other home appliances such as the washing machine and the telephone (see Marwick 1982: 120–1).

At the same time, the technology of television itself changed more perceptibly than at any other time in its history. The introduction during 1958 and 1959 of videotape recording, followed shortly after by the first techniques of electronic editing, revolutionized methods of production and contributed to the increasing industrialization of the medium. It is possible, of course, to overemphasize the significance of videotape as the magic key that gave sudden access to a new post-primitive age in television technology. Certainly, as far as audiences were concerned, the effects of the shift from the event of live television into recorded transmission may not have been very marked and, for some time anyway, programmes continued to be recorded continuously as if for live broadcast, so problematic were the demands of editing. Furthermore, the fact that, prior to video-tape, many programmmes had originally been made on film gives the lie to easy distinctions between the 'look' of television in the two decades; if anything, surviving footage from the 1950s now looks cleaner than the infant electronic material of the early 1960s. Nor should we assume that the taping of programmes for trans-mission was to provide anything like a comprehensive archive. Unlike film, anything recorded electronically can, in a matter of only seconds, be effortlessly wiped, leaving the medium available for re-use, and the 1960s saw a tragically casual obliteration of material, usually in the name of a minimalist economizing of resources. The haphazard survival of recorded programmes is one of the central problems in our understanding of the period and the even more arbitrary reprocessing of that material a critical factor in the popular mediation of the decade.

The most far reaching effects of videotape, however, were on methods of production. It brought more creative possibilities in the shaping of programmes, allowing a greater fluidity in the grammar of production, particularly in dramatic work; a creative control and independence that was to be enhanced and infused with an increasingly political significance in the hands of directors such as Ken Loach, as cameras became lighter and the integration of 16-millimetre location film footage allowed more contact with the world beyond the studio. Above all, videotape allowed a more flexible and efficient use of the costly resources of studio space and time – of paramount importance in the ever more competitive bid for quantity and variety. It was on the back of this technical and industrial flexibility that the creative opportunities of the new liberal patronage were to flourish.

Two further technical innovations, however, were to revolutionize the very image that television was able to offer its spectators. A decade that had begun in grainy black and white just managed to finish in not so glorious colour. With the launch of BBC2 in April 1964, the new 625-line broadcast standard was adopted, with its markedly enhanced image definition. Then in 1967 BBC2 began to transmit in colour, initially for specific programmes but within a few months (in time for Christmas, in fact) across the whole channel. By the end of 1969 colour had spread across the entire BBC and ITV output, though only, of course, for those fortunate enough to own or to be renting the right television set; at the very moment that the distribution of single sets appeared to be reaching saturation point, a new phase in the consumerist boom had well and truly begun.

Even beyond their obvious contribution to a second generation of television marketing, such technological developments were far from ideologically neutral. First of all, the sharper picture quality of 625 and the advent of colour served to enhance the image of BBC2 as a culturally exclusive channel, formally experimental in some areas of its work and, in others, serving highly specialized interests through minority programming. The title of BBC2's single play series at the time, *Theatre 625*, now seems to capture this ethos with remarkable precision – a cultural exclusiveness that in turn was essential in the populist redefinition of BBC1 as a rival to the commercial channels. Colour of course was not to remain the property of the few for very long, yet its ideological implications remained far from simple. Coinciding as it did with the onset of a far harsher economic climate at the turn of the decade – indeed, its own cost a contributory factor in the deficit experienced for the first time by the BBC – the advent of colour transmission provided a lifeline in the hitherto uncharted waters of competitive scheduling and international saleability that stretched into the 1970s and beyond. A central plank in the new strategy of 'commodity production' (Gardner and Wyver 1983: 119) was to be the prestige historical or literary serial, increasingly the winning formula as far as advertisers and international buyers or co-producers were concerned. The production values associated with colour and with image definition – lavish costume design, material authenticity and period atmosphere – all contributed to the essential texture of such production, though it was undoubtedly the unforeseen commercial success of *The Forsyte Saga*, made in black and white and first broadcast on BBC2 across 26 weeks in 1968, that set the tone for the genre. It is more than a little ironic that, in this of all years, the adaptation of a hitherto little known series of novels, at least partly devoted to a materialist critique of the late Victorian *haute bourgeoisie*, should have passed into the public consciousness as a celebration of the gentility and grandeur of a bygone age, and under the aegis of a head of drama, Sydney Newman, who had fostered some of the most radically contentious contemporary drama in the history of television. Yet it was here, if anywhere, that the *style retro* that would permeate historical television drama for the next decade and a half was firmly established. Its economic pre-eminence was reinforced in 1971 by the launch of London Weekend Television's centrepiece of post-Peacock populism, *Upstairs Downstairs* (a series whose uncontentious representation of the Edwardian establishment similarly seems to have belied the more radical intentions of its initial script – see Itzin 1972).

However, there can be no more graphic demonstration of the recuperative appropriation of the new experimentalism at the end of the 1960s than the blockbusting *Civilisation*, a 13-part series of trips by Sir Kenneth Clark around the archeological, literary and artistic artifacts of the west. Urbanely self-deprecatory in the 'personal' tone of its script, yet supremely confident in its high cultural assumptions, the series had been prompted by an invitation to Clark from the controller of BBC2, David Attenborough, merely to provide a series of colour films on art. In its unmistakable visual (and musical) triumphalism, it was to become a classic text in the reassertion, at the end of a contentious decade, of the BBC's underlying claim to the Reithian high moral and intellectual ground and in establishing the international reputation for the combination of cultural and technical 'excellence' upon which much of the export ethos of the 1970s would be built.

The technological spread of television in the 1960s was not only a matter of the image presented or the means by which it was produced. Extensive development was also taking place in the means by which images were transmitted or relayed, both on the ground and through space. In 1962 the first attempt was made to pick up pictures from the USA via the Telstar satellite, and by 1967 the BBC was able to mount the euphoric *Our World*, an extravaganza of entertainment relayed from each of the continents. News-gathering techniques began to edge towards the speed and immediacy now taken for granted, as direct link-ups and on the spot commentary became the order of the day. Television journalism took on aspects of dramatic spectacle, a linchpin in the growing competition for audiences. In 1958 the first television coverage of a by-election at Rochdale had revolutionized, literally overnight, the process of electoral politics, challenging existing rules of broadcast comment and discussion prior to an election, and promoting an unprecedentedly high turnout at the polling station into the bargain. As Kenneth Allsop wrote in the *Daily Mail*, 'The televoter is born. . . . Television is established as the hub of the hustings' (Buscombe 1981: 6). By the general election of 1964 the entire popular apparatus of tele-coverage was in place, complete with multiple on-the-spot reports, studio interviews and analysis, and the infamous swingometer. Major politicians became television personalities and were obliged, like it or not, to master the camera, the interview and the television process in general. Notwithstanding the natural television presence demonstrated by Macmillan, it was Harold Wilson who thus became the first prime minister to contend with television as a major determining force in the nation's political affairs. His reading of Theodore White's account, in *The Making of the President*, of Richard Nixon's 'heavy beard of the "bad guy" ' image in the famous televised contest with Kennedy, was a formative influence on his own virtuoso performance against the cadaverously untelegenic Alec Douglas Home during the presidentially styled campaign of 1964 (see Sked and Cook 1979: 217).

A SENSE OF URGENCY: PILKINGTON AND AFTER

Unease at the power of television to form opinion and at its position in the unmistakable ideological shifts taking place at every level of society was thrown into relief by unequivocal demonstrations of the new significance of the medium in matters explicitly political. It was the coverage of the upheavals of 1968 – the Grosvenor Square pro-Viet-Cong demonstration, the Paris *évènements*, the Democratic Convention in Chicago, the Soviet invasion of Czechoslovakia – that produced a watershed in attitudes to the relationship between television and political affairs. From here on the messenger, bloodstained from the thick of battle, could himself be blamed for the message. In 1971 the BBC faced the combined wrath of the political and newspaper communities, first over the scathing depiction of senior members of the recently deposed Wilson administration in the documentary *Yesterday's Men*, then over their decision to handle the matter through an internal inquiry. The following year the governors came under direct pressure from the Home Secretary, Reginald Maudling, to withdraw *A Question of Ulster*, in which representatives of the conflicting groups in Northern Ireland had been brought together in a television studio. In an attempt to forestall Conservative plans for a Broadcasting Council, the corporation set up their own Complaints Commission. Then, in 1973, an injunction was taken out by Norris McWhirter, temporarily banning the screening of a film by Associated Television about Andy Warhol on grounds of scenes likely to offend the viewer. Though the film was eventually transmitted, the unprecedented appeal to the obscenity laws in a matter of television broadcasting effectively left the Independent Broadcasting Authority with an implicit obligation to vet all possibly controversial programmes prior to transmission. Meanwhile, from the other end of the political spectrum, fundamental questions of access and democratic control were being raised as the TV-4 Campaign protested against commercial plans for the fourth channel and trade unions questioned the terms in which industrial affairs were covered on the screen. The 1960s, it seemed, was the era in which it became gradually apparent that, above all, in the public life of the nation, television mattered; a period in which the very nature of television and its position within the cultural life of the nation became a matter of public debate and involvement.

It was the setting up of the Pilkington Committee by the Conservative government in 1960, to consider the future of broadcasting in Britain, that marked the official recognition of a general unease, particularly concerning the perceived conflict between 'good broadcasting' and the immense financial profits reaped in the few short years since the first commercial licences had been awarded. The assumption governing the report (published two years later), that decisions concerning the constitution and organization of broadcasting would have 'a direct effect on the quality of the nation's total culture' (Smith 1974: 118), provided the springboard for debates and controversies around 'trivialization', 'sensationalism' and 'standards' that were to permeate public life over the next dozen or so years. As Stuart Hood points out, however, Pilkington's deliberations took place firmly within the context of a liberal consensus, signally avoiding more radical issues such as the question of impartiality, news value and the ideological assumptions governing public and commercial broadcasting (1980: 72–3). Voices on the Right were not to be quite as diffident. By 1963, at a conference in Birmingham, Mary Whitehouse had brought together the 'clean up TV' movement, begetter of the National Viewers' and Listeners' Association (NVLA), the fundamentalist voice of which was to harry the broadcasting community – principally the BBC – across the decade and beyond.

The increasingly problematic status of television as a perceived political force in public life is also reflected in the gradual emergence of critical and academic debate around the medium. The development of cultural studies as an academic field, institutionally inaugurated with the establishment of the Centre for Contemporary Cultural Studies at Birmingham in 1964, was to provide the framework within which, however tentatively, television as a form, practice and institution in the broader compass of the mass media was to begin to enter into the territory of scholarly discourse. The expansion of the field was marked by the establishment of two other key redbrick research centres in 1966: the Centre for Mass Communication Research at Leicester University; and the Centre for Television Research at Leeds.

It is not until the mid-1970s that a full theoretical discourse of television studies can be seen to emerge, crystallizing in particular around the twin poles of British cultural studies on the one hand, with its spectator-oriented emphasis on a democratic plurality of 'reading practices', and the harsher Althusserian structuralism of film theory on the other. The latter, associated particularly with the journal *Screen*, represents a conscious appropriation of post-1968 issues of signification and the subject, its most famous text being the debate around realism and the ideological positioning of the spectator in the Garnett/Loach series, *Days of Hope*. That these plays are addressed essentially as films within the broad critical framework of classic cinematic and literary realism, rather than in the institutional context of broadcasting, is but one indication of what can now be recognized as a crisis at the time in the critical discourse. The tradition of cultural studies, however, reaches back beyond the 1960s, to already significant interventions in the debate around the class nature of postwar British society – Hoggart's *The Uses of Literacy*, Williams's *Culture and Society* and *The Long Revolution*, and Thompson's *The Making of the English Working Class* (see Hall *et al.* 1980: 16).

If the mass media were to provide an important point of focus in a new, expanding and interdisciplinary curriculum that sought the rescue of culture from the Leavisite dichotomy of high and low, early scholarship in the field nevertheless clearly demonstrated a recourse to not wholly dissimilar systems of valorization. The collection of essays in Denys Thompson's *Discrimination and Popular Culture* (1964) show remarkable unanimity in their castigation of both the trivializing effects of television and the susceptibility of its audience. Even Hall and Whannel's *The Popular Arts*, published in the same year, reassuringly offers the sceptical schoolteacher a critical method for sorting wheat from chaff:

In terms of actual quality (and it is with this, rather than with 'effects', that we are principally concerned) the struggle between good and worth while and what is shoddy and debased is not a struggle *against* the modern forms of communication, but a conflict *within* these media. Our concern is with the difficulty which most of us experience in distinguishing the one from the other, particularly when we are dealing with new media, new means of expression, in a new, and often confusing, social and cultural situation.

(Hall and Whannel 1964: 15)

There is, then, a certain consonance between academic and public debate around the cultural significance of television during this period. The expansion of the medium, at a technological and a programming level, seemed to trigger a deep-seated sense of trepidation at the challenge of the new. Indeed, as the director Ken Loach was to suggest in 1990 (in an interview for the BBC's arts programme *The Late Show*), it was the impact of television on 'innocent eyes' – on a generation, in other words, who still could not be expected to take the medium for granted – that largely accounted for the shock waves set up by programmes such as *Cathy Come Home*. Little wonder, in such a climate, that the Pilkington Report was compelled to talk of a fundamental association between the public's concern with television and their anxiety about change in British society in general, or that the NVLA, in a manifesto presented as a petition to Parliament in 1965, could unflinchingly contend

that crime, violence and illegitimacy and venereal disease are steadily increasing, yet the BBC employs people whose ideas and advice pander to the lowest in human nature, accompanying this with a stream of suggestive and erotic plays which present promiscuity, infidelity and drinking as normal and inevitable.

NEW STORIES

The pre-eminence accorded to 'plays' in the demonology of the NVLA demonstrates perhaps the impact of the new television drama in the 1960s in relation to its position in the overall output. If there was a revolution in television's representation of the contemporary experience, it was along this front that the deepest incursions were made. Indeed, the very model of the 'progressive' single play, operating as a special force at the political cutting edge of the medium and couched dominantly in terms of a radical social realism, owes much to the pioneering programmes of plays that mark out that decade, from ABC's *Armchair Theatre* at the very end of the 1950s, to the BBC's two most politically contentious seasons of *Wednesday Plays* in 1965 and 1967. The genres that emerged and flourished during the 1960s have provided the foundations upon which the various traditions of television fiction have all developed. The single play, situation comedy, the drama series and the open-ended serial (or soap opera) are essentially products of the early part of the decade. Significantly, however, these new stories all capitalized upon – and, more importantly, subverted – dramatic modes inherited from the 1950s; a practice in which can be detected the conscious desire to dramatize new social and cultural shifts in the postwar era.

Ironically, this radical movement was fostered not only by the new liberal patronage of the Greene regime but by far more pragmatic imperatives. Notwithstanding its castigations of commercial television and its implicit leaning towards the values of public service broadcasting, Pilkington marked the tacit recognition that the duopoly was here to stay, and so heralded the beginning of a sense of competition that was to thrust the BBC into a new post-Reithian age of comprehensive and populist programming. Drama was at the centre of this initiative. For the 1958–9 season of *Armchair Theatre*, the new producer, Sydney Newman – a Canadian trained under the documentary film director John Grierson – had taken the ambitious step of replacing the repertoire of imports from America and Canada or from the West End stage with a programme dominated by new work written for television itself. Newman's championing of indigenous contemporary playwriting, and his leaning towards a new technical realism and social topicality, marked an important step forward, but it was rooted in an unabashed populism that recognized the importance of a new mass working-class audience. The success of this strategy (average viewing figures of 11 million, across 46 weeks a year, with over 6 million for an obscure play by Pinter called *A Night Out*), assisted, as Newman himself admitted, by the scheduling of *Armchair Theatre* after *Sunday Night at the London Palladium* (see Shubik 1975: 31), was clearly important for a company anxious for cultural prestige at a time of increasing anti-commercialism, but its effects quickly spread to the BBC. In 1963 Newman was poached to run the BBC's drama department, from where he launched not only the flagship *Wednesday Play* but a whole flotilla of serials, from *Dr Who* to *Dr Finlay's Casebook*, aimed at capturing a broad mass audience in the new ratings war.

The first heading in that new chapter of institutional rivalry and social awareness had already been clearly written with a now famous live transmission by Granada Television at 7 pm on Friday 9 December 1960. Conceived by a bright young producer, Tony Warren, just six months earlier, *Coronation Street* originally had a life expectancy of only 13 weeks, but within a year had become the top rating programme on the national network. Its origins may have been modest, but the sense of cultural significance that lay behind Granada's ambitions for the serial was clear. 'A fascinating free-masonry, a volume of unwritten rules. These are the driving forces behind a working class street in the north of England', wrote Warren in his original brief (Buscombe 1981: 79), while the genealogy of names floated by the executives – the original Florizel Street giving way to Jubilee, and Coronation, with Edward and Victoria also in the lists – suggested a national emblem of a rather different order. Debates around the ideological significance of the series have swung ever since between criticisms of its inherently conservative image of community and more optimistic readings of its narrative and character functions (see Dyer 1981), but there can be no mistaking the distance travelled between its original, popular and socially specific intentions and its eventual apotheosis, into a declassed and garishly exuberant national institution.

The predominantly celebratory and nostalgic tone of *Coronation Street*, depicting working-class life through a gallery of sharply drawn characters, obviously militated against its ability to explore contemporary reality in terms of social friction or tension. We might wish to acknowledge, however, an echo of the theme of the socially displaced scholarship boy – a recurring focus of cultural fracture in the more radical canon of Dennis Potter and David Mercer – in the early depiction of the homecoming trainee-teacher, Ken Barlow. Elsewhere, television drama in its various forms became the dominant means by which Britain in the 1960s came face to face with the disintegration of the postwar myth of social cohesion and homogeneity. Two early *Armchair Theatre* plays, Clive Exton's *Where I Live* and Angus Wilson's *The Stranger*, both dealt with the ironies of the new ethos of social mobility, one in terms of a tussle between a working-class couple and their 'successful' in-laws over responsibility for the care of the father, the other through a surreal satire of middle-class rivalry between new money and old.

It was under the umbrella of *The Wednesday Play*, however, that the new social realism was to flourish. Though by no means the dominant strand in the series, the astringently topical and formally innovative dramas produced under Newman by young mavericks such as Tony Garnett and James McTaggart quickly assumed the status of a *cause célèbre*. In 1965 alone, Nell Dunn's *Up the Junction* and Michael Hastings's *For the West* came under fierce attack from the NVLA and sections of the press, the former principally for its abortion scene, the latter for its story of a white woman raped by black children. Beneath these specific objections, however, lay a deeper hostility to the political depictions taking place, from Dunn's energetic picture of working-class life to Hastings's uncomfortable reminder of war in the Congo. Drama, and particularly the single play, quickly became the focus of the growing antagonism towards the supposed liberalism of the BBC, moral outrage not infrequently tipping over into objections of a more overtly political nature. '*The Wednesday Play*', wrote Mary Whitehouse (1971: 73), 'roamed clumsily, even subversively, amongst the most sensitive areas of human, social and international relationships, and was quite prepared to exploit its opportunities for propaganda'. Nor was such a vision of the corporation as 'the enemy within' confined to the Christian fundamentalist lobby. In 1989 we find the liberal Tory MP Julian Critchley, himself an advocate at the end of the 1960s for the establishment of a Broadcasting Council, attributing the abiding 'hatred' of his party for the BBC not to the satire of *That Was The Week That Was* or to the perceived bias of their political journalism, but to the 'grainy drama-documentaries which challenged the comfortable assumptions of those whom the electorate had, in its wisdom, chosen to govern us'. If a Tory was looking for left-wing bias at the BBC, Critchley recalls being told by Lord Swann, 'he need go no further than the drama department' (Critchley 1989: 21).

PERMISSION TO SPEAK

Such club-room banter may lose its comic edge when we rehearse the evidence of conspiracies in the early 1970s to dismiss filmmakers such as Garnett and Roland Joffé from the BBC. The boundaries of the possible have always been unequivocally marked out by specific moments at which the institution of television has found itself confronted by a drama whose formal complexity truly challenges political assumptions. The supreme example of such a crisis can be found in *The War Game*, Peter Watkins's film drama for the BBC, originally due to be screened in 1966 but withdrawn for the next 20 years. The real challenge of Watkins's film lay not so much in its convincing depiction of the aftermath of nuclear attack as in the implications of its dramatic technique. Rejecting the prevailing aesthetic of naturalism that underlay even the most challenging social plays of the period, it appropriated and subverted a range of non-dramatic conventions (documentary, actuality foot-age, public service announcement, interview, etc.) traditionally associated with the authority and authenticity of television as 'infor-mation'. In so doing, *The War Game* effectively added up to a deconstruction of the medium and institution of television itself and of its politically 'neutral' role of benign paternalism. Small wonder that the BBC was prepared to countenance the film's release for theatrical exhibition, where its intertextual potency would be safely neutralized. It was arguably the same self-reflexive rule-breaking that made *That Was The Week That Was* so hot to handle and that contributed to its early demise. Generated by the team responsible for the new current affairs magazine programme *Tonight* and pro-duced under the formal supervision of the Television Talks Depart-ment, *TW3* stirred the live theatricality of cabaret and revue and the new conventions of studio-based television (interviews, comment, direct-to-camera presentation, etc.) into a lethally unpredictable brew, the effects of which could not help but spill over into the way the rest of television might be watched and understood.

As their titles sometimes indicate, the satirical and revue pro-grammes that followed in the wake of *TW3* – *The Frost Report, Not So Much a Programme, BBC 3, Not Only But Also, Do Not Adjust Your Set* and, at the very end of the decade, *Monty Python's Flying Circus* – were partly dedicated to subverting the increasingly recognizable languages and formats of the more respectable end of television itself. Nothing, however, could quite recapture the tension that was essential to both the form of *TW3* and its up-to-the-minute writing, rehearsal and transmission schedule (conditions which, incidentally, allowed for the edition on the night of Kennedy's assassination to change at the eleventh hour into a far more sombre affair).

Beyond such explicit curtailments, however, and beyond the examples of censorship that pepper the history of television drama (the vetting of David Mercer's *A Climate of Fear* in 1962 for possible pro-CND propaganda, for example, or the last-minute refusal to transmit Dennis Potter's *Vote, Vote, Vote for Nigel Barton* without a rewrite of its final, anti-establishment speech), any sense of the new television drama as a site of truly radical opposition has to be measured in terms of the essential closures at work within the medium itself. By the end of the decade, it might be argued, the challenges of *The Wednesday Play* had been absorbed, its socio-political messages now familiar territory and its intensive realism no longer quite so alarming. In his stage play *The Party*, Trevor Griffiths's working-class writer, Sloman (loosely modelled, it has often been observed, on David Mercer himself), offers a typically lugubrious critique of the revolutionary permissiveness that popularly defines the culture of television during the period.

> The only thing you're allowed to put in to the system is that which can be assimilated and absorbed by it. Joe, this is a society that has 'matured' on descriptions of its inequity and injustice. Poverty is one of its best favoured *spectacles*. Bad housing, class divisive schools, the plight of the sick and the aged, the alienating indignities of work, the fatuous vacuities of 'leisure' – Jesus God, man, we can't get enough of it. It's what makes us so 'humane', seeing all that, week in, week out. Wednesday Plays? It's the Liberal heartland, Joe. Every half-grown, second rate, soft-bowel-led pupa in grub street is in there fighting with you. It's the consensus. It's the condition of our time. Impetigo. Pink. Itchy. Mildly catching.
>
> (Griffiths 1974: 67)

Written and first performed in 1973, but set during the events of May 1968, Griffiths's play is centrally concerned with the politics of intellectual and cultural production at the turn of the decade, its protagonist, Joe Shawcross, a left-wing working-class television drama producer struggling with the ideological contradictions of his social and professional position. While other institutions – academy, theatre, journalism, to name but three – come under scrutiny in the play, it is television that comes to represent the central crisis for the radical intellectual or artist in a potent yet repressively tolerant 'culture industry'. For Griffiths, the irony of Joe's occupation in this most glittering of careers is too good to miss. 'A socialist producer?' demands Sloman, 'What's that? It's irrelevant' (1974: 66).

Sloman, one suspects, has been reading his Marcuse and, particularly, it would seem, the essay 'The affirmative character of culture', itself published in 1968. For Marcuse, artistic production serves as a means of transposing the expression of inequality or suffering on to an aesthetic level, a cathartic process through which existing social relations, rather than being challenged, are merely reasserted (see Wolff 1981: 89). And in *One-Dimensional Man*, published four years earlier, we find him arguing in particular against the repressive effect of a mass culture that, in its very simulation of a communal experience, has the power to 'de-emphasize real class differences and to assimilate cells of resistance' (see Bigsby 1976: 15).

Of course, it is not difficult to imagine that one of the *Wednesday Plays* to which Sloman refers might be the celebrated *Cathy Come Home*, emblem of the radical realism of the 1960s and principal classic text in the canon of progressive television drama that has bequeathed respectability and gravitas to the medium. Yet, as Loach himself has since admitted, far from articulating a truly radical analysis that might have dealt with such fundamental ideological questions as the ownership of land, this was a play very much in the liberal tradition of social description. *Cathy Come Home* may have contributed to the setting up of Shelter, but in the light of an even deeper crisis of homelessness in the early 1990s, that achievement appears, at best, a modest index of political efficacy and, at worst, little more than a fragment in the wider strategy of ideological containment to which Sloman so scathingly testifies.

Any discussion of television during the 1960s then must take account of competing definitions of the medium as a cultural agent; between the consensual affirmations of a bourgeois commodity-driven institution and the challenges of what Dennis Potter had identified by the middle of the decade as this 'most democratic medium'. For the 1960s counter-culture, television as institution and as popular cultural product was incurably infected by the twin evils of commercialism and bourgeois officialdom. By the turn of the decade it had become even more graphically associated with an older, parental generation and – particularly through the pronouncements of such gurus as Charles Reich – with a profoundly anti-revolutionary culture of passive consumption and false needs (see Buxton 1990: 3). Yet, compared with the USA, where a heightened form of commercialism was more obviously inherent in the structure of broadcasting, the British countercultural rejection of television held far less sway. The reasons for this are primarily sociological. For a new post-1944 Education Act school of writers and directors, often intent on addressing the class from which they had emerged, television had been firmly recognized as a necessary site for political intervention and for the struggle over collective meaning at the heart of the capitalist culture industry. Potter's work since *Vote, Vote, Vote for Nigel Barton*, like the later work of Griffiths, Jim Allen, Alan Bleasdale and many more, is testimony to the legacy of that entryist challenge, complete with all its contradictions. For John McGrath, one of the initiators of *Z-Cars*, the end of the liberal experiment was less a matter of ideological purity and more a question of reasserted institutional control. A decade that had begun with the British ruling class in confident mood had ended with the first signs of economic collapse and political reaction: 'So the BBC, sensitive as ever, has altered its structure. Anarchy is over. Centralised control, elaborate systems of command, super-vision, check and review have been introduced. And on the personal level, the bully-boys have moved in to stay' (McGrath 1977: 104).

CONCLUSION

We began this account with a consideration of some of the dominant retrospective impressions of the 1960s as a distinct era in the history of television. It is worth pointing out the extent to which, by the very nature of the medium, our contemporary understanding of that moment is now mediated via television itself. At one level, the very continuity of television serves to anaesthetize us to a critical sense of its historical significance. *Coronation Street* and Alf Garnett, two of the most potent social creations of the 1960s, both live on into a politically evacuated old age, long after *Z-Cars* has been transformed, via its 1970s spin-offs, into just another police series. Even more invidiously, however, in a form of intertextual cannibal-ism characteristic of the mass media in general, television has increasingly fed on itself – and never more voraciously than in the wholesale reappropriation of the imagery of the 1960s. This occasional and highly fragmented re-screening by television of its own past has little to do with either a commitment to the informed attention to the historical transformations of the medium or an unlocking of the archives for public scrutiny. In the state-of-the-art world of the electronic media, the past is indeed a foreign country and they do things differently there. Seasons devoted to the early work of television dramatists selectively elevated to the literary canon – so far, David Mercer and Dennis Potter – rub shoulders with the occasional retrospective, the celebratory compilation and the unashamedly parasitic telly quiz in what often appears as a conspiracy to represent a television identifiably (and often, by impli-

cation, comically) other than that to which we are now accustomed
– black and white, acoustically flawed, crudely edited, largely studio
bound, maybe peopled with the younger faces of now familiar personalities and, of course, shot through with all the iconographic
excesses of the period for which a condescending amusement is
constructed as the expected response. Of the hundred or so extracts
idiosyncratically packaged into Channel Four's three-hour long cav-
alcade *The A-Z of Television* in 1990, all but a handful came from
between 1955 and 1975, a full 60 per cent originating from the
1960s themselves. It is a decade characteristically offered to us as
'yesterday's' television, its imagery plundered in the fetishization of
the ephemeral and the incidental that is part of a particular brand
of post-modern 'pop' culture.

Of course, in dealing principally with the field of dramatic or
fictional entertainment, we may ourselves distort the picture. Given
the appropriate archival resources, it may be that we could learn
more about the 1960s from the changing design of the BBC logo or
from a study of narrative and character developments in the Oxo
commercials. If the explosion of the mass media in the 1960s teaches
us anything, it is that our very definition of 'drama' must be wid-
ened, not only to include those other narrative forms, situation
comedy and popular serials and series, that were forged in the
crucible of the decade, but to address the more fundamental sense
of television as the means by which society in all its complexity is
itself mediated in a heightened form. Raymond Williams's idea of
a 'dramatised society', though promulgated in a lecture marking his
inauguration, in 1974, in a Cambridge chair of drama, is essentially
shaped by a critical engagement with the entire culture of television
– his attempt, mainly through a monthly column in *The Listener*,
to 'make sense of the more general television experience' during the
late 1960s (Williams 1989: x). If, as Williams argues, television is
the prime example of the intersection between drama as a formalized, occasional social activity and as a habitual experience at the
very centre of our cultural existence, then it is the gradual dawning
of this problematic as a central, often contradictory, function of the
medium that can be said to define the real revolution of television
in the 1960s. When, precisely halfway through the decade, Hugh
Greene spoke of the broadcaster's 'duty to take account of the
changes in society, to be ahead of public opinion rather than always
to wait on it' (Smith 1974: 183), charges of subversion and the
challenge to democracy began to be heard in the land. The great

'drama' of television during this period, it seems, is to be found in the critical struggle – inside the institution and in the public debate surrounding it – over the political status of broadcasting and its relationship with the whole unsettling process of cultural change.

BIBLIOGRAPHY

Alvarado, M. and Tulloch, J. 1983. *Doctor Who: The Unfolding Text.* London: Macmillan.

Bigsby, C. W. E. (ed.) 1976. *Approaches to Popular Culture.* London: Edward Arnold.

Buscombe, E. (ed.) 1981. *Granada: The First 25 Years.* London: British Film Institute.

Brandt, G. W. (ed.) 1981. *British Television Drama.* Cambridge: Cambridge University Press.

Buxton, D. 1990. *From 'The Avengers' to 'Miami Vice': Form and Ideology in Television Series.* Manchester: Manchester University Press.

Critchley, J. 1989. 'How the BBC provokes the Tories'. *Guardian*, 13 Feb. 1989, 21.

Dyer, R. (ed.) 1981. *Coronation Street.* London: British Film Institute.

Edgar, D. *et al.* 1982. *Ah! Mischief: The Writer and Television.* London: Faber & Faber.

Elliott, J. 1970. *Mogul: The Making of a Myth.* London: Barrie & Rockliffe.

Gardner, C. and Wyver, J. 1983. 'The single play; from Reithian reverence to cost-accounting and censorship'. *Screen*, vol. 24, no. 4–5, 114–29.

Garnett, T., Gould, J. and Hudson, R. 1972. 'Television in Britain: description and dissent'. *Theatre Quarterly*, vol. 2, no. 6, 18–25.

Gilbert, W. S. 1975. 'In and out of the box'. *Plays and Players*, vol. 2, no. 6, 11–15.

Goldie, G. W. 1977. *Facing the Nation: Television and Politics 1936–1976.* London: Bodley Head.

Griffiths, T. 1974. *The Party.* London: Faber & Faber.

Hall, S., Hobson, D., Lowe, A. and Willis, P. (eds) 1980. *Culture, Media and Language: Working Papers in Cultural Studies 1972–1979.* London: Hutchinson.

Hall, S. and Whannel, P. 1964. *The Popular Arts: A Critical Guide to the Mass Media.* Boston: Beacon.

Hewison, R. 1986. *Too Much: Art and Society in the Sixties 1960–75.* London: Methuen.

Hood, S. 1980. *On Television.* London: Pluto.

Itzin, C. 1972. 'Production casebook no. 6: *Upstairs Downstairs*'. *Theatre Quarterly*, vol. 2, no. 6, 26–38.

MacCabe, C. 1990. 'Death of a nation: television in the early sixties'. *Critical Quarterly*, vol. 30, no. 2, 34–46.

Maddern P. 1976. *British Television Drama 1959–1973*, Complete Programme Notes for a Season Held at the National Film Theatre, 11–24 October 1976. London: British Film Institute.

McGrath, J. 1977. 'TV drama: the case against naturalism'. *Sight and Sound*, vol. 46, no. 2, 100–5.

Marwick, A. 1982. *British Society Since 1945*. Harmondsworth: Penguin.

Milne, A. 1988. *DG: The Memoirs of a British Broadcaster*. London: Hodder & Stoughton.

Murdock, G. 1980. 'Radical drama, radical theatre'. *Media, Culture and Society*, no. 2, 151–68.

Shubik, I. 1975. *Play for Today: The Evolution of Television Drama*. London: Davis Poynter.

Shulman, M. 1973. *The Least Worst Television in the World*. London: Barrie & Jenkins.

Sked, A. and Cook, C. 1979. *Post War Britain: A Political History*. Brighton: Harvester.

Smith, A. (ed.) 1974. *British Broadcasting*. Newton Abbot: David & Charles.

Thomas, H. 1977. *With an Independent Air*. London: Weidenfeld & Nicolson.

Thompson, D. (ed.) 1964. *Discrimination and Popular Culture*. Harmondsworth: Penguin.

Whitehouse, M. 1971. *Who Does She Think She Is?* London: New English Library.

Williams, R. 1974. *Television: Technology and Cultural Form*; 2nd edn edited by Williams, E. 1990. London: Routledge.

Williams, R. edited by O'Connor, A. 1989. *Raymond Williams on Television: Selected Writings*. London: Routledge.

Wolff, J. 1981. *The Social Production of Art*. London: Macmillan.

FURTHER READING

Indispensable to a study of television in this period is Smith (1974), an authoritatively annotated selection of documents providing unparalleled coverage of the development of debate in and around the broadcasting institutions. Memoirs of broadcasters such as Milne (1988), Goldie (1977) and Thomas (1977) contain fascinating but understandably subjective accounts of the background to programme-making during the period. Drawing similarly on first-hand experience, Shubik (1975) examines the development of television drama, including the *Wednesday Play*. Studies of key television dramatists of the period can be found in Brandt (1981), the introduction to which also covers important developments in technology and dramatic form. For a sharply focused polemical analysis of the radical impulse in television drama during the 1960s, see Murdock (1980); for analytical case-studies of two popular drama series of the period, see Alvarado and Tulloch (1983) and Elliot (1970). Shulman (1973) gives a witty, informative, but somewhat jaundiced account of the populism of the BBC under Greene. Finally, no discussion of television during this period would be complete without reference to Williams (1974), a remarkably prescient critical study of the medium and its possibilities.

Chapter 8

British poetry and its discontents

Robert Sheppard

THE POETRY OF THE 1960s

To ask 'What was the poetry of the 1960s?' and to ask 'What is the poetry of the 1960s?' is not to ask the same question. The first could be answered neutrally; a bibliography of all books classified as poetry during that decade. It could be assumed that the 1960s is a certain 10-year period, and not the shorthand for a *zeitgeist*, whether that is the 'swinging sixties' of the popular imagination or the period of gestation of much post-structuralist, feminist or Marxist modes of our current intellectual histories.

To ask what the poetry is suggests that the vantage point of the 1990s offers an evaluative overview that might differ significantly from contemporary accounts. This is not just a conventional re-evaluation of forgotten or hidden talents, but it admits more honestly that, supplementary to our diligence as historians, our readings happen in the present. I prefer to ask the second of my opening questions, reframed as: What is the poetry that can be most clearly identified as relating to the 1960s as an era of attempted 'cultural revolution'?

To answer this question involves the abandonment of some familiar names. Ted Hughes and Sylvia Plath were clearly important figures during this period, though their work did not belong to the poetry reading and small-press publication network that I see as the material base for this poetry, and which I shall examine in the third section of this chapter. More popularly, the Liverpool poets, Adrian Henri, Roger McGough and Brian Patten, who emerged from this network into commercial success and minor stardom, represent another poetry of the 1960s. Their mild pop art inheritance, along with a borrowing from beat lyricism, rode on the

success of the Beatles, and is still popular with audiences. Meanwhile Hughes has been elected to laureateship and Plath has become
a legend as feminist heroine.

Despite these writers, the orthodoxy that has dominated British
verse since the Second World War was established in the 1950s in
the practice of the so-called Movement writers – Philip Larkin,
Donald Davie, John Wain, Kingsley Amis, Elizabeth Jennings and
others. Their ascendancy, which outlasted the turbulence of the
1960s, led to the obscuring and devaluation of much other work,
not just of emerging writers, but of older talents like W. S. Graham
and Basil Bunting, who were producing some of their best work in
the 1960s.[1] It was not just an anti-modernist poetic of social realist
irony, which I shall examine in the next section, but a self-conscious
publishing machine. Anthony Hartley at *The Spectator*, John Wain
at the BBC and Donald Davie in his critical work, helped establish
the orthodoxy through the promotion of Movement values, a process
recorded by Blake Morrison in *The Movement*. It is not surprising
that the poets of the 1960s saw these figures, and others, as the
establishment, from which they were excluded, and consequently
organized their own network of alternatives.

It is no accident that Blake Morrison, with Andrew Motion, is
also co-editor of *The Penguin Book of Contemporary British Poetry* (1982),
an anthology that, although it places ludic metaphorization at a
premium, promotes the latest Establishment writers. Andrew
Motion is also Larkin's biographer, as well as poetry editor of
Chatto & Windus, in which role he is Blake Morrison's publisher.
Along with Craig Raine, the chief 'metaphor man' and ex-poetry
editor of Faber, these poet-critics have followed the 1950s poets in
attempting to impose a taste on a decade. They favour a continuation of a poetic mode that was fully established by 1960. A little
flashier in its metaphors, a little laxer in its rhythms, a little more
open to a safely historical modernism, it nevertheless represents the
persistence of the Movement orthodoxy, and one that deliberately
asserts rejection of all the poetries of the 1960s.

My reading of the 1960s concentrates on four poets who remain
active at the radical edge of British poetry, a position that entails
both a late modernist commitment to breaking the paradigms that
define poetry, and a loose commitment to radical and marginal
political perspectives and causes. It is the antithesis of the dominant
orthodoxy. These four writers have produced some of the best work

since the beginning of the 1960s, and it is my hope that they will now seem less marginal than they have been made to appear.

DONALD DAVIE AND BRITISH POETRY: LARKIN AND FISHER

Donald Davie's *Thomas Hardy and British Poetry* (1973) was an attempt to argue that the most enduring influence on British poetry was Hardy. As such, it was the re-assertion of the poetic of the Movement, embodied, for Davie, in the work of Philip Larkin (and in the creative and critical practice of Davie himself). The so-called 'extremity' of Hughes and Plath is given short shrift. Underpinning this, the book's political manifesto is an attempt to counter the counter-culture of the 1960s – another 'extremity' – by asserting the necessity of a return to a social-democratic centrist and consensual politics, moderated by modesty and a willingness to lose one's nerve in potentially apocalyptic international confrontations such as Suez and Vietnam. Unfortunately consensus had broken down in both politics and poetry by the end of the 1960s, although Davie still sees his versions of both prefigured in Hardy's quietist scientific humanism and in 'Larkin's poetry of lowered sights and patiently diminished expectations' (Davie 1973: 71).

Larkin's poetry, and that of the Movement orthodoxy generally, favours narrative coherence and closure, taking over a number of devices from realist fiction. 'Mr Bleaney', from *The Whitsun Weddings* (1964), tells of a prospective boarder inspecting and finally taking an insufficient room with a landlady who continually reminds him of the former occupant (who cleverly remains both a focus and an absence). Its plot is reducible to paraphrase, its details easily naturalized. It is a poetry that atomizes the world into discrete, recognizable and consumable 'experiences':

This was Mr Bleaney's room. He stayed
The whole time he was at the Bodies, till
They moved him.

Why was he moved? It may be unfair to expect an answer, any more than to query Mr Bleaney's attitudes to industrial relations. But merely to ask such questions shows how areas of experience are – necessarily perhaps – excluded. Grammar and syntax are not open to modernist disruption and the Movement poems' common insistence upon the speaking voice strives to maintain the effect of a stable ego for the narrator, an individualized human personality. In 'Mr Bleaney' he is typical, exemplary; his calamities are banal: 'Stuffing my ears with cotton-wool, to drown/The jabbering set he egged her on to buy' (Larkin 1964: 10). The iambic base levels the speech of tonal levity, emphasizes presence, although the rhymes and pentameters are disguised by run-ons. It appears to deny its own artifice; its form is invisible. Likewise there is no modernist self-consciousness, or delving into what Larkin has called disparagingly the 'myth-kitty'. The narrator is not Tiresias, Mr Bleaney is not Mr Eugenides, and there are no quotations from Spenser to contrast his world to Bleaney's. There is, however, ironical judgement and moral questioning, if not quite affirmation, that remains rooted in this everyday world. The narrator meditates upon Mr Bleaney's condition; did he shiver 'without taking off the dread/ That how we live measures our own nature'? The narrator slides effortlessly from the 'I' of personal experience to the consensual 'we' of Davie's and Larkin's ambivalent sense of community.[2]

'Hardy and Larkin', Davie writes, 'may have sold poetry short but at least neither of them has sold it short so as to make the poet less than a human being' (1973: 73). Recognizable human values, as in Larkin's concluding questions, assure us the poet is 'a citizen of some commonwealth' (1973: 73).

Before examining writers excluded from this commonwealth (the term has a suitably post-colonial ring of fellowship about it), it is more instructive to see what has to be sacrificed if an important figure is to be granted admission.

Roy Fisher began to write seriously in 1955 but immdiately recognized that 'the commonwealth' excluded both his working-class experience of Birmingham and his commitment to European modernism The former drove him more into the city as his private poetic focus, while the latter provided an aesthetic. The fruit of this dual approach was *City*, a work in both prose and poetry, that was published as a mimeographed pamphlet in 1961 by Gael Turnbull's Migrant Press. More or less a lone enterprise in those days, before the exfoliation of little presses dealt with in my next section, Turnbull's press also published *Migrant*, a magazine which gave Fisher access to the Black Mountain poets, Olson and Creeley, *Origin*'s Cid Corman, and the British-born American poet Denise Levertov, as well as to Turnbull's own pioneering poetry.[3]

Davie identifies the prose of *City* as 'description at its most impressive' but is generally dismissive of the verse. Yet such a mixture of forms was still audacious by the standards of the orthodoxy (1973:158). His tactic in Fisher's case and, more extraordinarily, in his treatment of J. H. Prynne, is to assert the poets' closeness to Hardy and Larkin and to privilege recognition of, and identification with, narratives of personal experience. But the narrator of *City* is hemmed in by perceptual excess. He is most often an alienated observer rather than a character like Mr Bleaney, and never rises to the moral embrace of 'we'. The city is never named; it is yet another of the hallucinatory, defamiliarized, 'unreal' cities of modernism.

> In an afternoon of dazzling sunlight in the thronged streets, I saw at first no individuals but a composite monster, its unfeeling surfaces matted with dust: a mass of necks, limbs without extremities, trunks without heads; unformed stirrings and shovings spilling across the streets it had managed to get itself provided with.
>
> (Fisher 1988: 23)

Given this disembodied presentation of the citizens, it is interesting that Davie sees Fisher 'opting for pathos and compassion' on the grounds that 'political alternatives to social democracy . . . are too costly in terms of human suffering' (Davie 1973: 172). What the work is focused upon are subjective transformations of the city, particularly the tardy redevelopment of Birmingham after wartime bombing and decades of social deprivation. When *City* is explicit about social conditions it is sceptical of, even anarchistic towards, Birmingham's 'limited and mean' administration:

> It supplies fuel, water and power. It removes a fair proportion of the refuse, cleans the streets after a fashion, and discourages fighting. With these things . . . it is content. There is no mind in it, no regard.
>
> (Fisher 1988: 23)

Throughout Fisher's work, techniques of defamiliarization – ways of making strange to disrupt readers' automatic responses – deny the habitual and familiar that so often provide the Movement orthodoxy with its consensual strength. While the two characters of 'Mr Bleaney' share social conventions, in Fisher's 'Interiors with Various Figures', written in the early 1960s, two speakers interact obscurely in an undefined relationship; even gender is uncertain. The objects of their rooms, unlike Mr Bleaney's 60-watt bulb that circumscribes a particular kind of domestic deprivation, become threatening agents in the drama: 'That bulb again. It has travelled even here' (Fisher 1988: 40). That this sequence of ten poems is mostly not in verse, but in a prose line derived from the propositional form of Wittgenstein's *Tractatus*, and was conceived in a systematic painterly way, with motifs repeating between sections, marks it off from Movement practice. Sheets on a billiard table become transformed, even transfigured, into

> the actual corpse, the patient dead under the anaesthetic,
> A third party playing gooseberry, a pure stooge, the ghost of a
>   paper bag;
> Something that stopped in the night.

(Fisher 1988: 47)

The reader is not a consumer of a recognizable English narrative – Fisher has called his technique 'de-Anglicizing England' – but is participating in an act of imaginative subversion of social realist readings. As Marcuse has argued, such images of freedom, located in an autonomous art work, are the beginnings of a critique of social reality, not an escape from it. Davie was right to be suspicious of Fisher's formalism, and was bound to find his contrasting empiricism comforting. It is in the tension between these extremes that Fisher operates so well, the reader situated for both recognition and wonder.

SWINGING THE DUPLICATOR HANDLE

The most spectacular poetry reading of the 1960s was the Poetry Incarnation of 1965, when 7,000 people filled the Albert Hall for four hours of poetry from Allen Ginsberg and fellow American beats, Adrian Mitchell, the British political poet Harry Fainlight and from the Austrian sound poet Ernst Jandl, among others. There seemed a new respect for poetry – particularly oral poetry – among the young. Possibly it seemed a minor, though significant, act of imaginative insurrection against the instrumental reason of a world that they were to recognize increasingly as not theirs – the world of the atomic bomb and Vietnam.

This was not a one-off event. Michael Horovitz's 1969 Penguin anthology *Children of Albion: Poetry of the 'Underground' in Britain* documented hundreds of live New Departures 'shows' that Horovitz organized in the 1960s; venues ranged from the Marquee to the

ICA, with a laudable disregard of conventional divisions between high and popular culture. The anthology ranges from imitative British beat poetry to mature work by Roy Fisher and Gael Turnbull, from uneven selections of Lee Harwood and Tom Raworth to dozens of other 'unwean'd kids' and poets yet to produce their best work.

A problem in summarizing this period is the sudden but confusing profusion of networks of little magazines and presses, to which Horovitz's anthology was also attempting to do justice. The spontaneity of this community of exchange for writer-editors is noted by Jeff Nuttall in his valuable account of these years, *Bomb Culture*; when he and his friends, including Bob Cobbing, were 'swinging the duplicator handle throughout the long Saturday afternoons of 1963 we had no idea that the same thing was happening all over the world' (Nuttall 1970: 159).

Bob Cobbing, an indefatigible arts and workshop organizer and publisher, had intermittently operated under the name Writers Forum since 1954. From 1963 the press became a model of radical consistency, tirelessly producing cheap mimeo pamphlets of concrete and experimental poetry, much of it Cobbing's own. By the end of the decade he had published 54 titles. Often he presented new talent, as in the case of Lee Harwood's *title illegible* (sic) in 1965, which contained beat and surrealist work that had been aired at Cobbing's workshops. Cobbing became manager of Better Books, an important venue for London readings and an unofficial resource centre.

These sorts of personal contact – from performances at Better Books up to Tom Pickard's Morden Tower bookselling and reading venue in Newcastle – were vital in order to sustain a poetry so different from established forms. Visiting Americans, whether Robert Creeley talking to a young Barry MacSweeney in Newcastle, or Edward Dorn resident at the University of Essex, broadened horizons by their presence, readings and information. In 1963 Lee Harwood went further, and visited the dying Dadaist Tristan Tzara, whose work he was to translate throughout the decade, in Paris (collected in Tzara 1987). This was tantamount to visiting modernism at its source. In 1965 he made his first trip to experimental modernism's second home, New York, where he met John Ashbery and other 'New York' writers who had adapted surrealism to a discursive mode. The result of his submission to this aesthetic was that his second book, *The Man with Blue Eyes*, was published in New York and received the prestigious Poets' Foundation Award.

Throughout the 1960s Harwood was also the publisher of an irregular magazine. In a refusal to produce monuments and to negate the consistency of a subscription list or bookshop distribution, each issue had a different title; one was *Tzarad*. It introduced a small nexus of readers Harwood had built up through correspondence to new English, American and French work. Tom Raworth's *Outburst* and J. H. Prynne's and Andrew Crozier's *The English Intelligencer*, and hundreds of other virtually unrecorded poetry magazines, were organized on the same vital, evanescent principle, in this time of relatively easy and cheap printing.

At the other end of the spectrum were publishers such as Fulcrum and Cape Goliard. Fulcrum was founded in 1965 by Stuart and Deidre Montgomery, and published quality hardbacks and paperbacks, with an impressive range of both British and American writers. Editions of work by Fisher, Harwood, Raworth and others materially assisted their reputations, but perhaps Fulcrum is best remembered for the publication of Basil Bunting's *Briggflatts* (1965), one of the most important achievements of the 1960s, a late flowering of the objectivist poetics of the 1930s. Goliard, run by Raworth and Barry Hall, received the backing of Cape, and published Olson as well as Turnbull and Prynne. Interestingly, both operations ceased in the early 1970s, reflecting the end of economic expansion and, in Goliard's case, the withdrawal of vital patronage.

Since then fugitive presses, operating through mail order or a few shops, or selling at readings, have propagated the most formally inventive work. They have rejected the increased commercialization of poetry publishing, are often without Arts Council or regional arts association funding (which has never favoured innovative work) and have pursued an independent line in terms of work published and production formats. Poetry publishing is as much a passion as the writing of it.

LEE HARWOOD: TOWARDS THE OPEN WORK

Lee Harwood's modernist inheritance gave him both a sense of the complexity and interconnectedness of apparently unrelated experiences, and a realization of the potentialities of fragmented narrative structures. The results are collected in Fulcrum's *The White Room* (1968).

The heroes of Harwood's modern 'mythology' are gunslingers, gauchos or insecure consul officials in forgotten colonies, all of them questors without a grail, hopelessly haunted by images of lost love. They are meaningless men in artificially ornate narratives. In those with a colonial setting, the characters' meaning has been removed as much by history as by the sudden breaks in narrative continuity. Larkin could satirize colonial independence and post-imperial withdrawal from a right-wing point of view in his 1969 'Homage to a Government' ('Next year we are to bring the soldiers home/For lack of money') but Harwood's 'The Doomed Fleet' activates the affective mythic imagery behind Larkin's chilling disregard for the colonial peoples who 'must guard themselves and keep themselves orderly' now (Larkin 1974: 29).

> The entire palace was deserted, just as was
> the city, and all the villages along the 50 mile
> route from the seaport to the capital.
> It was not caused by famine or war –
> 'It was all my fault.'
>
> > (Harwood 1988: 58)

This childlike plea is the storyteller's, who guiltily intrudes into the fiction; he is the single 'commander-in-chief' of the operation and he is responsible for the narrative deteriorating into cliché.

> Maybe they never did get there and, instead,
> the whole expedition lay at the bottom.
> This already begins to sound like a very bad boy's story.
>
> > (1988: 60)

Self-consciousness is not simply a literary game, but is a way of emphasizing how experience is inevitably distorted, even as it is communicated, by discourse: 'Nothing that would disturb the carefully planned/vanity was tolerated. That was the new order' (58). The expedition and the narrative are both self-consciously manipulated, both doomed, as options narrow towards an eventuality. The final section opens:

> Age began to show . . . and the divisions widen
> and become even more resolute and rigid.
> 'What could have been' became altogether another story
> like the family photos in the captain's wallet
> – there was no room for sentimentality now.
>
> > (60)

'Power' and 'menace' operate not merely in the purpose and armoury of the battleships, but in the area of linguistic control. The sailors

> didn't understand 'pity'. The very word
> had been deliberately deleted from all the books
> scattered among the fleet.
>
> (59)

Following this Borgeian incident, the now inflexible characters are in the power of the fictions that have written them, fictions that operate functionally in Larkin's imagery of post-imperial stasis: 'The statues will be standing in the same/Tree-muffled squares, and look nearly the same' (Larkin 1974: 29). The characters are lost in static posturing, beyond 'what could have been': 'The heavy service revolver seemed somehow too/melodramatic to be real enough for its purpose' (Harwood 1988: 60). The helplessness that 'a feeling of finality' brings about is absurdly artificial and operates both at the level of storytelling and in the story. 'Finality' is a key word of a number of Harwood's fictions at this time: it is the undefined goal of the quest, but, as it approaches, unreality engulfs everything. The alluring promise of the fictional hangs suspended; in 'The Doomed Fleet' an atmospheric image of corrosion and purposeless movement is the equivalent of Larkin's stasis: 'Salt waves broke over the rusted iron decks' (Harwood 1988: 61).

By the time a third Fulcrum volume, *The Sinking Colony*, was published in 1970, the texts formally display semantic and syntactic indeterminacy and discontinuity. They are what Umberto Eco calls 'open works'. Harwood's own metaphor for the poem at this time was the catalyst; poems are objects that cause various changes within readers without themselves changing. Open works most obviously allow this by literally letting the reader complete them, like a puzzle. The first poem in *The Sinking Colony*, 'Linen', ends

> touching you like the
> and soft as
> like the scent of flowers and
> like an approaching festival
> whose promise is failed through carelessness
>
> (Harwood 1988: 113)

The poet is not afraid to supply his own concluding similes, but, as Harwood himself has explained of this passage, 'Each of us has

got a different concept of what touching is like . . . I should respect
your view (Bockris 1970: 9). Active readers can become the co-
producers of this poem, a strategy that, although not always
successful, avoids the narrational embrace of Movement discourse.
If there is to be a 'we', it is not one tyrannized into supposed
consensus but one formed through interaction. The open work is
not simply what anybody 'reads into' it. Eco makes a fine distinction: 'The *possibilities* which the work's openness makes available
always work through a given *field of relations*', in the case of 'Linen'
through a focusing upon the notion of touching. There is no single
view, but the poem is clearly 'not an amorphous invitation to
indiscriminate participation' (Eco 1981: 62).

'Animal Days' is Harwood's most radical open work in *The Sinking
Colony*. Narratives of colonial vanity are collaged with other discourses, in a way that avoids even the cohesion of 'The Doomed
Fleet'. The fragments, though, are mostly discursive, giving a sense
of disembodied voices, of continuities broken: 'it was as though your
eyes filled with glass tears/crying some strange'. This desperate
longing then 'cuts' in a manner analogous to the techniques of
avant-garde film-makers, such as Jean-Luc Godard, into other
'shots', and so on. There is imposture and posing:

> standing in the shadows or maybe in the distance
> he Like a long arcade or cloister.
> It was far from the grim scenes of the north
> In his red tunic

> (119)

The specificity of the imperial (or bloody) tunic contrasts with the
ghostly background of disembodied images. At one level, the colonial life is becoming what it always had been: a collective dream
of orientalists and administrators.[4] On another level it is the reader's
function to construct the 'he' who is only 'maybe' present, to con-
nect this character to the 'grim scenes'. This is at both levels
a world of incommensurables; something is being squandered in a
matter called 'the heat of the moment/not knowing what', yet
a jaunty sense of savagery ('The polo season would start early in
April/so there was no time to be wasted') exists alongside a refusal
to perceive (118/120). The poem ends:

> Like oppressors striking fear into people
> with threats of pillage and 'no quarter'

Inside the wall where
'No!'
too heavy on evenings like this
in the courtyard
'the battlements'

(121)

Beyond all this there still lies the otherness of the oppressed – 'the indian chiefs/what are the wounds, anyway, and their cost?' – though this voice may as well be in North America as India, so much do the narrative fragments refuse to constellate into a single reductive 'setting' for the reader. And there is still the question: Who pays the cost of the wounds?

TOM RAWORTH: IMPOSSIBLE OBJECTS

Where Harwood's fragments are held apart for the reader's intervention, Tom Raworth's work of the 1960s often elides details to create new and confusing wholes that then constitute new combinations, fresh perceptions. The result is at once more matter-of-fact and more surreal. His early poems conform to the Black Mountain dictum that in a poem 'ONE PERCEPTION MUST IMMEDIATELY AND DIRECTLY LEAD TO A FURTHER PERCEPTION', without reflection or qualification, but his refusal to descriminate and demarcate marks it off from the often literal American work (Allen 1960: 387–8).

'Six Days' presents itself as a diary, but it disorders as much as it orders:

in the *marais* we bought sweet cakes in the heat without shirts
                    there were still tattooed numbers
birds walk inside the dry pool the flowers are dark and even
on the wooden floor the cup broke quickly calvados a faint
                    smell of apples

(Raworth 1988: 27)

The extraordinary presentation of sharp detail and rapid re-location of point of view, in a rare long-lined open form measure, creates a semantic indeterminacy that resists, but doesn't defeat, naturalization. Raworth's practice of reciting his work very fast helps in this imaginative re-organization of social detail. The poem ends 'things are reflected several times', as though to confirm that the perceptions overlap rather than merely 'lead to' the next (Raworth 1988: 27).

> i made this pact, intelligence
> *shall* not replace intuition, sitting here
> my hand cold on the typewriter
> flicking the corner of the paper
>
> (Raworth 1988: 21)

Improvisatory intuition, as in jazz playing, rather than reductive reasoning, is entrusted with creative control; but Raworth's manifesto is no more important than the immediate sense data that follow. The words are never far from their moment of composition: 'blue gown – that's nice' (1988: 42). The work is the result of an activity, an event. It rejects the patterning of Movement forms and the circumscription of its discourses; it parodies or removes narrative frames. The result is not escapist bizarrerie but, in Raworth's words, a contact with 'other minds, who will recognize something that they thought was to one side or not real. I hope that my poems will show them that it *is* real, that it *does* exist' (Raworth and Watson 1989: 57). The political implications are that Raworth's texts, like Fisher's more orderly subversion of perception, are celebrations of difference and possibility; 'trust marginal thoughts' (Raworth 1988).

One of the key legacies of May 1968 has been to give consciousness and voice to the marginal, and it is clear in 'Tracking', a poem from 1972, that Raworth's privileging of intuitive linguistic attack was a plea for a re-location of reason: 'The words (knowledge, intelligence, etc.) must be re-defined, or new words coined' (Raworth 1988: 90). For Herbert Marcuse 1968 seemed a crucial point for the objective establishment of a new rationality. He saw art as a means and as a model for achieving this. Defamiliarization was politicized in the radical arts, which consist not merely of

> new modes of perception reorienting and intensifying the old ones; they rather dissolve the very structure of perception in order to make room – for what? The new object of art is not yet 'given', but the familiar object has become impossible, false.
>
> (Marcuse 1969: 45)

Raworth's poems enact this search for the new, argue the centrality of the marginal, while Movement practice valorizes the familiar.

'Stag Skull Mounted' of 1970 is a more ambivalent flirtation with the limits of Raworth's medium. The text is generated serially, in diary form, like 'Six Days', without external pattern or thematic cohesion; poetic form is the result of poetic activity; content is the perception of the moment. There are some familiar elements from early poems. There is, for example, the note of pathos and morbidity that often underlies even Raworth's oddest utterances, in the narrator's 'useless pity' for 'the girl with the twisted spine' (1988: 62). He is awkwardly self-conscious as he realizes

> i can not love her and her life
> may be filled with warmth i project my past
> sadness on to all the weight
> of my thought of her misery may add
> the grain that makes her sad
>
> (1988: 62)

Intimations of mortality lend urgency to the contemporaneity of perception and the concomitant irrecoverability of history:

> which is why today the roman wall is not the stones the romans saw
> (1988: 62)

As the narrator 'can not find my way/back to myself', he is increasingly absorbed by literary and conceptual self-consciousness (1988: 66). Instants are recorded as contentless ('*12:10 a.m. June 1st 1970/* the time is now'), and the text consists of its own meticulous, but pointless, correction: '12:256 a.m. June 1st 1970/looking at my watch'. (1988: 66). The poem becomes increasingly minimal and self-referential, textual rather than perceptual, until the poem is reduced to the inevitable entries 'poem' and 'word', and to a silent (blank) entry. The experiment ends dismissively on the brief entry for 29 June: 'this trick doesn't work' (1900: 68–9). But like other artistic 'dead ends' – Cage's *4' 3"* or Beckett's *Breath* – the 'familiar object' has been avoided, whatever the cost.

BOB COBBING: SONIC ICONS

Raworth's self-referential 'poem' took him almost into the area of concrete poetry, but it was Bob Cobbing who was the most important British concrete poet of the 1960s. The basic orientation that unites all forms of concrete poetry is that it foregrounds, by emphasis or distortion, one or more of the conventional elements of poetic structure (such as line and layout or rhyme and alliteration) and concentrates upon the resulting materiality of language. The link between the physical signifier and the conceptual signified of ordinary language is problematized or even suspended. Concrete poetry can be broadly divided into two types, visual and sound poetry, both of which are practised by Cobbing. However much this work looks like art or sounds like music, its origin is in the resources of poetic creation; indeed Cobbing asserts that his work belongs to a centuries-old tradition of graphological and phonological invention within conventional poetry, rather than simply being a continuation of dada or futurist experiment or of the Brazilian Noigandes group of the 1950s, or even of the Jack Kerouac of *Old Angel Midnight*, a particular influence on Cobbing.

In visual poetry the physical signs of print on paper assume prominence. At its simplest there are the pattern poems of George Herbert or Dylan Thomas. The more experimental calligrammes of Apollinaire or the typographical jests of Lewis Carroll lead on to words and letters arranged in patterns upon the page, whether it be the characteristic violence of futurist 'words in freedom' or the comparative stasis of Gomringer's 'constellations' (itself a term borrowed from Mallarmé's *Un Coup de dés* 1897). Letters and word-shapes can swirl into dancing patterns, as in Cobbing's suggestive *Three Poems for Voice and Movement* (1971) and it is only a short step to presenting fractured signs that look alphabetic but that are not actual orthographies, as in some of Max Ernst's paintings as well as in Cobbing's *Songsignals* (1972). At its most abstract, visual poetry can consist purely of printscapes or, as Dom Sylvester Houdedard's 1960s typewriter designs are called, 'typescracts', or in Cobbing's later use and misuse of the duplicator and photocopier, in which ink, rather than print, is the material.

Sound poetry has been divided into *poésie phonétique* and *poésie sonore*. Phonetic poetry, whether Kurt Schwitters's *Ur-Sonata* (1923–8) or Ernst Jandl's or Edwin Morgan's poems of the 1960s, works by making sound structures of syllables and words. *Poésie sonore*, such as the work of Frenchman Henry Chopin, resident in Britain during the late 1960s, uses the voice and electronic superimpositions and speed variations of tape recorders to create sound textures, from whispers to bellows. Some poets use the unaided voice; some make use of sophisticated electronics.

It is not simply Cobbing's achievement that he has practised all the forms outlined above, but it is crucial to his work that his visual poems are always scores for performance. Cobbing has performed in various ensembles, sometimes with improvising musicians and dancers, but often with other poets. A group can develop techniques and procedures, possibly even establish conventions of translating marks on the page into sound – even when the text is most abstract and apparently non-linguistic. What began as determinate notation became indeterminate suggestion, as in some of the open-work scores of John Cage or, in Britain in the 1960s, of Cornelius Cardew. One of Cobbing's Writers Forum titles of 1970, *Sonic Icons*, neatly and anagrammatically suggests the connection between the two types of concrete poetry – as well as reminding one that self-publication is also a necessary part of Cobbing's creative project.

Cobbing did not arrive at this freedom easily. His first work of sound poetry, *ABC in Sound*, wasn't written until 1964, after two decades of arts organizing, painting and literary experiment. Certainly, his contact with other writers and thinkers of the nascent 'underground' – he worked at the same school as Jeff Nuttall – seems to have helped him to achieve the authority to break artistic paradigms.

The *ABC in Sound*, originally called simply *Sound Poems*, was first performed at Better Books and published as a record and booklet in 1965 by Writers Forum. A second recording was made the same year at the BBC and it is this recording that I will refer to (Cobbing nd). Compared to later work it is uncertain in places, but the range of the 26 alphabetical poems is broad. There are semantic elements. 'J' seems to be an alliterative counterpointing of the forces of desire and law, and the indentation was translated into speed changes in the studio:

> Jugeur jugeur jugeur
> Jouer jouissance
>
> (Cobbing 1986)

There is a mock deathliness in the whispered 'G':

> grin
> grim
> gay green
> grey green
> gangrene
>
> (1986)

'S' is a sardonic commentary on the jargon of sociolinguistics:

Sociallyinstitutionalionized
Systematicwholeofspeechsounds
Shit

(1986)

As another Francophone text reminds us, 'Langage/Est mort'. More
abstract is 'M', an alphabetic list of 35 Scottish surnames, read at
double speed over a bagpipe-like voice drone:

Macbean
MacBrayne
MacBryde

(1986)

There are playful puns, in 'Q' ('Kew/Queue/Cue'), performed as
multitracked explosive whispers. 'N' and 'O' use letters as structuring devices, the former as though they were prefixes ('Ndure'), the
latter, again a list, of initials that become a 'quick, fairly high
pitched' rhythmic recitation in performance, that subtly rhymes
and alliterates:

OD
OE
OED
OEEC
OES
OF

(1986)

In 'R' there are the beginnings of individual performance routes
around a text, from 'Rebus' to 'Repeat'; a performer may choose
any direction along or across the four columns of seven words, all
of them titles of paintings by Rauschenberg, to whom the piece is
dedicated.

The best works are those that enable a virtuosic oral performance,
although some still use recognizable words. The use of Japanese for
non-speakers of Japanese tends towards pure sound: 'Da degeki
daka dai dai dido' (1986). Similar effects are present in 'P', which
rapidly alternates the music of the consonant 'p' with the various
pronunciations of 'o':

oll/ollapodrida oll/omeramergau oll/oll/potpourri
poc/pocahontas poc/popocatepetl poc/poc/opossum

(1986)

More complex is 'W', an alliterative palindrome that forces a slow reading (on the BBC recording, over low sounds derived from the text):

wordrow worn row
wombat tab mow
womb mow wort row
weser re-sew
wolf flow

(1986)

The finest piece is probably 'T', a complex re-arrangement of a six-word Veda song, 'ta(n) – di – na(n) – ne – are – ra – ro – (k)ri – tu', as a dance for t, d, n, r, k sounds.

tan tandinanan tandinane
tanan tandina tandinane
tanare tandita tandinane
tantarata tandina tandita

(1986)

The piece gains intensity by the use of an increasing and decreasing echo, a treatment that was later imitated in film-maker Steve Dwoskin's typographical re-arrangement of the text, using large letters for maximum echo.

It is interesting to compare the 1965 recording, which is a strict chant, with three 1968 variations by French sound poet, François Dufrêne, and the two men's wives, with which it is edited as 'Variations on a theme of Tan'. There is an added spontaneity, an interplay of the voices that gradually moves away from the chant into paralinguistic sounds, such as grunting, panting and coughing, that take over the rhythm of the poem.

It is this sense of variation and transformation that was to drive Cobbing prolifically on to his experiments of the late 1960s, allowing his radical foregrounding of poetic devices to disrupt the conventions of poetry and language. By 1969 Cobbing declared a political dimension to his work. He argued that the intellect had been bypassed by this new form of communication 'more natural, more direct and more honest than . . . the present-day voice of politics and religion' (Cobbing and Mayer 1978: 43). Whether this anti-intellectualism, with its appeals to nature, is a mystification or not, Cobbing's formal activity, like Raworth's, was again, in Marcuse's sense, asserting its refusal of the given social reality by destroying and re-creating its constituents, this time by rupturing the linguistic sign itself.

CONCLUSION

In a spectrum that runs from the defamiliarized fictions of Roy Fisher to the linguistic disintegrations of Cobbing, the poetry of the 1960s that I have identified here marks an ambitious continuation of the international modernism that the Movement orthodoxy sought to eclipse; the work itself was a repudiation of that orthodoxy as well as a constituent part of the general revolt in the arts during the 1960s. However, in terms of poetry, if not in politics, given the crisis of both Labour and Conservative parties in the 1970s, and the dominant Thatcherism that followed, Davie's 1973 argument was partly predictive. The fashionable poets of the 1970s and 1980s have largely kept to the Movement orthodoxy and its illusory consensus; indeed, perhaps that poetry belongs less to a time of Davie's hoped-for 'consensus' (Thatcher has poured scorn on the term) than to the time of Thatcher herself, with its re-assertion of conformity in style and empirical content. This has not stopped the four poets considered here going on to produce excellent work since the 1960s; indeed each has had collected or selected poems published. Nor has it stopped younger writers building on their adventurous achievements, ensuring that the Movement orthodoxy will never achieve monopoly control of British poetry.

NOTES

1 See *Poetry Information: Basil Bunting Special Edition*, Autumn 1978, and Lopez 1989.
2 The terms in which I discuss the Movement orthodoxy are largely derived from Crozier (1983), Easthope (1983) and Forrest-Thomson (1978).
3 For a selection of Turnbull's work see Turnbull (1986).
4 For a critique of orientalism, see Said 1978.

BIBLIOGRAPHY

Allen, D.M. (ed.) 1960. *The New American Poetry 1945–1960*. New York: Grove Press.
Allnut, G. (ed.) *et al.* 1988. *The New British Poetry 1968–1988*. London: Paladin.

Bockris, V. 1970. 'Extracts from a conversation with Lee Harwood'. *Pennsylvania Review*, 1, 11–14.

Cobbing, B. 1970 'Variations on a theme of Tan' (1964(sic)/1968). On *Sound Texts/?Concrete Poetry/Visual Texts*. Amsterdam, Uitgave: Stedelijk Museum (LP record).

Cobbing, B. 1976. *Bill Jubobe, selected texts 1942–1975*. Toronto: Coach House Press.

Cobbing, B. 1986. *ABC in Sound*. London: Writers Forum.

Cobbing, B. 1988. *Changing Forms in English Visual Poetry – The Influence of Tools and Machines*. London: Writers Forum.

Cobbing, B. nd. *An ABC in Sound/Trilogy*. Balsam Flex (Cassette Tape).

Cobbing, B. and Mayer P. (eds) 1978. *Concerning Concrete Poetry*. London: Writers Forum.

Crozier, A. 1983. 'Thrills and frills: poetry as figures of empirical lyricism'. In A. Sinfield (ed.), *Society and Literature 1945–1970*. London: Methuen.

Crozier, A. and Longville, T. (eds) 1987. *A Various Art*. Manchester: Carcanet.

Davie, D. 1973. *Thomas Hardy and British Poetry*. London: Routledge & Kegan Paul.

Easthope, A. 1983. *Poetry as Discourse*. London: Methuen.

Eco, U. 1981. 'The poetics of the open work'. In *The Role of the Reader*. London: Hutchinson, 47–66.

Fisher, R. 1988. *Poems 1955–1987*. Oxford: Oxford University Press.

Forrest-Thomson, V. 1978. *Poetic Artifice*. Manchester: Manchester University Press.

Harwood, L. 1988. *Crossing the Frozen River: Selected Poems*. London: Paladin.

Horovitz, M. (ed.) 1969. *Children of Albion: Poetry from the 'Underground' in Britain*. Harmondsworth: Penguin.

Larkin, P. 1964. *The Whitsun Weddings*. London: Faber & Faber.

Larkin, P. 1974. *High Windows*. London: Faber & Faber.

Lopez, T. 1989. *The Poetry of W. S. Graham*. Edinburgh: Edinburgh University Press.

Lucie-Smith, E. (ed.) 1985. *British Poetry Since 1945*. Harmondsworth: Penguin.

Marcuse, H. 1969. *An Essay on Liberation*. Harmondsworth: Penguin.

Mayer, P. (ed.) 1974. *Bob Cobbing and Writers Forum*. Sunderland: Ceolfrith Press.

Morrison, B. 1980. *The Movement: English Poetry and Fiction of the 1950s*. Oxford: Oxford University Press.

Morrison, B. and Motion, A. 1982. *The Penguin Book of Contemporary British Poetry*. Harmondsworth: Penguin.

Nuttall, J. 1970. *Bomb Culture*. London: Paladin.

Raban, J. 1971. *The Society of the Poem*. London: Harrap.

Raworth, T. 1988. *Tottering State: Selected Poems 1963–1987*. London: Paladin.

Raworth, T. and Watson, D. 1989. 'The big green day'. *City Limits*, 23 Feb. 1989, 57.

Said, E. 1978. *Orientalism*. Harmondsworth: Peregrine.

Soar, G. and Ellis, R. J. 1983. 'Little magazines in the British Isles today'. *British Book News*, Dec. 1983, 728–33.

Thurley, G. 1974. *The Ironic Harvest*. London: Edward Arnold.
Turnbull, G. 1986. *A Gathering of Poems 1950–1980*. London: Anvil Press.
Tzara, T., trans. Harwood, L. 1987. *Chanson Dada*. Toronto: Coach House/ Underwhich.
Weatherhead, A. K. 1983. *The British Dissonance*. Columbia and London: University of Missouri Press.
Williams, E. (ed.) 1967. *An Anthology of Concrete Poetry*. New York: Something Else Press.

FURTHER READING

Anthologies containing relevant work include Lucie-Smith's *British Poetry Since 1945* (1985), Allnut's *The New British Poetry 1968–1988* (1988) and Crozier and Longville's *A Various Art* (1987). For a contemporary collection Horovitz (1969) is still useful, while Nuttall (1970) is an impassioned inside account of the social and literary underground. I have been greatly indebted to Crozier (1983) for my analysis of the Movement, but for a general account see also Morrison (1980). Davie (1973) is unavoidable for strength of argument on behalf of the orthodoxy. Alternative poetries and poetics are, as yet, not so coherently surveyed. Raban's *The Society of the Poem* (1971) outlines the confusing variety of poetry appearing in the late 1960s. Thurley's *The Ironic Harvest* (1974) is an eccentric account of twentieth-century British poetry, but his final chapter deals with Lee Harwood and Mark Hyatt as well as the Liverpool poets. Weatherhead's *The British Dissonance* (1983) offers an explication of British poetry of the 1960s and 1970s outside the Movement orthodoxy, including Fisher and Harwood; it is recommended as an introduction to the poetics of indeterminacy. Cobbing and Mayer (1978) is an invaluable source book of concrete poetry, and Mayer (1974) itemizes Cobbing's contribution to it.

Chapter 9

The return of the repressed: Gothic and the 1960s novel

Bart Moore-Gilbert

INTRODUCTION

There are a number of obvious developments in the British novel
of the 1960s through which the concept of 'cultural revolution' could
be explored. For instance, in the early part of the decade especially,
a distinctive group of writers – including Storey, Barstow and Williams – built on the foundation provided by Sillitoe and Braine in
the late 1950s to provide challenging explorations of the changing
identities of class.[1] Of equal note was the tentative emergence of a
new aesthetic in women's writing, prompted by increasing mobiliz-
ation round issues of gender – of which Doris Lessing's *The Golden
Notebook* (1962) is the prototype. However, such writing only gathers
momentum at the end of the decade. Fresh kinds of 'experimental'
writing also began to appear, providing a radical challenge to established narrative conventions and, more debatably, to the social
assumptions supporting them.[2] B. S. Johnson was possibly the most
interesting domestic writer attempting to reorient the genre in light
of reconsiderations of modernism and experiments abroad such as
the *nouveau roman*.

But perhaps the most significant development was a sharply
accelerated cross-fertilization between 'popular' and 'serious' narrative forms in the 1960s. As the dominant postwar mode of neo-
realism, favoured by figures like Snow, Cooper and Wain, came
increasingly to be seen as a dead-end, a number of writers looked
to 'popular' narrative as a way of re-animating an apparently atro-
phying genre. Science fiction received serious critical attention with
Kingsley Amis's *New Maps of Hell* (1960), and achieved new audiences and levels of excellence through the work of figures like Brian
Aldiss, Michael Moorcock and J. G. Ballard. The genre also

provided fresh inspiration for 'mainstream' novelists. Anthony Burgess abandoned the realism of *The Malayan Trilogy* (1956–9) for science fiction in *A Clockwork Orange* (1962) and *The Wanting Seed* (1962), and there is a steadily developing interest in the genre between the early novels of Doris Lessing and her later work, beginning with *The Four-Gated City* (1969). And while Fowles's *The French Lieutenant's Woman* (1969) is usually considered a reworking of historical romance through the prism of the *nouveau roman*, Waugh (1984) points out the narrator's description of it as a science fiction journey back in time (123).

But science fiction was not the only 'popular form' seen to contain such potential. Amis's *The James Bond Dossier* (1965) made large claims for spy fiction. While his *Colonel Sun* (1968) does not, perhaps, fully substantiate his case, the genre was transformed into an instrument of penetrating social criticism by Len Deighton's *The Ipcress File* (1962) and John Le Carré's *The Spy Who Came in from the Cold* (1963). And Le Carré gave a similar new direction to the detective novel in *A Murder of Quality* (1962).

Gothic is one instance of this process of cross-fertilization that has received insufficient attention.[3] For example, the genre is absent from the list provided by Waugh of the 'popular' forms that excited the interest of 'serious' writers in the new decade (Waugh 1984: 86). While critical studies of Gothic have proliferated recently, their focus has usually been on its romantic and modernist phases, and this volume provides an opportunty to consider its resurgence in the 1960s. Many of the problems addressed by 1960s Gothic, including violence, gender politics, sexuality and culture's role as an instrument of social control and discrimination, are connected with some of the wider issues at the centre of political and cultural debate – and indeed are still very much alive. Moreover, since Gothic re-emerged as a serious literary resource in the 1960s, an increasing number of British writers, including Carter, Bainbridge, Weldon, Tennant, Martin Amis, Sinclair, McEwan and Ackroyd, have used its conventions with varying degrees of emphasis.

Between the modernists (James and Conrad experimented with the mode, and Virginia Woolf wrote sympathetically about it) and the 1960s, Gothic lost much of its appeal for the modern novelist, with the notable exception of Mervyn Peake. (Though elements remain in Lowry, Henry Green and Evelyn Waugh.) None the less, Gothic continued to thrive as a 'popular' mode in the postwar era, taking forms as diverse as the 'horror' fiction of bestsellers like

Dennis Wheatley and, above all, cinema. *The Hammer House of Horror* series began in 1957, inspired by the success of Hollywood Gothic in the 1930s, and versions of the Dracula and Frankenstein stories helped Hammer become one of the most successful British film houses over the next 20 years. With *Psycho* (1963) and *The Birds* (1963), moreover, Hitchcock demonstrated that 'horror' retained the potential for psychological investigations of considerable power.[4]

Since little work has been done on modern British Gothic,[5] it is first necessary to establish that the mode did indeed make a return in the 1960s, before proceeding to consider the cultural/political implications of its renaissance. In this chapter it will only be possible to look at the work of Iris Murdoch, John Fowles and Muriel Spark in even superficial detail. But one should be aware of the wider range of work centrally influenced by Gothic in the decade. These include Colin Wilson's *Ritual in the Dark* (1960) and *Adrift in Soho* (1961); David Storey's *Radcliffe* (1963) (the title invokes one of the great figures of romantic Gothic, and Storey also wrote a screenplay of *Wuthering Heights*); and Jean Rhys's retelling of *Jane Eyre* to include the first Mrs Rochester's point of view, in *Wide Sargasso Sea* (1966). The end of the decade brought J. G. Farrell's *Troubles* (1970) and Angela Carter's emergence as a dominant figure in contemporary Gothic with *The Magic Toyshop* (1967) and *Heroes and Villains* (1969).

However, Fowles's first two novels, much of Spark's fiction from *The Comforters* (1957) to *The Hothouse by the East River* (1973) and most of Murdoch's output between *A Severed Head* (1961) and *The Nice and The Good* (1968) constitute the major evidence of a return to Gothic in the decade. While some of these novels have already been identified as having Gothic elements – for instance *The Unicorn*, by Scholes (1967: 106); *The Prime of Miss Jean Brodie* and *The Driver's Seat*, by Stevenson (1986: 184–5); and *The Magus*, by Kane (1988: 120ff) – this body of work is usually considered as responding to foreign influences such as the French existential novel and/or the *nouveau roman*.

These writers were undoubtedly aware of continental developments. *The French Lieutenant's Woman* (1969), for instance, refers to Barthes and Robbe-Grillet (85). Even this novel, however, has strong Gothic elements; the model for Sarah's elusive 'double' identity is *Dr Jekyll and Mr Hyde*, which is identified as 'the best guidebook to the age' (319). And the preface to the revised edition of *The Magus* (1977) acknowledges no debt to French contemporaries. Similarly,

Stevenson's concentration on links between Spark's *The Comforters* and the *nouveau roman* (1986: 182–3) ignores her considerable research on the Brontës and Mary Shelley in the 1950s. In *The Mandelbaum Gate* (1965), the protagonist Barbara Vaughan, at least, is antagonistic towards the *nouveau roman* (177). In 'The sublime and beautiful revisited' (1959) Iris Murdoch's praise for Emily Brontë, Hawthorne, Melville and Dostoevsky, 'to whom we would not want to deny a first place' (258), is recognition of the achievement of a marginalized tradition that she herself was to explore in the next decade. (Murdoch's title echoes not just Kant, but Burke, whose *Inquiry into the Sublime and Beautiful* (1756) facilitated the emergence of the original Gothic aesthetic, in reaction to the Augustan values of order, harmony and clarity. These, interestingly, were often invoked nostalgically by postwar neo-realists like Cooper, Amis and Wain, whose main critical interests and narrative models lay in the eighteenth century.)

In any case, many of the novels in question link themselves on a variety of levels with Gothic precursors. For all three writers, James's *The Turn of the Screw* is an important point of reference. In Murdoch's *The Italian Girl* (1964), for instance, the narrator at first idealizes the ambiguous Flora in a manner that recalls the governess's initial response to her identically named charge. The revised edition of the *Magus* (1977) acknowledges the inspiration of James's tale (5), and in Muriel Spark's *The Public Image* (1968) Frederick works on a script that reminds Annabel Christopher of the novella. An equally important source is Charlotte Brontë. The reviewers describe Spark's Annabel as 'a twentieth-century Jane Eyre' (20), and the fires in Murdoch's *The Italian Girl*, Storey's *Radcliffe* and Carter's *The Magic Toyshop* all owe something to Brontë's novel. Individual works have more specific affiliations. For instance, the ominous opening of Murdoch's *The Unicorn* recalls Harker's approach to the Count's castle in *Dracula*, and a series of scenes link Hannah Crean-Smith to Dracula himself (40, 219). Similarly, Murdoch's *The Time of the Angels* (1966) recalls M. G. Lewis's *The Monk*, with its focus on a demonic priest involved in incest with a relative whom he has imprisoned. Spark's *The Ballad of Peckham Rye* (1960) echoes *Confessions of a Justified Sinner* by Spark's fellow Scottish writer James Hogg; like Gilmartin, Dougal Douglas is a 'diabolical agent' (81) who has the power to change appearance at will.

At the level of motif, too, these novels reveal their generic lineage.

The Unicorn and *The Magus* involve governess figures (or their male equivalents) who are made to confront the limitations of their self-knowledge. Both Fowles novels and Carter's *The Magic Toyshop* are centred on orphans. 'Mad' figures appear in Storey's *Radcliffe*, Murdoch's *The Italian Girl* and Spark's *Not to Disturb*. The architectural tropes of earlier Gothic return, including Chateau Klopstock in *Not to Disturb*, Beaumont in *Radcliffe* and Gaze mansion in *The Unicorn*. Even the more modest buildings in Murdoch's *The Time of the Angels* or Fowles's *The Collector* (built in 1625) have isolated claustrophobic settings and rooms that function as dungeons. Suspense and horror, so characteristic of earlier Gothic, are heightened in its contemporary equivalent by similar plot conventions, including kidnap (*The Magus* and *The Collector*) and imprisonment – mental as well as physical (both Fowles novels, *The Unicorn*, *The Time of the Angels*). Finally, as in romantic Gothic, violence of manifold kinds and sexual 'deviancy', including incest, voyeurism and sado-masochism recur throughout the trio's work.

But there are important differences, too, between contemporary Gothic and its earlier forms. Modern Gothic usually has a surface realism that allows the reader to suspend disbelief in the face of apparently extreme events and situations. It tends to 'domesticate' many of the genre's established conventions, so that the settings are distanced in time or space only vestigially or symbolically. While *The Unicorn* is set amongst 'the gentry' (11), as is Spark's *Not to Disturb*, most 1960s Gothic prefers a more ordinary social milieu than the religious orders or aristocracy favoured by romantic Gothic. Most obviously, except in the case of Spark, the supernatural aspect of earlier Gothic disappears; ghosts, vampires and monsters survive only metaphorically, within a psychologically realistic framework. Possession, for instance, is transformed into obssession. Thus, in *The Italian Girl*, the 'Gothic' Otto (34), with his bestial appetites and 'exceptional physical strength' (39), behaves 'monstrously' without ever threatening to become superhuman. The 'domestication' of modern Gothic relates to one of its most important insights, that the everyday and the 'normal' may be sources of horror and terror quite as potent as anything conceived of by earlier Gothic. In its contemporary variant, domestic violence can be as sickening as any of the torture scenes in romantic Gothic; an apparently innocuous neighbour or friend may become a 'monster'; and family and friends can be emotional vampires.

ATROPHY OR INNOVATION?

As a broad generalization, the 1960s have usually been seen as a period in which the British novel was unable to match the range and quality of writers in Europe and America, or even the Third World. Bergonzi (1970) argues powerfully that it was, by and large, formally conservative and preoccupied with relatively mundane local themes. Alter (1975), Scholes and Waugh argue that experimentation with the genre was notably lacking in Britain. Despite the efforts of Bradbury and Palmer (1979) and Stevenson, such pessimism about the achievement of the 1960s has persisted. Patrick Swinden's essay (1989) is particularly scathing; like Bergonzi, he sees 'cultural decline' (277) in the decade as symptomatic of wider decay. (The comment that 'Britain's economic power was being sapped by the insidious demands of a parasitic social democracy' (254) indicates the political affiliations of his argument.) Swinden particularly deplores the turn to 'popular' culture, concluding that it only 'exerted a pressure towards the juvenile, the irresponsible' (263). Lamenting the demise of the 'elegant' (a recurrent buzzword) social comedy favoured by Pym, Powell and Amis, Swinden asserts that the British novel of the 1960s, 'by seeking to be earnest and relevant . . . ceased to be serious without being comic' (270). Swinden is able to construct his hostile image of the decade only by studiously avoiding much of its characteristic literature; he concentrates instead on 'old hands, trained in the pre-1960s schools of common-sense realism and respect for their craft' (283). He overlooks 'experimental' writing, ignores Fowles and Spark (and Lessing) completely and complains that Murdoch was 'pouring out unnecessary and uninspiring novels at the rate of one a year throughout the 1960s' (279).

Swinden's essay provides a useful opportunity to reconsider the nature and quality of the British novel in the 1960s. Far from agreeing that it entered a state of atrophy or decadence, I would suggest that the turn to 'popular' narrative forms helped lay the foundations for a major revival in the fortunes of the domestic novel in the subsequent two decades. Moreover, I would argue that 1960s Gothic can legitimately be seen as a local version of the technical innovations that earned such praise for the new European and American novel in this period and constitute an equally radical challenge to dominant novelistic practice in Britain between 1945 and 1960.

Contemporary 'experimental' fiction is characterized most obviously by its formal self-consciousness, the foregrounding of convention to stress its fictionality. This problematizes the relationship between language and its referents and, more broadly, between the conventions of representation and 'reality'. In this sense, 'experimentalism' may be understood as a symptom of what Bergonzi describes as the era's 'pathological uncertainty about the nature of reality' (198). An increasing sense of the strangeness of the contemporary world and the breakdown of consensually determined definitions of 'reality' led many 'experimentalists' to see it sceptically as, at best, a 'collective fiction, constructed and sustained by the processes of socialization, institutionalization, and everyday social interaction, especially through the medium of language' (McHale 1987: 37).

But 1960s Gothic, too, is beset by the ontological doubt that McHale sees as 'the dominant' of 'experimentalism'. In *The Unicorn*, for example, the play with binoculars, mirrors, and the name 'Gaze' draws attention to Murdoch's exploration of how far subjective vision constructs reality, particularly the identity of others. *The Magus* centres on the struggle of Urfe (and the reader) to separate illusion from 'reality', and in *The Ballad of Peckham Rye* Douglas's metamorphoses make other characters (and the reader) 'hesitate' between natural and supernatural explanations of his identity. As in earlier periods, hallucination, nightmare and paranoia stalk the protagonists of contemporary Gothic, emphasizing the unstable and elusive nature of the boundaries between subjective and objective reality.

Self-consciousness is manifested at another level in the number of artist figures in 1960s Gothic, including the (failing) poet Urfe in *The Magus*, and the sculptor Alexander in Murdoch's *A Severed Head*, whose comments on the problems of rendering personality reflect on Murdoch's own preoccupations with construction of character in the novel. Spark's fiction contains many artist protagonists; in *The Comforters*, most obviously, Caroline researches 'Form in the Modern Novel' and records her 'difficulty with the chapter on realism' (57). Moreover, the characteristic avoidance of intrusive omniscient narrative often shifts responsibility (on one level) from the author to a narrating character who has to wrestle with the problems of shaping the structure of his/her story and elucidating its significance. Urfe in *The Magus* (which at a different level is about another storyteller, Conchis), and Lynch-Gibbon in *A Severed*

Head, are obvious examples. The Prospero-like Lister in Spark's *Not to Disturb* is a variation on this trope.

Indeed, most of the techniques used by 'experimental' fiction to foreground its problematic relations to 'reality' are also found in 1960s Gothic. Thus, in keeping with Murdoch's dictum that good texts 'provide lucid commentaries on themselves' (cited in Conradi 1986: 121), it flaunts its intertextual relations with earlier phases of the genre, as noted earlier. Language is consistently foregrounded as constructive rather than simply reflective of 'reality'. This is one function of Spark's use of bizarre metaphor; *Not to Disturb* describes lightning as 'like a zip-fastener ripped from its garment by a sexual maniac' (86), and in *The Comforters* there is 'a silence so still you could hear a moth breathe' (127). Murdoch's perception of language's arbitrary and conventional qualities is dramatized in her use of 'empty' symbols that fracture conventional notions of linguistic transparency. An example is the unicorn in the novel of that name. Conjuring up a creature that does not exist, the symbol fails to 'match' its referent. Max's description of Hannah in terms of medieval associations of the unicorn with Christ obscures as much as it clarifies. To see Hannah simply as suffering redeemer ignores her antithetical role as would-be murderess and her associations with Dracula.

While 1960s Gothic characteristically follows generic precedent in its emphasis on suspense, it also plays with conventions of plot in the manner of contemporary 'experimental' fiction. In *The Driver's Seat*, Spark subverts the reader's expectations of murder mystery by revealing the denouement early on, in order to concentrate attention on how the events leading up to Lise's death are organized. Similarly, Murdoch sometimes provides a whole series of 'turns of the screw' to her plots, in a deliberate challenge to conventional realist notions of probability. In *The Unicorn* this is done with particular emphasis. Two-thirds of the way through, Marian comments 'It was like a comedy by Shakespeare. All the ends of the story were being bound up in a good way' (208). But the seven major twists that follow serve to deconstruct the conventional purposes of plot; it is revealed as, above all, a device habitually producing consolatory resolutions and containments that *The Unicorn* itself studiously resists.

A further parallel between 1960s Gothic and 'experimental' fiction lies in their conception of character and the problems posed in its representation. Unlike neo-realism, which generally sees character as psychologically 'legible' and morally definable, modern Gothic portrays human personality as contradictory, fragmented and elusive on both levels. Murdoch's 1960s novels embody much of the argument of her seminal essay of 1961, 'Against dryness', in which she called for a renewed recognition of the 'opacity of persons', as against realism's 'consoling myth' of its accessibility and clarity (30). Spark's novels consistently dramatize the radical oddness and mystery of seemingly average people like Georgina Hogg in *The Comforters*. To some degree, the ambivalence of characters like Gerald Scottow in *The Unicorn* is reminiscent of the Byronic villains of romantic Gothic, who are at once repulsive and attractive. But Honor Klein, Dougal Douglas and Conchis are more radically contradictory characters, supporting interpretations that are mutually irreconcilable and establishing a plurality of meaning that is finally impossible to stabilize.

This manoeuvring towards a more 'realistic' (but anti-realist) conception of character is paradoxically accompanied by a self-conscious display of the fictionality of even this new paradigm. In 1960s Gothic, characters are often aware of themselves as actors/ actresses in a plot they do not control. This cannot simply be seen as a psychologically credible response to their situation, nor is it merely expressive of their creators' characteristic rejection of the more extreme versions of existential voluntarism. Their self-awareness draws the reader's attention to their status as linguistic constructions, effects of textual practice, in a manner that corresponds to play with the 'absence' of character in 'experimental' fiction. In *The Unicorn*, for instance, an insistent pattern highlighting characters' awareness of 'role' serves to undermine the illusion of realism encouraged by the surface texture of Murdoch's prose. Early in the novel, for example, Marian has a revelation: 'Her own place in the story occurred to her for the first time. The ghastly tale had become a reality. . . . And it was a tale in which nothing happened at random' (64). In *The Comforters*, Spark achieves similar effects when Caroline hears the sound of the typewriter coming from the adjoining room and rebels against the web into which she is woven by both Georgina and the author: 'I won't be involved in this fictional plot' (117).

'EXPERIMENTAL' OR RADICAL?

The claim is often made on behalf of contemporary 'experimental' fiction that its formally radical nature involves an equally progressive set of social values. Beginning with Barthes in *Writing Degree Zero* and Robbe-Grillet in *Towards a New Novel*, an increasing number of contemporary critics have argued that realism is ideologically coercive and socially regressive. This is seen as the consequence of its assumption of shared perceptions of what 'reality' consists of, its belief in 'the innocent eye' of a monologic authorial persona, its conviction that the self is unitary and its false optimism about human history. Above all, by taking for granted its conventions of representation, realism has been seen by such critics as 'mythologizing' what is in fact cultural as natural. Thus, whatever disturbs the discourse of realism has been taken to be, *ipso facto*, 'progressive'. Waugh claims that the more fiction 'experiments . . . at the level of the sign', the more 'fundamentally' it interrogates an everyday 'reality' that is in itself structured by disguised systems of oppression. For many such theorists, according to Waugh, realism is 'the mode most threatening to full civilisation, and metafiction becomes the mode most conducive to it' (41).

This is a position that needs reconsideration because the modern British novel is usually conceived by such critics, more or less explicitly, to be less radical, politically as well as formally, than its 'experimental' counterpart abroad. The issues are complex. While taking Conradi's point, that realism has probably been the most socially critical novelistic mode over the last century as a whole (1986: 25), it is also true that in postwar Britain, at least, it became in some respects a conservative mode. If one examines the attacks made by 1950s neo-realism on the committed literature of the 1930s, it is not just the hostility to mixing art and politics that needs noting. The form of address to the reader in which these attacks are couched leaves no space for disagreement (or even interpretation), so that the (coercive) form of the attack supports the politically conservative ideas being expressed. A good example occurs in William Cooper's *Scenes from Provincial Life*:

> Unfortunately it is very difficult to write about politics in a novel. For some reason or other political sentiment does not seem to be a suitable subject for literary art. If you doubt it, you have only to read a few pages of any novel by a high-minded Marxist.
>
> (Cooper 1950: 20)

Thus while 1950s neo-realists like Snow, Cooper and Amis celebrate the freedom of their characters to make sense of or shape the world they inhabit, the role they construct for their readers is often a passive one, in which response to the text is limited by a monologic narrative voice.

The Gothic of the 1960s reverses these emphases. In many cases the characters' freedom in fact lies in discovering the degree to which they are constrained by a variety of determinants. The reader, meanwhile, is placed in a far less stable position by the formal disorientations characteristic of the genre, including the use of faulty narrators such as Martin in *A Severed Head* or Edmund in *The Italian Girl*, framing devices like the tale within the tale (in both Fowles novels), problematic 'closures', and interrogation of received ideas about character (and conventions of characterization). As with much 'experimental' fiction, these effects not only disorient but enfranchise the reader to construct the text's meaning. Just as *The French Lieutenant's Woman* produces the author within the text (thereby revealing authorship as the effect of textual practice rather than as something transcendent and prior to it), *The Magus* does the same for the reader, by merging his/her position *vis-à-vis* the events with Urfe's. Both are similarly challenged to make sense of events; both experience anxiety and exhilaration as they attempt to do so. Spark may seem an exception in this respect, but the habitually extreme detachment and irony of her authorial personae refuse interpretation on the reader's behalf. In *The Ballad of Peckham Rye*, for instance, the radically ambivalent characterization of Douglas and the equally problematic ending prevent the kind of complicity between narrative voice and reader characteristic of much postwar realist fiction.

In attempting to assess how radical 'experimental' writing really is, one should remember how much it draws on the example of modernism – often deeply suspicious of mixing politics and literature – and the French *nouveau roman*, which was a reaction against the *littérature engagée* of the existentialists. The limitations of Waugh's argument become apparent in her comments on Fowles and Sukenick respectively. She points out the contradiction between Fowles's sympathy for feminism and the reproduction within his novels of oppressive stereotypes of women (1984:126–7). By comparison, Waugh is curiously neutral when she discusses Sukenick's introduction of real acquaintances as a way of disturbing conventional narratalogical decorum. She cites *98.6*: 'Beside the roommate is a girl who claims to be the lover of Richard Brautigan; maybe she knows something . . . I mean here is a girl saturated with Richard Brautigan's sperm.' Comment on the tone or gender-political implications of the passage is suppressed by the desire to advance Sukenick as one of the most 'radical' recent 'experimentalists' (132).

There is no need to share the hostility of Bergonzi (1970: 210) or Alter (1975: 222–5) to certain kinds of 'experimentalism', which they interpret not as signs of renewal in the genre but of its decadence. Yet it can sometimes seem self-absorbed and obssessively formalistic. A good example of this might be Perec's *La Disparition* (1969), the result of a determination to write a whole novel without using the letter 'e'. By comparison, 1960s Gothic, though less self-consciously 'radical' at the level of form, seems a good deal more engaged with some of the decade's most troubling cultural/political issues.

There is, for instance, persistent exploration of the accelerated fragmentation of traditional class hierarchies. *The Unicorn, Radcliffe* and *Not to Disturb* all exploit the convention of the 'great house' in order to challenge the characteristic optimism of 1950s neo-realism that the 'classless' society was at hand. *The Collector* is perhaps the most interesting example, in terms of the focus of this chapter, for its exploration of the way in which 'culture' is a field of conflict articulating wider class tensions. Miranda's consistent attempts to 'correct' and develop Clegg's aesthetic taste are aspects of her hostility to the somewhat indeterminate class to which Clegg's windfall now affiliates him. She is at her least sympathetic when using the heroic rhetoric of World War Two, describing herself as one of 'the Few' (220), defending a tradition of 'breeding' and 'high' culture against the barbarians represented by Clegg. In the end, she loses confidence, asserting that 'there's nothing to hold back the New People, they'll grow stronger and stronger and swamp us' (242). By articulating such prejudices, Miranda loses the reader's sympathy – with the troubling consequence that she can no longer be seen simply as victim, despite the appalling ordeal that Clegg forces her to undergo.

Indeed, perhaps the most troubling insights of 1960s Gothic derive from exploration not of class, but gender relations. Murdoch and Fowles, in particular, repeatedly explore the variety of oppressions that women continued to experience in a decade that deluded itself that 'sexual liberation' offered equal benefits to men and women. The traditional motif of the imprisoned heroine is adapted to explore some of the ways in which contemporary women are psychologically and emotionally positioned within patriarchal society. Representations of domestic or 'romantic' violence against women are common in 1960s Gothic, and constitute an important source of its horror and terror, but the principal focus of such fiction is on the more subtle gender coercion exercised by the symbolic order, especially via cultural narratives and codes. The degree to which negative images of women are mediated and reproduced by culture, in the narrow sense here of artistic heritage and practice, is an important preoccupation of 1960s Gothic. This leads to serious doubts about the status and function of culture, and a blurring of boundaries between culture and politics, which is symptomatic of the decade.

Miranda's attempt to provide Clegg with an aesthetic education is founded on the delusion that access to the 'right' kind of culture will liberate him from the destructive attitudes to women that have led to her imprisonment. Much 1960s Gothic is sceptical that any distinction can be drawn between 'high' and 'popular' culture in this respect. While the treatment of the film industry in Spark's *The Public Image* and of televison in *The Collector* suggest how 'popular' culture exploits and coerces women, Angela Carter's *The Magic Toyshop* applies a similar critique to 'high' culture. Melanie's early gender identity and expectations are constructed just as much from internalizing 'attitudes' and 'poses' (1, 14) derived from painters like the pre-Raphaelites, Toulouse-Lautrec and Cranach – and writers like Lawrence – as from advertisements (2) or the 'women's magazines', the normative values of which finally coerce her house-keeper into pretending to be married.

Gothic of the 1960s like *The Unicorn*, however, demonstrates that while such cultural narratives reinforce women's oppression, they are also damaging to men. Trapped in the discursive and ideological patterns of the literature of courtly love, Effingham Cooper 'reads' Hannah as a victim so that he can become the hero of the 'spiritual adventure story' (99) that he constructs out of their circumstances. This, ironically, makes him complicit with Scottow in prolonging her imprisonment and powerfully makes the point that the idealiz-ing tendency of the male gaze deprives its victim of freedom and autonomy just as surely as its pornographic counterpart: 'And as he sat in his office dreaming of Hannah he found himself feeling a certain strange guilty pleasure at the idea that she was, somehow, for him, shut up, reserved, sequestered' (73). But since every jailer is in some sense a prisoner of his charge, Cooper's controlling gaze denies him the opportunity to have the very thing he apparently yearns for, a real and free relationship with Hannah.

Even the most self-consciously fictive aspects of such works are incorporated into this kind of cultural/political critique. Thus Murdoch's unicorn image does not merely draw attention to language's difficulty in registering the full presence of its referent, but makes the point that the faulty gaze of Hannah's male companions empties her of her truly complex, contingent identity. The same is true in more substantial areas like characterization. 'Experimentalism' often regards character quite patently (and finally) as no more than a product of discourse, not only on the textual level but ideologically, too. As Bradbury has suggested, 'the model of a cybernetic world has led to an art in which the human figure exists itself as a . . . role-player, a formless performer, a cardboard cut-out' (Bradbury and Palmer 1979: 203). Gothic of the 1960s, while rejecting the supremacy of the individual will celebrated in much postwar realist and existentialist fiction, usually retains some sense of its characters' independence. At one level, this is registered in the fact that the more contradictory characters like Hannah and Honor remain 'other', unconsolingly inassimilable to conventional interpretive schemes. But this symbolic independence from the 'system' of text also represents the possibility of liberation from other coercive discourses; for some of the female characters, in particular, the possibility of liberation from the analogous 'symbolic system' of patriarchy.

The refusal of conventional notions of 'closure' is a another example of subordination of formal 'play' to cultural/political critique in 1960s Gothic. The open-endedness of Murdoch's *A Severed Head* and the circularity of Fowles's *The Magus*, for example, deny the reader the satisfactions of resolution apparent in much realist fiction. Both novels are first-person narratives and each raises the problem of the degree to which the narrating 'I' diverges from the narrated 'I'. But this emphasizes the crucial question of the degree to which, if at all, the central protagonists have transcended their initial patriarchal vision.

In *The Magus*, for instance, it is arguable that Conchis's attempt to educate Nick Urfe has failed. On his return to London, Urfe retains traces of the patriarchal blindness identified earlier as being, perhaps, his chief limitation. The desire for revenge on Alison remains to some degree, and there are flashes of his old predatory

sexual instinct. On the other hand, Urfe has come to a truer realization of Alison's separateness and value as a human being. He is
also able to relate to his landlady simply as a friend and refuses
the opportunity to exploit the young Scottish bohemian Jo-Jo who
mistakes her vulnerability for genuine freedom of sexual choice. *A
Severed Head* is equally 'open'; Gindin argues that Martin and Honor
will never be reconciled (193) and Kane is equally confident that
they will (43). Honor concludes at the final meeting, ' "This has
nothing to do with happiness, nothing whatever" ' (205). This could
be interpreted as a comment on Martin's failure to attain a level
of self-awareness that would make love between them possible. On
the other hand it might mark her recognition that Martin has at
last transcended his initial expectations of gender interaction.

CONCLUSION

The cultural/political critique provided by modern Gothic is not
without its contradictions, perhaps the most deep-seated of which
involves its treatment of the themes of liberation. There is a profound paradox whereby characters like Hannah, Urfe and Miranda
are liberated (if they are) by extreme forms of coercion. The problem is acute in respect of gender relations. As Waugh points out,
Fowles's apparent reproduction of female stereotypes that are ostensibly identified as the source and index of Urfe's limitations is
troubling. Murdoch's relation to feminism is also problematic;
Johnson (1987) has deplored her fiction's 'often *explicit* assumption
of "masculinist" perspectives and values, and its curious
reluctance . . . to deal directly or non-ironically with women's
experience' (xi–xii). While the preceding discussion has argued that
Murdoch assumes the male gaze in order to deconstruct it, it is
also true that Hannah and Honor are close to the witch/Circe
stereotypes traditionally used to contain the empowered woman. In
the former case this cannot be ascribed to the limitations of a male
narrator, since *The Unicorn* is not a first-person narrative.

   There may be analogous doubts about the degree to which 1960s
Gothic enfranchises the reader. Bergonzi criticizes Murdoch for
surrendering to the very 'consolations of form' that 'Against dryness'
warns against and suggests that her fiction remains 'far from the
Tolstoyan openness to which she aspires' (1970: 47). Byatt's scepticism about *The French Lieutenant's Woman* raises similar questions
about Fowles's earlier work. Its apparent 'openness' is an illusion,

she argues, because the alternative endings 'cancel each other out, rendering Fowles as arbitrary a puppet-maker as he declared his desire not to be' (1979: 28). Just as the characters are finally contained in and controlled by the text, so the reader's freedom of interpretation is similarly curtailed. Both authors are aware of the problem. Murdoch records only partial 'willingness to hand over the interpretation to the reader', and Fowles, too, realizes that the liberation he offers is limited: 'I do not think a novelist can offer freedom to his readers, however aleatory his technique' (Ziegler and Bigsby 1982: 217 and 118).

None the less, Fowles's defence of his method holds good for much 1960s Gothic, particularly in comparison with the role constructed for the reader by 1950s neo-realism. It 'suggests to the reader a possible mode of escape in terms of her or his own life and its fictions and realities. It can't, of course, offer the actual escape itself' (Ziegler and Bigsby 1982: 118). As Bigsby comments, 'The author unavoidably has his thumb in the scale, but his gestures of deconstruction, his offer to let the text go where it will, are not wholly unreal or deceptive' (113). By rejecting the monologic authority of neo-realist narrative voice, 1960s Gothic encourages plurality of meaning, enlarging the role of the reader in 'producing' the text. From a purely formal perspective, lack of 'closure' may be a convention as arbitrary as its presence, but the actual experience of reading an 'open' rather than a 'closed' text is quite different.

In other respects, too, 1960s Gothic marked a distinct break with the novelistic practice dominant between 1945 and 1960. The self-awareness and frankness of its treatment of sexuality makes the work of many of the novelists of the 1950s seem puerile in this respect, though to be fair the *Lady Chatterley* trial made the climate much more favourable for later writers. A new maturity is particularly evident in the way 1960s Gothic was able to represent 'deviant' sexuality in non-judgemental ways, as in Storey's *Radcliffe* and Carter's *The Magic Toyshop*, for example.

The use of 'popular' form enabled much 1960s writing to bridge markets and audiences (all three writers under discussion were bestsellers). It also helped undermine the authority of accepted notions of what constituted 'good' literature. The Leavises, still a dominant force in English criticism at the beginning of the 1960s, had been hostile throughout their careers towards Gothic. *Fiction and the Reading Public* (1932) railed against its 'clumsy call for pity, shudders and so forth' (134), and *Revaluation* (1956) dismissed 'the trashy fantasies and cheap excitements of the Terror school' (134). Charlotte Brontë and Dickens were excluded from the 'great tradition' partly because their work diverged from the *Scrutiny*-derived discourse linking 'realism' to social and moral responsibility in fiction, but also for incorporating 'popular' narrative forms into their fiction – Gothic perhaps being the dominant one for both. That aesthetic canons such as these supported discriminatory, even coercive, social values is ably demonstrated by 1960s Gothic novels such as *The Collector* and *The Magic Toyshop*. In this area of debate, as well as in its admittedly problematic treatment of sexuality, gender and freedom, 1960s Gothic consistently probed at and articulated some of the central anxieties of the decade. The innovatory form with which these problems were expressed bears comparison with some of the more obviously 'experimental' writing in Europe and America at the time, and may do something to counterbalance one habitual belief about British culture in the modern period, that when experiments or formal developments did appear, they were always imported from abroad.

NOTES

1 Jeffrey Richards's chapter in this book explores film versions of many of their novels.
2 Alternatives to the term 'experimental fiction' in criticism of the contemporary novel include 'the anti-novel', 'metafiction', 'the postmodern novel', 'irrealism', etc.
3 Recourse to 'popular' form, while a characteristic of the 1960s novel, was not, of course, exclusive to it. *The Turn of the Screw* and *The Secret Sharer* remind us that even 'high' modernism was interested in the possibilities of Gothic.
4 Hammer is discussed further by Jeffrey Richards in chapter 11.
5 A welcome exception is Randall Stevenson's chapter 'Contemporary Gothic' (Stevenson 1986), but, apart from a few lines on Spark, he focuses on writers more recent than those addressed by this chapter.

BIBLIOGRAPHY

Editions cited are those from which page references are taken.

Alter, Stephen 1975. *Partial Magic: The Novel as Self-Conscious Genre*. California: University of California Press.

Barthes, Roland 1970. *Writing Degree Zero*. Trans. Annette Lavers and Colin Smith. London: Cape.

Bergonzi, Bernard 1970. *The Situation of the Novel*. London: Macmillan.

Bold, Alan 1986. *Muriel Spark*. London: Methuen.

Bradbury, Malcolm (ed.) 1977. *The Novel Today*. London: Fontana.

Bradbury, Malcolm and Palmer, David 1979. *The Contemporary English Novel*. London: Edward Arnold.

Byatt, A. S. 1979. 'People in paper houses; attitudes to realism and experiment in English postwar fiction'. In Bradbury, M. and Palmer, D., *The Contemporary English Novel*. London: Edward Arnold.

Carter, Angela 1967. *The Magic Toyshop*. Reprinted 1981, London: Virago.

Conradi, Peter 1982. *John Fowles*. London: Methuen.

Conradi, Peter 1986. *Iris Murdoch: The Saint and the Artist*. London: Macmillan.

Cooper, William 1950. *Scenes From Provincial Life*. Reprinted 1983, London: Methuen.

Dipple, Elizabeth 1982. *Iris Murdoch: Work for the Spirit*. London: Methuen.

Farrell, J. G. 1970. *Troubles*. London: Weidenfeld & Nicolson.

Fowles, John 1963. *The Collector*. Reprinted 1976, London: Triad/Granada.

Fowles, John 1969. *The French Lieutenant's Woman*. Reprinted 1977, London: Triad/Granada.

Fowles, John 1977. *The Magus*, Revised Version. Reprinted 1988, London: Picador.

Gindin, James 1962. *Postwar British Fiction: New Accents and Attitudes*. Cambridge: Cambridge University Press.

Johnson, Deborah 1987. *Iris Murdoch*. Brighton: Harvester.

Kane, Richard 1988. *Iris Murdoch, Muriel Spark and John Fowles: Didactic Demons in Modern Fiction*. London: Associated Universities Press.

Laing, Stuart 1983. 'Novels and the novel'. In Sinfield, Alan (ed.), *Society and Literature 1945–70*. London: Methuen.

Leavis, F. R. 1956. *Revaluation: Tradition and Development in English Poetry*. London: Chatto.

Leavis, Q. D. 1932. *Fiction and the Reading Public*. Reprinted 1965, London: Chatto.

Loveday, Simon 1988. *The Romances of John Fowles*. London: Macmillan.

McHale, Brian 1987. *Postmodernist Fiction*. London: Methuen.

Murdoch, Iris 1959. 'The sublime and beautiful revisited'. *The Yale Review*, XLIX, winter 1959, 247–71.

Murdoch, Iris 1961. 'Against dryness'. Reprinted in Bradbury, M. (ed.) 1977. *The Novel Today*. London: Fontana.

Murdoch, Iris 1961. *A Severed Head*. Reprinted 1987, Harmondsworth: Penguin.

Murdoch, Iris 1963. *The Unicorn*. Reprinted 1977, London: Triad/Granada.

Murdoch, Iris 1964. *The Italian Girl*. Reprinted 1987, Harmondsworth: Penguin.

Murdoch, Iris 1966. *The Time of the Angels*. Reprinted 1968, Harmondsworth: Penguin.

Murdoch, Iris 1968. *The Nice and the Good*. London: Chatto & Windus.

Page, Norman 1990. *Muriel Spark*. Basingstoke: Macmillan.

Pearce, Spencer and Piper, Don (eds) 1989. *Literature of Europe and America in the 1960s*. Manchester: Manchester University Press.
Robbe-Grillet, Alain 1970. *Snapshots, and Towards a New Novel*. Trans. Barbara Wright. London: Calder & Boyars.
Scholes, Robert 1967. *The Fabulators*. Oxford: Oxford University Press.
Sinfield, Alan (ed.) 1983. *Society and Literature 1945–70*. London: Methuen.
Spark, Muriel 1957. *The Comforters*. Reprinted 1987, Harmondsworth: Penguin.
Spark, Muriel 1960. *The Ballad of Peckham Rye*. Reprinted 1988, Harmondsworth: Penguin.
Spark, Muriel 1961. *The Prime of Miss Jean Brodie*. London: Macmillan.
Spark, Muriel 1965. *The Mandelbaum Gate*. Reprinted 1987, Harmondsworth: Penguin.
Spark, Muriel 1968. *The Public Image*. Reprinted 1988, Harmondsworth: Penguin.
Spark, Muriel 1970. *The Driver's Seat*. Reprinted 1988, Harmondsworth: Penguin.
Spark, Muriel 1971. *Not To Disturb*. London: Macmillan.
Spark, Muriel 1973. *The Hothouse by the East River*. London: Macmillan.
Stevenson, Randall 1986. *The British Novel Since the Thirties: An Introduction*. London: Batsford.
Storey, David 1963. *Radcliffe*. London: Longmans, Green.
Swinden, Patrick 1989. 'Literature at home'. In Pearce, S. and Piper, D. (eds), *Literature of Europe and America in the 1960s*. Manchester: Manchester University Press.
Waugh, Patricia 1984. *Metafiction: The Theory and Practice of Self-Conscious Fiction*. London: Methuen.
Ziegler, Heidi and Bigsby, Christopher 1982. *The Radical Imagination and the Liberal Tradition*. London: Junction Books.

FURTHER READING

Little has been published on the novel in the 1960s specifically, though Swinden in Pearce and Piper (1989) and Laing in Sinfield (1983) are useful starting points. Bergonzi (1970) takes a pessimistic perspective on the postwar period up to the end of the decade. There is also interesting material in Stevenson (1986). Scholes (1967), Waugh (1904) and McHale (1987) provide good discussions of 'experimental' writing in the decade. Bradbury (1977) and Bradbury and Palmer (1979) contain essays by or on the principal writers discussed in this essay. Ziegler and Bigsby (1982) provide important interviews with Murdoch and Fowles. Recommended criticism of Fowles includes Conradi (1982) and Loveday (1988); Conradi (1986) is good on Murdoch, as are Johnson (1987) and Dipple (1982); for Spark one might consult Bold (1986) and Page (1990). Kane (1988) discusses all three writers on whom this essay focuses, but is limited. Pearce and Piper place British writing in the decade in an international context.

Chapter 10

Step by step: the cautious revolution in dance

Judith Mackrell

INTRODUCTION

During the early 1960s the aesthetics of classical ballet still dominated the world of British dance; in fact the term 'dance' scarcely
figured in the language of serious art. Folk dance or ballroom
dance were generally regarded as activities for cranks and amateurs
respectively, while modern dance – the distinctively twentieth-
century form of choreography that emerged from central Europe
and America during the late 1920s – had scarcely been seen on the
British stage.

By the late 1960s, however, a series of carefully considered
manoeuvres had effected the transplantation of American modern
dance to British soil. In 1966 a school had been formed for the
training of British dancers; by 1967 there were two native modern
dance companies; and a public had emerged that was curious, even
avid, to see more of this 'new' form. What makes these developments appear so rapid is not just the brevity of the time scale,
however. It is the fact that only a decade earlier, Martha Graham,
seminal figure in American modern dance and creator of the style
that would inform the growth of British modern dance, had performed with her company for the first time in London – and met with
near universal rebuff.

The profound conservatism that had settled over British culture
during the early 1950s was nowhere so blanketingly evident as in
the dance world. In the space of two decades ballet had graduated
(or hardened) from being one of the most chicly experimental of
the arts into a national institution, famous for its magnificent rec-
reations of late nineteenth-century classics.

Under the instruction of Serge Diaghilev, European audiences

during the second decade of the century had come to associate ballet
with the ritzier and more fashionably daring aspects of modernism,
appreciating it as a sophisticated form of *Gesamtkunstwerk* (artistic
synthesis) that involved composers like Stravinsky, Poulenc and
Satie; painters like Picasso and Míro; and choreographers like
Massine, Nijinsky and Balanchine. The fledgling British companies
that developed just before and after Diaghilev's death – Ballet
Rambert (1926) and the Vic-Wells Ballet (1931) – certainly couldn't
afford to work with artists of that stature. Yet their small-scale
shoe-string repertoires continued to feed the public's appetite for
innovation, producing a new generation of British choreographers
like Frederick Ashton and Antony Tudor who worked with composers like Lord Berners and William Walton and designers like Sophie
Fedorovitch and Cecil Beaton.

As these companies became established, however, a certain fossil-
izing process set in, more perhaps in audience expectation than in
the companies' own attitudes. The nationwide touring undertaken
by both companies during the Second World War had created a
new audience for ballet, broader and less self-consciously sophisticated in its tastes than the fashionable milieu of the 1920s and 1930s.
Ballet Rambert, which had displayed a particularly strong commitment to new work, found it could only survive during the postwar
years with a repertoire dominated by the recognized classics. And
once the Vic-Wells ballet had moved to Covent Garden in 1946 and
was given its Royal charter in 1956, it had obvious responsibilities to
its new status and was less ready to take the risks that had characterized its early years.

The changes in the ballet scene did not, of course, involve a total
abandonment of new or contemporary work; Ashton made *Scènes de
Ballet*, one of his most radically austere and abstract works, in 1948.
Yet the climate was heavily weighted towards safety and familiarity
– so much so that 1954 could not have been a more unpropitious
year for Martha Graham to give London its first serious viewing of
modern dance.

Both public and press reacted to her two-week season with bewilderment, condescension and distress. The critics, failing to see any
significant form in the work, insisted on calling it 'barefoot' or 'free'
dance, viewing it as an obscure ritual devoid of familiar theatrical
pleasure. The *Sunday Times* fretted that 'The unceasing effort
required to deduce from the dance dramas even a hint of Miss
Graham's abstractions and philosophies leaves one exhausted rather

than entertained'. Some perceived dimly that Graham had developed a new language in which she was saying 'new things'. But only one critic, the *Observer*'s Richard Buckle, defended the work with any conviction (McDonagh 1973: 229).

This general panning was similar to the response that Graham had aroused in America during the 1920s and 1930s, when most people could see no further than the disobliging 'ugliness' of her movement. (A favourite joke at the time was that if Graham gave birth it would be to a cube.) Yet both reactions were predictable, given that Graham's whole approach had been forged in opposition to classical ballet, the form that provided the dominant dance aesthetic in both periods.

MARTHA GRAHAM AND THE BREAK WITH CLASSICAL TRADITION

Graham's attack on academic classicism sprang from three basic premises: she regarded the fairytale subject matter of nineteenth-century ballet as an insult to modern intelligence; she dismissed the technical virtuosity of ballet as little more than mechanical gymnastics; and thought its ornate and aristocratic elegance inexpressive of twentieth-century life. Dance, she believed, had to be stripped to its most basic elements in order to communicate the reality of modern conditions: 'Life today', she wrote in 1929, 'is nervous, sharp and zig zag, the old expressions could not give it form' (McDonagh 1973: 113).

Graham looked to primitive ritual and classical myth as source material for her works, finding in them potent symbols of the contemporary unconscious. In her early work she took inspiration from Nietzsche, and during the 1940s and 1950s began to explore classical myth, enthused partly by those decades' preoccupation with Jung. Out of this came the fascination with archetypal female imagery that was to dominate her work: St Joan as Maid, Warrior and Martyr; Jocasta as Victim, Sensualist, Mother.

The intense inward dramas that Graham choreographed were utterly unlike the simply plotted stories of nineteenth-century ballet. Not only was the material allusive and heavily symbolic; it was often communicated via cinematic techniques – narrative flashbacks, or montages of action. Thus in *Deaths and Entrances* (1943), based on the lives of the Brontë sisters, one sister appeared to journey through the past lives of all three women, a journey in which reality was freely distorted by memory and fantasy.

What added to the public's discomfort with Graham's dances and the fact that they seemed like so much hard work was their staging, which was passionately antithetical to the tutus-and-tulle image of traditional ballet. Never concerned with beguiling her audience, Graham's dancers performed in bare feet and in scrupulously plain costumes, the action taking place against starkly symbolic sets and accompanied by music as stripped down and dissonant as the choreography.

But it was of course her movement that was hardest for balletomanes to stomach. The vocabulary of modern dance as developed by Graham, Mary Wigman, Doris Humphreys and others, appeared worlds away from the confident symmetry and legibility of classical ballet. Abrupt, extreme or 'distorted' physical gestures were used to express extremes of emotion, so that a dancer might convey anger through violently percussive jerks of the body, despair in a sharp curve of the spine, anguish in a heavy fall to the floor. Movements rarely blossomed into seamless phrases as they did in ballet but would often be executed as single uncompromising physical statements.

One of the physical premises on which Graham's own technique was based was the contraction and release of the torso, a movement that derived from the release and inhalation of the breath. This curving action could be slow and resonant or abrupt and agonized, this freely expressive use of the upper body contrasting directly with the lifted vertical spine of ballet. Graham found sources of dramatic expression in other physical gestures, too, that were unavailable to ballet at that time: in flexing as well as pointing the feet; in having legs and feet turned in rather than rotated outwards; in angling the limbs rather than disposing them in graceful lines or curves. While ballet dancers concealed both the weight of their bodies and their struggle for control (the 'effortless' split jeté, the 'serene' multiple pirouette), Graham also made dramatic play of gravity, inventing a language of rolls, falls and crawls where the dancer was rooted or abandoned to the ground.

Two of the works that Graham brought to London in 1954 exemplified the emotional range of this style, the earliest of which, *Appalachian Spring* (1944), was made at the peak of her 'American' period. Set to a score by Aaron Copland and taking its title from Hart Crane's epic American poem *The Bridge*, it portrayed the life of early pioneer settlers – the challenge of wild prairie spaces to a newly married couple. For Graham the dance also dramatized the conflict between piety and passion, resolve and doubt in which the whole American dream was rooted. But it demonstated, too, the detailed characterization of which her style was capable. In the danced soliloquies of the Bride and Husbandman, images of past and future meshed with the emotions of the present. The Husbandman moved with his feet settled firmly into the ground, as if drawing sustenance from it, his delving, shooting motions showing his preoccupation with his newly acquired land. In contrast, the Bride's fussy steps and hand movements suggested her nervousness at the vastness of her environment. The whole work took place in a setting designed by the sculptor Isamu Noguchi: a section of fence indicating with lean economy the territory possessed by the young couple; the 'house' suggested by a peaked entrance and a clapboard wall.

Dark Meadow (1946) was one of the first works in which Graham took myth as her subject matter; not the great Hebraic and Greek stories she was to use later, but a much less specific myth of her own devising. In a programme note, Graham wrote that '*Dark Meadow* is a re-enactment of the Mysteries which attend the eternal adventure of seeking' (McDonagh 1973: 188). Her characters had generic names like 'The One Who Seeks', the comforting earth-mother figure 'She of the Ground' and the godlike male 'He Who Summons'. There was no specific plot or incident but a sense of ritual that engaged the characters in a cycle of quest and return; thus the work opened with Graham (the Seeker) meditating quietly on a rock before moving into a long solo with a black cloth that represented the thoughts that darkened or troubled her mind.

Such was the style of work that so puzzled British audiences in 1954 – uncompromisingly serious and passionately expressionist in its approach. It was in essence, however, a style that had been forged out of the artistic climate of the first quarter of the century. (When, for instance, Graham commented in 1927 that 'out of emotion comes form' she was closely echoing Kandinsky's remark of 1912 that 'the form is the outer expression of the inner content' (Jowitt 1988: 164).) And by the mid to late 1950s choreographers in America, responding to a new climate of abstract expressionism, pop art and the aleatory theories of composition propounded by John Cage, were already dismissing Graham's work as old fashioned.

In the light of this growing impatience with Graham's work at home, it may seem strange that when she returned to Britain in 1963 she was not only received with fervent adulation by press and public alike, she was also embraced as all that was modern in dance. Indeed when schools and companies were established in this unfamiliar form, it was Graham's choreographic approach that was emulated rather than one of the more obviously contemporary alternatives coming out of the States.

CAPITULATION TO THE MODERN

Before articulating the reasons for this choice, a word or two should be said about this sudden conversion of the British to modern dance. Clearly the general economic and cultural climate of the 1960s was very different from that of the previous decade and one of the most significant changes for dance was the emergence of a young audience with money to spend and a will to discover its own tastes. Yet there were important rumblings from within the dance world, too; a quiet push towards a more contemporary image that actually took place within the major ballet companies and helped to prepare the acceptance of modern dance proper.

The dominant image of 1960s dance remains, of course, the superstellar reign of Fonteyn and Nureyev, who made headlines out of ballet and wowed the public in their performances of the great classic roles. Yet a handful of younger choreographers were beginning to flirt with a new modernity in their work: exercising a fascination for psychological motivation and urban realism; dispensing with the notion of ballet as a vehicle for stars. Kenneth MacMillan's *The Invitation* (1960), for instance, was a tense uncomfortable ballet about adolescent sexuality and rape, while Peter Darell's *The Prisoners* (1957) explored notions of imprisonment in a story of two men who escaped from jail, only to be trapped by their passion for the same woman.

Among this group was Norman Morrice at Ballet Rambert who, working with a pared-down version of the classical vocabulary, made dances portraying aggressively modern people in pointedly real situations. *Cul de Sac* (1964) was set in the London Underground; *Travellers* (1963) in an Iron Curtain airport; while his first ballet, *Two Brothers* (1958), was influenced by *East of Eden* and resulted in Morrice (who played the James Dean character) being mobbed at the stage door. Morrice however was aware that American choreographers were working with a vocabulary that was far better suited to this sort of material than ballet, and during the early 1960s went to New York to study modern dance.

He was most impressed by Graham's work (not surprisingly, since it echoed his own narrative bias), but he also studied the work of Merce Cunningham, Anna Sokolow and Glen Tetley. So absorbed did he become with these various branches of the form that when he returned to Britain in 1966 it was with the conviction that Ballet Rambert ought to cut its losses as a classical company and become a modern dance group, re-training its dancers in modern technique and taking the work of modern choreographers into its repertoire. Marie Rambert, the company's founder, agreed, not only because she herself had been deeply impressed by the Graham season of 1963 but also because she was conscious that the company could no longer support the unwieldy expense of a classical repertoire, with its demands for a full corps de ballet and orchestra. Teachers were thus imported to school those dancers who remained in the company, and by 1967 Rambert had its first modern works in the repertoire.

Evidence of the drastic change in the company's identity and its wholesale commitment to new and modern work can be seen in the increase of new productions and/or new choreography in its repertoire. Between 1960 and 1966 there were four new productions of nineteenth-century classics – La Sylphide (1960), Don Quixote (1962), Les Sylphides (1963) and Giselle (1965) – plus six new works by Morrice – Wise Monkeys (1960), A Place in the Desert (1961), Conflicts (1962), The Travellers (1963), Cul de Sac (1964) and Realms of Choice (1965). In 1967 alone the list contained John Chesworth's Time Base plus four works from Glen Tetley, all of which were new to Britain – Pierrot Lunaire, Ricercare, Freefall and Ziggurat. A particularly bold innovation was a collaborative work, Collaboration I (1967), made by various choreographers, set to several pieces of music and designed by students from the Central School of Art and Design.

The period of Rambert's transformation (1966–7) also saw the creation of an entirely new company with its own school, London Contemporary Dance Theatre and the London School of Contemporary Dance, whose existence was largely due to the efforts of one man. Robin Howard, a businessman, had been one of the few converts to the Graham company during its first season in 1954, and when he heard she was returning to Edinburgh in 1963 he put up the money for her London season. Reviewers in both cities duelled with superlatives, performances were sold out and, fired by the public's enthusiasm, Howard persuaded Graham to take several British dancers back with her, the idea being that once trained in her technique they would return to London to help set up a school and eventually establish a company.

According to plan, the school opened its first classes in 1966, attracting a small group of students who ranged from disaffected ballet dancers to art students who had barely danced a step. Impressively, however, it was only a year later that Howard was ready to form a company, asking one of Graham's own dancers, Robert Cohan, to become its artistic adviser, teacher and choreographer.

The challenges that LCDT faced were, of course, daunting, as were those confronted by the restructured Rambert. English dancers had to work against their natural grain to develop the powerfully accented, dramatic style of Graham's movement – so different from the restrained lyricism of the British style. And if London audiences had been won over by modern dance, most of the rest of the country still had to be convinced. Both companies toured exhaustively, giving lecture demonstrations in colleges and community centres, as well as straight theatrical performances. Some sections of the public still came to see Rambert on the assumption that they would be fed the old diet of *Coppelia* and *La Sylphide*, and were deeply affronted to see dancers in leotards moving to electronic music.

Significantly, Howard's first name for the trust that supported his company and school was Contemporary Ballet Trust. He felt that in 1966 the term 'dance' did not carry sufficiently serious connotations in Britain, particularly among those from whom he was anxious to draw money and support. The speed with which he and his organization changed that perception may be judged from the fact that the trust was renamed Contemporary Dance Trust in 1970.

As far as repertoire went, it was too early to discern a clear British style, although most new works (as opposed to American imports) tended to deal with serious quasi-moral 'themes' and were quick to reflect fashionable trends in either music or design. The choreography itself tended to be strongly influenced by Graham technique, although this was sometimes diluted by classical ballet.

LCDT had been given one work by Graham, the 1940 piece *El Penitente*, but most of its repertoire was choreographed by Cohan, with his 1969 piece *Cell* emerging as a classic of the period. The title referred literally to the white walls in which the dancers were enclosed, metaphorically to the frequent signs of mental and emotional alienation that they exhibited. Contractions of the torso and falls, clawed or tensed movements of the hands, suggested an intensity of emotion, wound to a greater pitch by Ronald Lloyd's score. Yet *Cell* did not present the kind of mythic psychological drama of Graham's work. As the dancers sought comfort or repulsed each other, they seemed like very contemporary people, dressed in ordinary street clothes.

The *Sunday Telegraph* opined that it 'was little short of a masterpiece', and that the company 'should become one of our major dance assets'. Significantly, though, it did not yet regard such work as British: 'If we are to see American modern dance, then we need to see major achievements with first rate dancers, and the Contemporary Dance Theatre is in a position to give us both'.

Cell has subsequently remained in the repertoire of the company, but for many works of this period we have to rely on contemporary descriptions, memories and reviews to supply information and description. These are clearly subjective at best, at worst inaccurate or biased. Even the most neutral description inevitably veers towards metaphor, inevitably passes some judgement. The best one can do is extrapolate from as many sources as possible, using personal knowledge to identify lurking prejudice or over-enthusiastic rhetorical flight.

An added complication is that many sources contain only sketchy description of the actual movement. When critics have seen a work only once (which is the rule rather than the exception), their memory of specific choreographic content is often weak and may be padded out with narrative or descriptions of the set. Thus works that may contain only an implicit plot, message or theme may be recorded/remembered as being far more theatrical, didactic or plot-heavy than they actually appeared in performance.

Most of Rambert's rep in the 1960s and early 1970s was taken from American choreographers like Glen Tetley, but there were significant British experiments, too, including Norman Morrice's *Blind Sight* (1969) and John Chesworth's *H. H* (1968) was constructed as a series of impressionistic images related to the then pressing H-bomb threat, and helped to establish a new genre of semi-dance drama. It was set on an antiseptic white stage from which two spotlights glared blindingly on to the audience. Figures in white coats moved aside white sheets to reveal heaps of bodies lying on the floor, some apparently lifeless, some mourning or comforting their fellows. Other discarded sheets revealed not people, but cylindrical bombs, ready for use. As the piece progressed, the victims began to fall limply back on to their original piles while the white-coated 'scientists' consulted their watches and made notes. The piece was accompanied by Pendercki's *Polymorphia* – an assemblage of noises like spasms of pain. But the boldest element in the piece was the movement, which eschewed any recognizable, formal technique, replacing 'steps' with stylized everyday gesture.

Morrice's *Blind Sight* was a much more dancerly piece, blending natural gesture with classical and modern movement; but it displayed an equally grim determination to shock. Set in what looked like a silvery jungle and accompanied by a jazz score by Bob Downes, the piece presented various episodes relating to physical and moral blindness. At the opening, 12 dancers gathered round a charismatic figure who emerged clearly as their leader. At his instigation they persecuted an outcast figure, a blind woman, who was finally raped. One man tried to defend her but was in turn attacked and, as the curtain fell, the sightless girl was seen kicking blindly at her protector's corpse.

Apart from *H*, with its simplified non-dance choreography, most of the works performed by Rambert and LCDT stood obviously in line with the standard Graham repertoire. Their subjects may have been more contemporary than hers, but they used a recognizable version of her technique and adopted the same intensely theatrical methods – symbolic sets and costumes, powerfully evocative music. What united them most obviously was the assumption that dance was essentially a dramatic medium, a way of telling a story or delivering a message. Yet, ironically, it was this principle that was marking Graham out as passé in America; this principle that a new generation of choreographers, busy with a new politics and a new formalism of dance, were singling out as naive. The British might have finally accepted modern dance, but they were about 20 years out of date.

THE AMERICAN AVANT-GARDE

Briefly, what was going on across the Atlantic was a radical questioning of all the terms under which dance had previously been defined. Responding in part to the anti-elitist *Zeitgeist* of the period, choreographers of the 1960s had begun to explore the idea of dance as a natural rather than virtuosic activity. Bravura classical moves, even the severely eloquent gestures of Graham's choreography, were rejected in favour of unadorned, unstressed human movement. And just as Graham had rejected the fairytale heroes and heroines of nineteenth-century ballet, so choreographers of the 1960s turned their backs on the intense, mythic protagonists of Graham's work, creating dances that had no plot, theme or characters, but stated merely neutral facts about the movement and the mover.

Thus a new vocabulary of pedestrian, unstudied movement entered the dance language; performers walked, ran, crawled or danced in a deliberately low-key manner. The glamorous, gymnastic body image of the dancer was replaced by a demotic, casual look. Sneakers, jeans and tee-shirts replaced recognizable dance 'costumes'; trained dancers were rarely asked to flaunt their suppleness and control; and non-dancers were often used in performance to prove that the quirks of the untrained mover could be just as interesting, choreographically, as sleekness and coordination. (Yvonne Rainer once performed a shaky version of her seminal work *Trio A* (1966) just after a long illness, calling it *Convalescent Dance*.)

Many works were organized around simple tasks and structures, the point being to give a workmanlike ordinariness to the dance and present the performer, not as an otherworldly being, but as a practical decision-making individual. In Trisha Brown's *Rulegame* (1965), for example, the dancers had to follow a path that travelled up and down rows of masking tape. Each tape determined the level at which the dancers could move (varying from standing to prone) and as different dancers crossed on to different tapes they had to check that the 'person crawling along row 6 was at the correct height in relation to the dancer who was crouch-waddling along row 5' (Jowitt 1988: 306).

To emphasize the non-exclusivity, the 'ordinariness', of these concerns, certain works were conceived for non-theatre spaces such as parks, streets and rooftops. In Lucinda Child's *Street Dance* (1964) an area of the street was marked off and two dancers moved anonymously among the crowd, gesturing towards various buildings. The audience, watching from an upper-storey window, listened to a taped commentary on the architecture and the weather.

Towards the end of the decade, certain choreographers began to blend dance with other activities – everyday tasks, mime, song, the playing of instruments – in order to blur the distinction between one art-form or one occupation and another. In *Juice* (1969) Meredith Monk moved the audience around the Guggenheim Museum and the island of Manhatten. In part of the first instalment the spectators strolled up the museum's spiral ramp, past tableaux of dancers, with an exhibition of Roy Lichtenstein's paintings in the background. Three weeks later the second part of the performance took place at a theatre with the scale of events significantly reduced. It included four characters giving information about themselves in recitatives while frying chops and mixing chemicals. Monk herself whirled like a dervish and sang; a log cabin was gradually dismantled to reveal a violinist with books, a quart of milk and a print of a Lichtenstein painting. In part three, a week later, the audience assembled in Monk's own loft where they wandered through an exhibition of artefacts from the previous two instalments and watched four dancers on video quietly discussing their roles.

Monk's work had clear affinities with Artaud's theatre, its claim to 'present to the eye certain tableaux, certain indestructable, undeniable images that will speak directly to the mind. . . . There will not be a single theatrical gesture that will not carry behind it the fatality of life and the mysterious encounters of dreams' (Artaud 1976: 160). The more scrupulously movement- and task-based work of Rainer and Brown reflected the influence of Cage's music – the composition of music out of everyday sound and the work of minimalist artists who made sculpture out of found objects.

Of course it would have been too much to expect British audiences in the mid-1960s to plunge straight from the familiar pleasures of classicism to dancers crawling round gyms in old track suits, even if this new avant-garde work had been shown over here. Yet Graham was not the only alternative to ballet with which the public had been presented, and was certainly not the only possible school for a new modern dance to emulate.

MERCE CUNNINGHAM – GODFATHER AND GURU TO POSTMODERN DANCE

Merce Cunningham, the other great luminary of American modernism, had also enjoyed a highly successful season in London in 1964. And while his work struck many people as difficult or odd (his ideas had in fact sparked off some of the more radical energies of the 1960s), there were some reassuringly familiar elements to it; his choreography was obviously based on disciplined movement, while his dancers were visibly and reassuringly skilled technicians.

It was also based on completely different (and more fashionable) premises than Graham's, since Cunningham had rejected the latter's belief that dance should always tell a story or articulate a theme and proposed instead that it could and should be simply about itself. Cunningham's style, too, was based less on a personally orthodox technique than on the idea that any kind of movement could count as dance. Having performed with Graham's company, but having also taken ballet classes, he developed an approach that blended the vertical spine, the high leg extensions and fleet rhythmic footwork of classicism with the free curving torso of modern dance – a Cunningham dancer may balance in a classical attitude, leg angled high at the front or back, but have the torso bent sidewards or forwards. Tirelessly curious about movement from any source, Cunningham also slipped street gestures, animal movements and ordinary runs, walks or crawls into his choreography. So, in the 1965 work *Variations V*, he danced a solo in which he pulled the leaves off a plastic plant and rode a bicycle, while in *Septet* (1963) one of his dancers sprang energetically up and down while waving his arms like a traffic policeman. In a limited way this openness to found movement was an extension of John Cage's interest in the compositional potential of natural sound – a predictable connection since the two had been close collaborators from the late 1940s onwards.

Cunningham also juxtaposed several apparently disconnected movements on the same body at once. While a Graham movement was frequently a single emphatic gesture, and a ballet step aligned the body in one symmetrical design, a Cunningham dancer could be asked to execute a slow circling of the leg while the hands were tucked up to the shoulders, elbows rotating like propellors and the head turning this way and that. No part of the body and no single movement were regarded as more important than any other.

This sometimes bizarre density of physical information was also reflected in the moment-by-moment construction of his works. Classical ballets nearly always followed the laws of Renaissance perspective, the main action taking place at the centre of the stage, everything else acting as a kind of frame. Even Graham's work tended to be organized around the same principle, so that there could be no mistaking who were the main protagonists and what was the main action. But Cunningham argued that it was more interesting to have several equally absorbing events happening on stage at once, so that viewers had to decide for themselves what group of dancers, what duet, what space they would watch.

His logic was based not only on the belief that dance should reflect the dense information overload that is the condition of daily twentieth-century life, but also that it should be in tune with modern theories of the universe. (He once remarked that when he read 'that sentence of Einstein: "There are no fixed points in space", I said to myself if there are no fixed points, then every point is equally fluid and equally interesting' (Jowitt 1988: 289).) There are, again, significant parallels with Cage's music and its eschewal of the traditional organizing principles of harmony; also with painters like Rauschenberg and Johns (both collaborators with Cunningham), in whose works every image, form or colour compete equally for attention.

This deconstruction of the traditional stage picture extended to the way Cunningham used music and design. Believing that movements should be governed by their own timing and rhythm, he dispensed with the traditional practice of choreographing to a score. The dancers would rehearse to stop watches and the music, usually a fairly abrasive electronic composition, would be added at the last minute – sometimes as late as the first performance. If the score coincided with, echoed or contradicted the 'feel' of the movement, that was just part of the independent 'interest' that it contributed to the piece.

Cunningham also chose to have his designers work independently of his own composition. In *Rainforest* (1968) he used a Warhol installation of bobbing helium-filled balloons that were allowed to interfere freely with the already-choreographed movement, colliding with the dancers, scudding across their path or disappearing out of the wings. It was, he argued, more interesting to have three separate elements working together on stage than one carefully orchestrated spectacle; it left the audience free to make whatever connections they chose between dance, music and design, knowing they couldn't have been intentionally planned.

The operations of chance were also central to Cunningham's method of composition. While he developed the movement ideas for each work with immense care and rigour, he would allow chance to determine aspects of their organization, tossing coins to determine the order of certain sections of movement, or, as in *Suite for Five in Space and Time* (1953–9), marking the imperfections on a piece of paper to decide the path of a dancer through space. In 1955, he wrote:

> The feeling I have when I compose in this way is that I am in touch with natural resources far greater than my own personal inventiveness could ever be, much more universally human than the particular habits of my own practice, and organically rising out of common pools of motor impulse.
>
> (Jowitt 1988: 286)

The final sense in which Cunningham's work courted chance was his refusal to attach a public meaning or message to it. Whatever private significance a work held for him, he insisted that viewers were free to read into it whatever they chose. He has spoken with pleasure of the varying interpretations placed on a piece like *Winterbranch* (1965) – some people seeing images of the holocaust in it, others a concentration camp, others a storm at sea. The whole stage event admittedly invited grim interpretation, given La Monte Young's score – two piercing sounds coming at high volume from two speakers – the dancers' dark clothing, and the extremes of glare and darkness in Robert Rauschenberg's lighting. Yet Cunningham's own starting point was not disaster, so he claims, but a purely technical interest in the choreographic potential of falls. The dancers did a lot of collapsing in the piece and, because Cunningham was interested in having them exit without getting up again, they often fell on to pieces of cloth that the other dancers then dragged off stage – all possible images of catastrophe and rescue.

If Cunningham's fascination with chance and the more extreme quirks of his collaborators were too much for the staidly innocent British to absorb, the disciplined range of his choreography and his fascination with the body as an independently articulate instrument might have encouraged the dance world to see him as an important model. They did not, however. Although the 1964 season (and subsequent visits) attracted immense curiosity, it came more from the visual arts and music public than from dance audiences. Cage, Rauschenberg and Johns were the serious crowd pullers, rather than Cunningham himself. And there certainly seems to have been no question of anyone sending dancers to train at Cunningham's studio in New York (not in the 1960s, at least) or of a company being founded on the Cunningham style.

DANCE AND THE BRITISH ATTITUDE

Aside from the obvious fact that Graham's work had (and still has) a more direct and comprehensible appeal than Cunningham's, one reason for its more immediate popularity in Britain is that dance this side of the Atlantic has always been seen as an adjunct to theatre. Plot and characterization have consistently played a major role in British classical choreography, from Ashton, Tudor and de Valois through to MacMillan; we have not developed the kind of abstract tradition initiated by the Russian choreographer George Balanchine (founder both of New York City Ballet and of American classicism), whose work has always elevated the pleasures of pure movement and form over narrative.

Graham, who often referred to her dance dramas as plays and who believed that all movement should spring from an expressive motive, was clearly more in line with traditional British tastes than Cunningham, with his unprogrammatic, playfully intricate dance structures. The latter's thesis that dancing should be about itself rather than carry an intellectual or emotional meaning was a particularly difficult concept for the British to swallow, since for centuries our culture has been far more comfortable with verbal than physical expression.

Despite the so-called dance explosion of the late 1970s and the fashionable status of ballet during the prewar years, dance has never been taken as seriously as the other arts in Britain. Its lack of specialist representation at the Arts Council – until 1980 it was dealt with by the Music Panel – has contributed to its relative under-funding, while its lack of hard commercial potential has not helped it to gain coverage from the media. Ballets can't be sold over the counter the way books, prints and records can; they don't run for long continuous seasons like art exhibitions and plays, though the very recent growth in video recordings of dance may slowly help to redress the balance. Dance has also only recently been accorded a place in higher education. Clearly, the lack of primary sources make it difficult to study dance history – but not impossible, as the course at Surrey University demonstrates. And though much of the critical writing, both theory and history, attached to the subject still comes from America, British writers are slowly getting published.

It seems inevitable, then, that Graham should have been adopted as the basis of our national style and that Cunningham should have been viewed for several years as a difficult, even marginal, choreographer. But once the old classical hegemony was broken, attitudes in the dance world changed at an accelerating pace. By the late 1970s LCDT and Ballet Rambert had become firmly established as mainstream companies and, though their repertoire was fairly eclectic, the Graham-based style of much of their work was already being seen as limited and out of line with current trends. By the mid to late 1980s both companies changed their technical base, Rambert moving towards a mix of Cunningham and classicism, LCDT to a range of of Graham, Cunningham and some post-modern schools of dance.

During the 1970s, as these two 'pioneering' companies came to occupy establishment ground, so a fringe scene developed to form a genuine, British avant-garde. Richard Alston, one of the first students of the London Contemporary Dance School, reacted against the Graham-based approach of its training and in 1972 formed his own company, Strider, playing with movement that derived from the cooler, more analytic Cunningham school, and also with the more radical notions of the 1960s choreographers in America. By the mid-1970s he was making work with minimal low-key movement and spare formal structures, one programme significantly touring with an exhibition of work by Jasper Johns.

Rosemary Butcher visited the States in the early 1970s and came back with similar ideas, making work out of pedestrian, often improvised, movement that was often designed to appear in non-theatre spaces – a gallery, an open field, London's Paternoster Square. Other choreographers began to investigate the politics of dance, making multi-media performance work that tackled issues like the representation of women in dance; for example, in a re-write of *Giselle* the great tragic heroine of romantic ballet cast off her passive status as victim and became a conscious self-motivating woman.

As the number of small independent companies and solo artists proliferated, British dance fractured into a hitherto unimaginable pluralism and volatility. Choreographers invented their own techniques, collaborated with performers from the other arts and performed in whatever spaces took their fancy. Gradually the British public became initiated into the idea that dance was not a single form but a multiplicity of languages and activities.

The public's sturdy resistance to anything modern in 1954 thus took less than a couple of decades to dent. Though British dance in the 1960s was hardly ruffled by the decade of radical experiment in America, and though the first years of our own modern dance scene were largely imitative and conservative, it was none the less a crucial period for the form. Without the towering influence and the popularity of Martha Graham, without the setting up of one school and two companies in her image, and without the consequent breaking of the classical mould, genuinely native, genuinely innovative modern dance could not have happened in Britain. During the 1960s, it may not have been cultural revolution on the scale that galvanized music, theatre or the visual arts, but it laid all the foundations for the much publicized 'explosion' that took place in the following decade.

BIBLIOGRAPHY

Artaud, Antonin 1976. *Antonin Artaud: Selected Writings*, edited by Susan Sontag. New York: Farrar, Straus & Giroux.
Banes, Sally and Alexander, Robert 1980. *Terpsichore in Sneakers*. Boston: Houghton Mifflin.
Brinson, Peter and Crisp, Clement 1970. *Ballet For All*. Newton Abbot: David & Charles.
Jowitt, Deborah 1988. *Time and the Dancing Image*. New York: Morrow.
McDonagh, Don 1973. *Martha Graham – A Biography*. Newton Abbot: David & Charles.
Percival, John 1970. *Modern Ballet*. London: Herbert Press.
Robertson, Allen and Hutera, Donald 1988. *The Dance Handbook*. London: Longman.
White, Joan W. (ed.) 1985. *20th Century Dance in Britain*. London: Dance Books.

FURTHER READING

National newspapers provide contemporary review articles and interviews, as do the periodicals *Dancing Times* and *Dance and Dancers*, both published in London. *Ballet for All* by Peter Brinson and Clement Crisp, gives some description of the repertoire, as does *Modern Ballet* by John Percival. Other relevant works of reference are *20th Century Dance in Britain*, edited by Joan W. White, and *The Dance Handbook* by Allen Robertson and Donald Hutera. For the American scene *Time and the Dancing Image* by Deborah Jowitt has excellent chapters on Graham, Cunningham and the 1960s avant-garde. *Terpsichore in Sneakers* by Sally Banes and Robert Alexander covers the 1960s in greater detail, with good illustrative photographs.

Chapter 11

New waves and old myths: British cinema in the 1960s

Jeffrey Richards

INTRODUCTION

The 1960s witnessed a revitalization of British cinema and the emergence of a flourishing and diverse film culture, after what was widely perceived to be the doldrums era of the 1950s. The 1950s had seen the two great cinematic traditions of the 1940s – Ealing and Gainsborough – gradually running out of steam and expiring. Many of the great directors of the 1940s (Lean, Reed, Powell, Dickinson, Hamer, MacKendrick) declined, retired or removed to America. There was a sclerotic sense of old formulae being unimaginatively followed, of a failure of nerve and invention. The characteristic products of the decade reflected this: the war films that relived old glories; the Norman Wisdom comedies that trod in the footsteps of George Formby; the anaemic 'international' epics that aimed futilely to break into the American market, and which misused the sensitive talents of such stars as Dirk Bogarde and Peter Finch. In ethos and outlook, in technique and approach, mainstream 1950s films were essentially conservative, middle-class and backward looking.

The 1960s brought a small but influential body of films that captured the attention of critics by tackling the lifestyle and aspirations of the young and working class in a fresh unpatronizing way. They adopted an approach that was to be seen and proclaimed as sexually liberated, politically radical and socially committed. They marked a definite advance on 1950s cinema, but, seen from the perspective of the 1990s, seem more limited, particularly in their treatment of race, sex and gender, than critical orthodoxy has allowed. Over-concentration on these films at the expense of the many other cinematic products of the decade has also tended to distort the received picture of the age. This was perhaps inevitable, given the fact that British film-makers now operated in the context of an expanding British film culture. Hitherto this had consisted largely of the British Film Institute, *Sight and Sound*, the Academy Cinema and a belief in the superiority of continental 'art' films. The 1960s witnessed a mushroom growth of film societies, film magazines and film books, creating a whole generation of film-literate young *cinéastes*, willing to take an unprejudiced look at everything, notably the hitherto critically despised genre products of both Britain and Hollywood.

THE NEW WAVE 1959–63

British New Wave cinema was born out of the social and cultural upheaval of the late 1950s that embraced the death of the empire, the rise of working-class affluence, the emergence of a distinctive youth culture and the revival of the intellectual left. In form, it took its lead from French New Wave cinema, which preferred location-shooting to studio work, natural lighting to formal lighting and a fragmented impressionist approach to traditional linear narrative. But in content, British New Wave cinema was deeply rooted in, and strongly influenced by, the social-realist novels of writers like Alan Sillitoe and John Braine, the theatre work of the Angry Young Men like John Osborne and the 'kitchen-sink' working-class dramas that were a feature of Sidney Newman's *Armchair Theatre* on ATV.

The principal mood of the New Wave was one of discontent and dissatisfaction, a rejection of things as they were, a powerful sense that Britain was hopelessly mired in a hierarchical Victorian world of outdated values, disciplines and restrictions. The key year had been 1956 – the year of Suez and *Look Back in Anger*. It was also the year when a group of aspiring young film-makers – Tony Richardson, Karel Reisz and Lindsay Anderson – banded together, calling themselves Free Cinema in a conscious act of reaction against the cosiness, complacency, consensus and class consciousness that they saw characterizing 1950s cinema. But in fact, in personnel, approach and philosophy, they resembled nothing so much as the 'documentary boys' of the 1930s grouped around John Grierson; there was the same middle-class romanticization of the working class, the same commitment to a realist aesthetic, the same belief in location-shooting, the same rejection of studio artifice. This group graduated from short documentaries to full-length feature films in the 1960s.

They did so at a time of major change in cinema. The peak year for British cinema attendance had been 1946, with a record 1,635 million attendances at 4,709 cinemas. Thereafter there was a slow decline in the early 1950s that became precipitate after 1955 with the introduction of commercial television. Between 1955 and 1963 over two-thirds of the audience and over half the cinemas disappeared. This led to an increase in the proportion of young people in the audience. The old family audience at whom the cinema had aimed its product transferred its allegiance to television. Although the industry continued for some time to produce family films, and with some success – the top British box-office successes of 1960 and 1961 were *Doctor in Love* and *Swiss Family Robinson* – there was a greater emphasis on productions with an appeal to the young.

The British New Wave films shared common characteristics: black and white photography, melancholy jazz scores, northern locations (Blackpool, Salford, Bolton, Bradford, Wakefield, Morecambe, Manchester). The recurrent images of steam trains, cobbled back-streets, gasometers and railway viaducts gave the films the feeling of taking place at the fag-end of the nineteenth century. The bus ride around Manchester that opens *A Taste of Honey* (1961) captures perfectly this oppressive and decaying world of time-worn military statues, smoke-grimed buildings and weather-beaten Victorian iconography. Out-of-season seaside resorts and empty railway stations at night, recurrent locales in New Wave films, visually encapsulate the mood of despair and desolation that suffuses many of them.

But most of all, perhaps, the New Wave films were about sex and class. *Room at the Top* (1959) inaugurated the New Wave. It achieved sensational critical recognition. But the immediate popular reaction was to its sexual content. Film censor John Trevelyan put it in context:

> In retrospect one can see that Jack Clayton's *Room at the Top* was a milestone in the history of British films. . . . At the time its sex scenes were regarded as sensational and some of the critics who praised the film congratulated the Board on having had the courage to pass it. Ten years later these scenes seemed very mild and unsensational. . . . There was no nudity or simulated copulation, but there was rather more frankness about sexual relationships in the dialogue than people had been used to.
>
> (Trevelyan 1973: 106)

Honesty about sex was only one side of the picture. As John Braine, author of the original novel put it:

> The new dimension of the film was in presenting a boy from the working classes not as a downtrodden victim, but as he *really* was. It wasn't important that Joe Lampton was honest about sex, what was important was that Joe was honest about the whole business of class. Most ambitious working-class boys want to get the hell out of the working class. That was a simple truth that had never been stated before.
>
> (Richards, 1981: 1,134)

Room at the Top showed how, under the existing system, a working-class boy with the desire to succeed could only do so at the cost of his self-respect, peace of mind and personal happiness. The forces ranged against Joe are representative of the patronizing upper class, the self-made middle class anxious to preserve the status quo and a conservative and conformist working class, pressing him not to rise above his station.

So in a sense *Room at the Top* could be construed as a 'state of England' film, paralleling the plethora of books and articles appearing in the late 1950s and early 1960s on the subject of 'What's wrong with Britain'. So, too, could the two films made from John Osborne's plays by Tony Richardson, *Look Back in Anger* (1959) and *The Entertainer* (1960), though neither enjoyed the box-office success of *Room at the Top*. *Look Back in Anger*, the prototype Angry Young Man film, has not worn well, partly because of Richard Burton's monumental self-pitying bombast in the role of Jimmy Porter, a working-class university graduate running a market stall. The play itself is also a problem, dominated by a disgruntled and deracinated intellectual delivering a wearying succession of tirades against the middle class, the system, things as they were, symbolized by his upper middle-class wife whom he cruelly ill-treats and abuses.

Intellectually Jimmy is against the old value systems, declaring the age of chivalry dead and mocking the heroic imperialism of the 1939 film *Gunga Din*, which he sees at the cinema. Emotionally he is nostalgic both for the music hall, which is seen as a symbol of working-class irreverence, vitality and solidarity, and for an idealized lost Edwardian golden age ('high summer, long days in the sun, slim volumes of verse, bright ideas, bright uniforms'). But, with both gone, he has nothing to put in their place. Despite a bleak reunion with his wife at the end, the future seems to hold little prospect of change or improvement. Jimmy has no constructive philosophy, no social vision. The film, like the play, merely represents a cry of frustration against the system and as such struck a chord with young middle-class left-wing intellectual theatre-goers – though not with cinema-goers, who were alienated by its unrelenting biliousness.

The ideas in *Look Back in Anger* were elaborated in *The Entertainer*. Britain's greatest actor, Laurence Olivier, who as the wartime Henry V had become a symbol of the nation, now took on another symbolic role. Third-rate variety artist Archie Rice is England in the 1950s, seedy, bankrupt, rundown, at the end of a great tradition. His father Billy (Roger Livesey), dignified, elegant, patriotic, is a retired music-hall star who dies trying to make a comeback. His world and his values are gone beyond recall. While Billy sings nostalgically 'Don't let them scrap the British navy', his grandson is killed at Suez in the last imperial adventure.

But if Jimmy Porter and Archie Rice did not command the affection of cinema-goers, Arthur Seaton in Karel Reisz's *Saturday Night and Sunday Morning* (1960) did, making the film, according to producer Harry Saltzman, a box-office success. Alexander Walker aptly describes Arthur as 'unrepentantly sexy in a repressive community, sharper than his mates, tougher than the pub brawlers he worsts, anti-romantic in his view of women as providing a night's pleasure, reconciled to paying the penalty for his pleasure, but resistant to all life could do to him' (1974: 83–4). Arthur has a philosophy: 'Don't let the bastards grind you down. What I'm out for is a good time; all the rest is propaganda'. He is an authentic product of working-class affluence. He denounces the system (the taxman, the bosses, national service). He denounces the idea of the 'good old days' (the sentimentalization of the slums). But he is no radical or revolutionary. He is a totally self-centred wage-earning individualist with money to spend, who drinks himself silly, seduces a workmate's wife and shows no concern for anyone but himself. The film is a robust celebration of the 'rough' working-class ethic of immediate gratification (through sex, drink, sport and fighting).

Alan Sillitoe, who scripted *Saturday Night and Sunday Morning* from his own novel, also wrote the more ambitious 'state of England' film *The Loneliness of the Long Distance Runner* (1962), directed by Tony Richardson. Its central figure, Colin Smith (Tom Courtenay), shares Arthur Seaton's philosophy – 'I don't believe in slaving my guts out for the bosses to get all the profits' – and turns to crime.

He is sent to Borstal, the kind of total institution that classically functions as a symbol of the nation – repressive, socially controlled, run by a public school élite and headed by a paternalist governor. The film details Colin's rebellion against, and rejection of, the values they try to instil, winning his own battle by deliberately losing a cross-country race. Courtenay's Colin with his pinched 1930s features, grim and deprived home life and irrepressible bloody-mindedness looks back to the proletarian heroes of the past, social rebel rather than juvenile delinquent.

These and the other films of the New Wave centred almost exclusively on the discontents of the young urban working-class male (Albert Finney, Tom Courtenay, Alan Bates). Often they were employed and not short of money. They were willing to engage in extra-marital sex, but anxious to avoid marriage. But most of all they chafed against the weight of restriction and repression imposed by the combination of the class system, traditional Victorian morality and social convention.

But if the young male's pursuit of freedom was approvingly charted, there was no similar treatment of the young female. One of the continuing elements of the New Wave cinema, seen in, for instance, *Look Back in Anger* and *Saturday Night and Sunday Morning*, is a pervasive misogynism: the idea of marriage as a trap and the end of freedom for the male; the maltreatment of women by violence or exploitation, abuse or neglect.

John Schlesinger's *A Kind of Loving* (1962), based on Stan Barstow's novel, explores the nature of a 'shotgun marriage' between Alan Bates, romantic respectable working-class lad with an unsatisfied wanderlust, and his conventional unimaginative girlfriend (June Ritchie), tied to the apron-strings of her snobbish, reactionary, houseproud mother (Thora Hird), symbol of everything the New Wave detested. Lindsay Anderson's *This Sporting Life* (1963), based on David Storey's novel, memorably examines the predicament of a brutalized inarticulate working-class rugby player (Richard Harris), unable to express his affection for and need for the widow he has a relationship with.

Sidney Furie's *The Leather Boys* (1963), based on Gillian Freeman's novel, although often described as a film about homosexuality, is not. It is more centrally about the problems of a working-class marriage. Reggie (Colin Campbell) is married to Dot (Rita Tushingham), but sex is the only link between them. They row continually and Reggie finds greater fulfilment in his mateship with

Pete (Dudley Sutton), based on a shared love of motorbikes, the pub and having 'a good laff'. But the mateship is soured by the discovery by Reggie that blond and epicene Pete is gay. Reggie, having left Dot, now leaves Pete.

Dot is depicted as shallow and heartless; Reggie as decent and sensitive. He works; she idles. He looks after his widowed gran; she neglects her. She has sex with other men; he does not. But the root of the problem is that she does not conform to his view of a wife as an obedient demure home-creating woman. She outrages his working-class puritanism by her tarty hair style, telling dirty stories, neglecting her housework and devoting herself to a regime of 'the pictures', the hairdresser and *True Romances*. It is thus a film about the mismatch between the rough and respectable working classes; but it is also about the joys of mateship, emotionally fulfilling but ultimately flawed by the need to avoid sexual expression. Rita Tushingham in *The Leather Boys* represents one of the two main female types in the New Wave, where women are either 'silly tarts' (June Ritchie, Shirley Ann Field, Tushingham) or 'selfish old bags' (Thora Hird, Dora Bryan, Avis Bunnage).

The only New Wave film to centre on a woman is Tony Richardson's *A Taste of Honey* (1961), adapted by Shelagh Delaney from her stage play. It explores the uneasy relationship between a vulnerable gamine Jo (Rita Tushingham) and her tarty, self-centred mother (Dora Bryan). Jo becomes pregnant, but rejects adulthood, womanhood and responsibility, retreating into a childhood signalled throughout the film by recurrent children's songs and chants, and becoming reconciled with her mother. It is perhaps significant that it is this woman-centred film that contains representatives of two other groups largely absent from the New Wave, and little seen in the cinema of the 1960s. Rita Tushingham has a black lover, a cheerful Liverpudlian sailor whom she idealizes as an African prince, and an effeminate homosexual friend and confidant Geoff, whom she treats as a sister. But all three – the black, the gay and the single mother-to-be – are seen as marginal to mainstream society.

This is also true in Bryan Forbes's impressive *The L-Shaped Room* (1962), based on the novel by Lynne Reid Banks. A pregnant unmarried French girl (Leslie Caron) moves into a seedy London lodging house and is bracketed with its population of sympathetically observed but indisputably marginal inhabitants – a homosexual black trumpeter, an elderly lesbian music-hall artist and two prostitutes. Her pregnancy alienates the struggling young writer (Tom Bell), with whom she has fallen in love. In the end she rejects an abortion, but also gives up life as a potential single parent to return to her parents. Although this ending has been criticized subsequently, it is an authentic response for the period, and made entirely believable by Leslie Caron's beautifully judged interpretation of love, loneliness, despair and resolution.

Both Murray Melvin's sexless Geoff and Brock Peters's Johnny, with his very understated affection for the young writer, are sympathetic and unthreatening gays. But they are peripheral. Despite the liberation of young men, British cinema was not yet ready to liberate gays, women or blacks. However, it was Britain that produced the first commercial feature films to plead for tolerance for homosexuals since the German film *Anders als die Anderen* in 1919. Two films in 1960, *Oscar Wilde* and *The Trials of Oscar Wilde*, showed Wilde as a noble tragic hero, victim both of personal infatuation and of social and judicial prejudice. But the events took place safely in the past, and involved a Bohemian literary genius. It was Basil Dearden's *Victim* (1961) that showed homosexuals existing at every level of contemporary society, and illustrated the prejudice against them. Dirk Bogarde gave a courageous and moving performance as a married barrister and non-practising homosexual, who lays his career on the line to expose the plight of homosexuals under the existing law, a blackmailer's charter. As Vita Russo (1981: 131) points out, the careful characterization of the barrister meant that liberals could accept him as a non-threatening figure and gays as a crusader. It was not until *Sunday, Bloody Sunday* in 1971 that homosexuality could be presented as a valid alternative lifestyle. But then, neither Gay Liberation nor Women's Liberation really got underway until the 1970s.

Racial minorities were largely absent from New Wave films, as they were from British cinema in general in the 1960s. Jimmy Porter defends an Asian stallholder against racism, and Rita Tushingham has her black lover in *A Taste of Honey*, but the classic anti-racist statement comes in Ted Willis's social-realist drama *Flame in the Streets* (1961), directed by Roy Baker. Highly schematic and didactic, it showed English society permeated with racism, and highlighted the dilemma of a trade union shop-steward (John Mills) with impeccably liberal views, confronted by the prospect of his daughter marrying a black man. Hollywood's supreme exemplar of the noble black man, Sidney Poitier, came to Britain for the sentimental and predictable, but popular, *To Sir, With Love* (1965), directed and written by James Clavell from the novel by E. R. Braithwaite. Poitier plays a Guyanan teacher who wins over a class of tough unruly cockney kids – introducing them to good manners, culture and self-respect, and eliminating colour prejudice, mindless violence and scruffiness along the way. But no black British star emerged capable of emulating Poitier as charismatic standard-bearer of racial equality.

So New Wave films had little positive to say about blacks, gays and women. In fact the attitudes of the male characters of the New Wave films were generally negative. They were against a good deal but not for very much, except themselves. Colin Smith wants to line up the Establishment and shoot them; Arthur Seaton denounces the bosses and the system. But what did the New Wave heroes want in its place? 'Everything . . . nothing', says Jimmy Porter.

Along with hostility to the system in New Wave films went hostility to the new materialism, to affluence and to the homogenizing effect of the mass media. This had been the keynote of Richard Hoggart's seminal book *The Uses of Literacy* (1957), and it haunted the mainly left-wing writers and directors of the New Wave. Arthur Seaton claims that most people are content to conform, as long as they can get 'their telly and their fags'. Jimmy Porter denounces the Americanization of culture and celebrates the dying indigenous art of the music hall. Thora Hird's obsession with tawdry TV quiz programmes in *A Kind of Loving* is part of her monstrousness. In *Loneliness of the Long Distance Runner*, Colin Smith's family splurge on consumer goods, the compensation for their father's death, a sequence parodically shot as a TV advertising magazine. But there is a major paradox here. One of the objects of the Labour movement's long struggle had been to ensure a share of the national prosperity for the working class. But now that the working class had achieved affluence, they had used it to endorse and participate in a consumerist world, a situation summed up and satirized in *Live Now, Pay Later* (1962).

The positive side of the films is sexual frankness, the willingness to acknowledge and depict sexuality in a way previously rare in British cinema; and respect for the traditional pattern and texture of working-class life as it was lived – the seaside holiday, the pub, the football match, the dance, the family party. These were integral to New Wave cinema, and part of the Hoggartian nostalgia for a warm old working-class culture of communality. But it was a world that was vanishing, even as it was being filmed. Society was becoming steadily more privatized, with television, individual and home-centred, eclipsing the communal activities of the cinema, the football match and the pub; with private cars replacing public transport, and Spanish package holidays superseding the domestic holiday camp. In a sense New Wave films were part of this process, centring as they did on individual predicaments, and particularly highlighting sex and self rather than work and class. As John Hill (1986: 174) points out, this emphasis tends to make the films more conservative than radical, stressing individual fulfilment rather than social change. Certainly the individualism of the New Wave films is in marked contrast to the communality that was such a feature of wartime and postwar films, whether it be the service films about groups of men and women banding together to defend the nation; the Ealing comedies, in which small communities join forces to defeat some outside power; or the films about holiday camps (*Holiday Camp*, 1947), dance halls (*Dance Hall*, 1950) and cycling clubs (*A Boy, A Girl and a Bike*, 1949), in which the people as a collectivity are the hero.

FROM REALISM TO FANTASY 1964–70

A dramatic change came over British films after 1964, a change that coincided with the victory of the Labour government, with its emphasis on youth, progress and innovation, and the birth of 'Swinging London'. The film that symbolized this change and caught the mood of the moment was *Tom Jones* (1963). Henry Fielding's picaresque eighteenth-century novel, with its story of the rise of a poor boy to fame and fortune amid an uninhibited celebration of sex and conspicuous consumption, was brought to the screen by John Osborne, Tony Richardson and Albert Finney. The style they adopted was far from the reverent naturalism of previous classic novel adaptations. It was jokey and knowing, and it employed slapstick comedy, speeded-up action, captions, asides to camera and an urbane narration. This irreverent eclecticism, inspired by the techniques and ethos of pop art, set the tone and style for the rest of the decade. *Tom Jones*, bawdy and funny, celebrated a previous permissive age of gusto, gourmandizing and zestful free living, appearing at a time when the Labour election victory promised '100 days of dynamic action' and a programme of social reform in an era of full employment and growing affluence.

It signalled, in its subject, its style and its attitude, the end of the old order against which the New Wave heroes had chafed. Restraint and restriction, both personal and institutional, were in retreat, and a new world was emerging, a consumerist world of colour supplements and pirate radio, glamorous television commercials, discos and boutiques, a cult of the new and the now. The accent was on youth. For the first time in history it became fashionable to be young and working class. Looks, style and attitude, rather than birth and breeding, became the keys to success. Rock musicians, fashion photographers and pop artists were the role models of the moment. Sexy roistering Tom Jones was the symbol of this age. The cinema box-offices confirmed the truth of the poster slogan 'All the world loves Tom Jones'.

It was the involvement of New Wave stalwarts Osborne, Richardson and Finney in *Tom Jones* that was the most significant development. It signalled almost overnight the end of the New Wave. It was as if the unspoken agenda behind the discontent powering the New Wave – the desire for a life of total and unrestrained freedom – had been met by the crumbling of the old order. So in films sober realism and earnest social comment gave way to fantasy, extravaganza, escapism; black and white photography to colour; the grim north to the glittering metropolis; puritanical self-discipline to hedonistic self-indulgence; plain truthful settings to flamboyant unrealistic decorativeness. Where the emphasis had been on the dark side of the self – discontent, repression and deprivation – it switched to the bright side, to self-assertion, personal fulfilment and the good life.

John Schlesinger's *Billy Liar* (1963), based on the play by Keith Waterhouse and Willis Hall, was the transitional film for the New Wave. Black and white, and shot in Manchester, it highlighted the frustrations of early 1960s youth – a dull job, critical parents, a possessive conventional girlfriend. But Manchester youth Billy Fisher (Tom Courtenay) finds escape from all this in fantasy daydreams. Julie Christie represents the icon of escape. Totally liberated, she is his soulmate, sexually free and secure. At the end, she leaves for London: he cannot bring himself to go.

But the stars and directors who had made their names in New Wave films all forsook the pressures of working-class life in the north of England for the frenetic gaiety of the metropolitan maelstrom – Alan Bates in *Nothing But the Best* (1964), Rita Tushingham in *Smashing Time* (1967) and Tom Courtenay in *Otley* (1968). Julie

Christie became the chief symbol of 'liberated' womanhood in Swinging London, starring in *Darling* (1965), *Far From the Madding Crowd* (1967), *Petulia* (1968) and *The Go-Between* (1971). But there continued to be limits to, and ambiguities about, her liberation.

Tom Jones inspired imitations – *The Amorous Adventures of Moll Flanders* (1965), *Lock Up Your Daughters* (1969), *Sinful Davy* (1969) and, in more serious vein, *Where's Jack?* (1969) – confirming the view that the eighteenth century was the preferred model for the 1960s. Tony Richardson emphasized this by producing an historical counterpart to *Tom Jones* in *Charge of the Light Brigade* (1968), as unsparing an indictment of the nineteenth century as the earlier film had been an uninhibited celebration of the eighteenth. *Light Brigade* characterized Victorian society as squalid, repressive, brutal and irredeemably class-ridden, implying that it had survived into the twentieth century and was in need of final sweeping away. But the film was also importantly anti-war and anti-military, a direct response to the Vietnam War that dominated the thinking of many of the creative and the young, who saw it as an affront to the new age of freedom, peace and love, as a reminder of great power politics and of archaic imperialism. The nineteenth century was deemed useful only for providing the modish bric-a-brac for the new age, everything from hussars' jackets to Boer War biscuit tins; Victorian decor was utilized as the high camp and grand kitsch backgrounds for the comic capers of *The Wrong Box* (1966), *The Assassination Bureau* (1968) and *The Best House in London* (1968).

Fantasy never lurked far below the surface of many 1960s films. It even featured in the work of the New Wave veterans. Karel Reisz went on from *Saturday Night and Sunday Morning* to direct *Morgan – A Suitable Case for Treatment* (1966), based on David Mercer's play, which hinged on the fashionable Laingian idea that the mad were saner than the sane. Morgan (David Warner) dresses up in a gorilla suit and has fantasies of himself as Tarzan and King Kong. But he prefers his fantasies to reality and does nothing to bring about the Marxist revolution his father sought. Reisz next went for the fashionable historical parallelism with *Isadora* (1967), a lengthy and indulgent celebration of one of the 'bright young things' of an earlier era, the 1920s, a pioneer of sexual liberation and defiance of convention. Both films were typical tracts for the times, highlighting individuals who retreated into themselves and created their own world around them like a comforting cocoon rather than engaging with wider social issues.

If Richardson, Reisz and Schlesinger had been the characteristic directors of the New Wave, the celebrants of Swinging London were Dick Lester, Michael Winner and Clive Donner. Michael Winner's films encapsulated the most prized characteristics of the new era, coolness (*Play it Cool*, 1962; *The Cool Mikado*, 1963) and jokiness (*You Must be Joking*, 1965; *The Jokers*, 1966; *I'll Never Forget Whatsisname*, 1967) – the decade's prime directive being that nothing was to be taken seriously. Clive Donner's *Nothing But the Best* (1964) was the new era's black comedy mirror-image of the New Wave's *Room at the Top*. *What's New Pussycat?* (1965) satirized the sex obsession of the 'Swinging 60s', while *Here We Go Round the Mulberry Bush* (1967) was a suburban *Knack*, with inexperienced teenager Barry Evans attempting to lose his virginity amidst the shopping precincts and parks of Stevenage New Town.

Dick Lester's films were mercurial, modish mosaics, his style fragmented and breathlessly fast-moving, an amalgam of influences, from silent comedy, television commercials, comic strips, Marx Brothers and Goon Show surrealism. His was the quintessential visual style of the second half of the decade, a daring and dynamic form of montage gleefully embracing parody, pastiche and pop art. His career is emblematic of the way British cinema developed in the decade. In 1963 he directed the charming, whimsical *Mouse on the Moon*, which, with its antique monarchy, hereditary prime minister, medieval flummery and pretensions to great power status, looked back to the Ealingesque England of the 1950s. But in 1964 he directed *A Hard Day's Night*, followed by *The Knack* (1965) and *Help* (1965). All three films show provincial youth coming into their kingdom, conquering London and refashioning the world in their own image.

A Hard Day's Night is a celebration of the decade's greatest cult figures, the Beatles, and their music. The film is built around their image as cool, youthful, irreverent, quirky and quick-witted provincials. They were the first pop idols not to be processed into safe 'family entertainers' and in the process emasculated. Both Tommy Steele and Cliff Richard, initially viewed as threateningly sexy, had been carefully transformed into 'the boy next door', a Mickey Rooney *de nos jours*. Cliff in particular, who had starred in *Expresso Bongo* (1959) as a sexy working-class teen idol on the make, entered the 1960s as the distinctly unthreatening hero of a series of highly traditional screen musicals (*The Young Ones*, 1961; *Summer*

Holiday, 1962; *Wonderful Life*, 1964). The Beatles, however, were securely anchored by Lester in the new pop art and pop culture.

Help, the second Beatles film, is a brightly coloured pop collage, a *mélange* of Marx Brothers comedy, cod oriental mayhem, inventive sight gags and imperial bric-a-brac. The film bubbles with Lester's feeling about the era:

> There was an enormous sense of optimism that I felt in England from 1962–63 until 1967, which is when it started to go wrong, it seems to me. During that time, the films had a sense of a response to a feeling that anything could be achieved, that the class structure was breaking down, that there was a new opportunity for the structure of life in England.
>
> (Sinyard 1985: 19)

GENRE SUCCESSES

At about the same time as *Tom Jones*, James Bond, the other great cult figure of the 1960s, hit the screen. *Doctor No* (1962) was the first of what became a series stretching to the present day; it starred Sean Connery as Bond, and set the pattern for an unbeatable blend of conspicuous consumption, brand name snobbery, technological gadgetry, colour supplement chic, exotic locations and comic-strip sex and violence. Although Bond was, in Raymond Durgnat's words, 'the last man in of the British Empire Superman's XI' (1970: 151), pitted against Fu-Manchu (*Doctor No*) or travelling on the Orient Express (*From Russia With Love*, 1963), there were crucial differences between Bond and Richard Hannay or Bulldog Drummond – both of whom experienced cinematic revivals around this time, Hannay in *The Thirty-Nine Steps* (1959) and Drummond in *Deadlier Than The Male* (1966) and *Some Girls Do* (1968). Bond was both a sexual adventurer and essentially classless, Connery's Glaswegian accent distancing him from the upper-class English gentlemen who customarily played secret agents. This put him firmly in line with other 1960s icons. The films were classically in the 1960s style – cool and knowing, sharing with comic-strip adaptations like *Barbarella* (1968), *Batman* (1966) and *Modesty Blaise* (1966) an ironic sense of distancing from the nature of their source material. The combination of form and content proved so appealing that the Bond films provided the top box-office successes in Britain in 1963 (*From Russia With Love*), 1964 (*Goldfinger*), 1966 (*Thunderball*) and

1967 (*You Only Live Twice*). Bond's success sparked off a whole series of American imitations – Matt Helm, Derek Flint, Napoleon Solo – all informed by the same approach, though on rather lower budgets.

There was also a series of caper movies made in Britain, with titles like *Masquerade* (1965), *Kaleidoscope* (1966), *Arabesque* (1966) and *Fathom* (1967), in which form was all. They revelled in bright colours, flip dialogue, spectacular stunts, speed, style and sensation. Their complicated and irrelevant plots, in which no one is what they seem, everyone is engaged in elaborate role-playing, life is a game, and both loyalties and relationships are flexible and shifting, effectively summarized the 1960s philosophy that saw immediate gratification, individualism and self-assertion as paramount.

It is, however, arguable that such genre films were more subversive of the previous value-system than more overt, serious and intellectual 'state of the nation' films. In that event, we should set alongside the espionage thrillers both the long-running 'Carry On' comedies and Hammer's horror films.

The 'Carry On' series, which spanned the years from 1958 to 1980, allegedly included 29 films, but in fact were the same film made 29 times. The series deployed a talented cast of farceurs repeating in a variety of settings a familiar repertoire of sketches, jokes and characterizations derived from music-hall skits and routines and from the saucy seaside postcard world of Donald McGill – a world of fat ladies and overflowing bosoms, nervous honeymoon couples and randy jack-the-lads, chamber pots and bedpans. They constitute a 20-year act of defiance against every canon of taste, decency, decorum and responsibility, but they operate in territory mapped out in the 1930s and 1940s by the likes of Frank Randle and Max Miller. Yet, in a real sense, appearing when they did, they functioned almost as comic counterparts both of the New Wave and Swinging London. As Marion Jordan notes:

> Despite denying any place to women in their pantheon – portraying them, indeed, as gaolers, sexual objects, or unnatural predators – they nonetheless asserted by their themes, and by the gusto with which they were presented, a lower-class, masculine resistance to 'refinement'; an insistence on sexuality, physicality, fun; on the need for drink in a kill-joy world, for shiftiness in an impossibly demanding industrial society, for cowardice amid the imposed heroism.

> (Jordan 1983: 327)

Hammer, on the other hand, provided a symbolic and mythological counterpart to the New Wave and Swinging London. Beginning in the key year of 1956, and continuing throughout the 1960s, Hammer remade and then provided sequels to the Universal horror classics of the 1930s. Hammer films consistently pointed up the contrast between the ordered bourgeois normality of Victorian England and the forces of unreason and excess lurking below the surface. In particular, their films celebrated the single-minded gratification of their desires by outlaw anti-heroes. In film after film the conscience-less fanatical dandy Baron Frankenstein (Peter Cushing) pursued his scientific experiments in defiance of the laws of God and Man, and the virile arrogant indestructible Count Dracula (Christopher Lee) slaked his sexual desire on the bodies of a succession of mainly female victims who, after the initial contact, became his willing confederates in pursuit of sensation. Initially symbols of a ruthless and exploitative upper class, they soon became transformed into the heroes of an era of sex, style and 'anything goes'.

CONCLUSION

The Swinging London era of cinema had been mainly London-centred, male-centred, style-centred, self-centred, fatally self-indulgent. The issues of class, race, region and gender had taken second place to the exaltation of a classless consumerist self. All this, reflected in cinema, tends to validate the interpretation of the 1960s advanced by Bernice Martin in *A Sociology of Contemporary Cultural Change* (1981). She sees the 1960s as the latest manifestation of romanticism and the decade as a parallel of the late eighteenth and early nineteenth centuries. Romanticism seeks to destroy boundaries, reject conventions, undermine structures and universalize the descent into the abyss and the ascent into the infinite. Its matrix is material prosperity that releases people from the immediate disciplines of survival, and that concentrates their attention on their 'expressive' needs – self-discovery, self-fulfilment, experience and sensation. Romantics of the 1960s reacted against a world that was highly structured, traditional and conventional, still in essence Victorian. In its place they advocated a culture of liminality, in which the outsider, the rebel and the deviant were heroes, the self was exalted, spontaneity was everything, and rules, restrictions, conventions and traditions, both in art and life, were ditched. In films this had the effect of highlighting fantasy and sexuality rather than serious political engagements.

Eventually, however, there comes a reaction to romantic excess, a return to structure. It happened after the first romantic period with the rise of evangelicalism and the formation of Victorian values. It happened, too, after the 1960s with a return to structure and eventually the rise of Thatcherism. But it was not the same order and the same structure that had existed before the 1960s; the cultural revolution had long-term effects. Surrealism, particularly in comedy, became widely acceptable. The dominance of the old linear narrative was broken; audiences were willing to accept much more fragmented narrative techniques. The cinema took the lead in extending the limits of what was permissible in the depiction of both sexuality and violence. Throughout the 1960s audiences became used to more nudity, simulated sex and profanity than they had ever seen before. Violence became more graphic and more frequent. Authority was no longer accepted as beneficent and paternalist. Most noticeably, the chivalric ethic that had been central to British culture since the mid-nineteenth century was rejected. The twin processes of disillusionment with the status quo and liberation from restraint are reflected fully in the characteristic products of 1960s cinema: in the violence and cynicism of the spaghetti westerns; in the disgruntlement of the working-class anti-heroes in social realist dramas; in the hedonism and self-indulgence of the Swinging-London films. The ubiquitous spy films embodied the twin facets of the 1960s stance: in the anti-Establishment tone of the Le Carré brand, in which suave heartless upper-class spymasters manipulated and exploited proletarian agents; and in the cool classless consumerist style of the Bond brand. What all these genres and forms and films have in common is the exaltation of the individual, the unrestrained self, in pursuit of gratification. When there was affluence, that gratification took the form of sex, drink and drugs. During recession this was replaced by the pursuit of money, and this new direction taken by individualism was, in due course, to plunge the nation into the abyss of Thatcherism.

BIBLIOGRAPHY

Barr, Charles 1986. *All Our Yesterdays*. London: British Film Institute.
Curran, James and Porter, Vincent (eds) 1983. *British Cinema History*. London: Weidenfeld & Nicolson.

Durgnat, Raymond 1970. *A Mirror For England*. London: Faber & Faber.
Gaston, Georg 1980. *Karel Reisz*. Boston: Twayne.
Hill, John 1986. *Sex, Class and Realism: British Cinema 1956–1963*. London: British Film Institute.
Jordan, Marion 1983. 'Carry On – follow that stereotype'. In Curran, James and Porter, Vincent (eds), *British Cinema History*. London: Weidenfeld & Nicolson.
Laing, Stuart 1986. *Representations of Working Class Life 1957–1964*. London: Macmillan.
Leahy, James 1967. *The Cinema of Joseph Losey*. London: Zwemmer.
Martin, Bernice 1981. *A Sociology of Contemporary Cultural Change*. Oxford: Blackwell.
Marwick, Arthur 1984. '*Room At The Top, Saturday Night and Sunday Morning* and the "cultural revolution" in Britain'. *Journal of Contemporary History*, 19, 127–52.
Philips, Gene 1981. *John Schlesinger*. Boston: Twayne.
Pirie, David 1973. *Heritage of Horror*. London: Gordon Fraser.
Richards, Jeffrey 1981. '*Room at the Top*'. *The Movie*, 57, 1,134.
Robertson, J. C. 1989. *The Hidden Screen*. London: Routledge.
Russo, Vito 1981. *The Celluloid Closet: Homosexuality in the Movies*. New York: Harper & Row.
Sinyard, Neil 1985. *The Films of Richard Lester*. London: Croom Helm.
Stead, Peter 1989. *Film and the Working Class*. London: Routledge.
Sussex, Elizabeth 1969. *Lindsay Anderson*. London: Studio Vista.
Trevelyan, John 1973. *What The Censor Saw*. London: Michael Joseph.
Walker, Alexander 1974. *Hollywood, England*. Reprinted 1986, London: Harrap.

FURTHER READING

For a clearsighted overview of the cinematic decade see Alexander Walker, *Hollywood, England* (1974). Various aspects of the decade are covered in essays in two illuminating collections, Charles Barr's *All Our Yesterdays* (1986) and James Curran and Vincent Porter's *British Cinema History* (1983). The best analyses of the British New Wave are John Hill, *Sex, Class and Realism: British Cinema 1956–1963* (1986) and Arthur Marwick's (1984) article. Raymond Durgnat's, *A Mirror for England* (1970), individual and idiosyncratic, is indispensable for all aspects of British cinema. On the working class in cinema, see in particular Peter Stead, *Film and the Working Class* (1989), and Stuart Laing, *Representations of Working Class Life 1957–1964* (1986), which also covers television and theatre. The definitive study of the British horror film is David Pirie, *A Heritage of Horror* (1973). There are a number of useful monographs on individual directors: Neil Sinyard, *The Films of Richard Lester* (1985); James Leahy, *The Cinema of Joseph Losey* (1967); Elizabeth Sussex, *Lindsay Anderson* (1969); Gene Phillips, *John Schlesinger* (1981); Georg Gaston, *Karel Reisz* (1980). On developments in censorship, see J. C. Robertson, *The Hidden Screen* (1989) and John Trevelyan, *What the Censor Saw* (1973).

Chapter 12

Still crazy after all these years: what *was* popular music in the 1960s?

Dave Harker

INTRODUCTION: EVERYBODY KNOWS

'Nothing', writes Peter Wicke in *Rock Music*, 'has changed . . . the music culture of the twentieth century more fundamentally than the meteoric rise to fame of the Beatles.' And nothing, he believes, has changed the 'context' of popular music consumption so much, either. What the 'now forty-five-year-old Beatles generation' has helped to achieve is an enormous change that amounts to 'the formation of a new everyday culture, influenced by the media' (Wicke 1990: viii). And it happened in the 1960s.

These are powerful ideas, but are they true? Why does a 38-year-old German popular-music critic – perhaps the best popular musicologist at work today – believe that 'Rock Music' is and was anglophone and, according to the rest of his book, predominantly male? And why did it happen there, then?

The problems facing the serious student of 1960s popular music begin with this difficulty; everybody knows the music, empirically, but nobody has yet offered a sustained and theoretically consistent account of its history or significance. The popular music fan is well catered for, with book after book of data on chart performance and biographical detail; and with the seemingly continuous re-presentation of material produced in the 1960s, not only on re-released singles and compilation LPs, but spliced film, TV and radio tape, on juke-boxes, radio programmes and as film sound-tracks. Whole albums are remastered, repackaged and remarketed. Old stars continue to win new audiences (sometimes); and even dead people get commercially 'revived'. All this may be a problem for someone born after 1970; but it is an even bigger problem for those of us who lived through that decade. Some of my friends have never left it; others try to 'buy back' into their youth, retrospectively; while young fogeys I know, almost like antiquarians, behave similarly, but with more scepticism, in relation to the music their parents say they used to like.

What, then, gets bought? Of the 25 best-selling reissued LPs in the UK in 1989–90, four were first released in the 1960s. At number 8 is the Beatles' *Sergeant Pepper*. So far so good. But at numbers 17 and 25 we find *Led Zeppelin II* and *Led Zeppelin*; and number 28 is *Phil Spector's Christmas Album (BPI Yearbook 1989–90*: 92). What are they doing there? Who are they, anyway? Is the past all some people have to look forward to? But why that past? And why, as with these albums, do some years in the 1960s seem to get privileged? Is it that this history, like most autobiographies, has been written backwards, so that the 1960s begin with 1969 and Woodstock, develop through student militancy and the Rolling Stones' 'Street Fightin' Man' in 1968, and culminate in 1967 with *Sergeant Pepper*, with a glance back to the Beatles' early singles (and an embarrassed silence about 'My Bonnie lies over the ocean')?

There are all sorts of problems with Wicke's 'common-sense' perspective. If the Beatles' success was 'meteoric', as he claims, why did it happen two years later in the USA than in the UK? Can flat discs of black vinyl really have the kinds of fundamental cultural effects he claims for them? Can the products of capitalist commerce be in any but the slackest conversational sense 'revolutionary'? There are, also, other interesting questions. What were the connections between, say, the Tory and Labour governments in Britain in 1964, and what multinationals like EMI shifted in the market-place? And to what extent, if at all, were the songs of a Baez, a Dylan, a Lennon or a Jagger connected with the student activity in the US and Europe in 1968, let alone with the far more important movements amongst the blacks in US inner cities and the working class on an international scale (Harman 1988)? One chapter cannot hope to deal with these issues satisfactorily; and I have dealt with some of the crasser myths and idealist errors elsewhere (Harker 1980: *passim*). What I want to do here is to show how complex and contradictory the 'popular' was in the 1960s, and how inadequate are the conventional accounts of 1960s popular music from both left and right populists in the 20 years that followed.

THE YEARS OF THE BEATLES, THE YEARS OF THE STONES?

It is important to put the 1960s capitalist music industry in some economic perspective. As far as the overall functioning of the capitalist mode of production is concerned, popular music hardly mattered. After the end of the 1960s, sales of recorded music in the UK accounted for 0.2 per cent of all UK spending, and only 1 per cent of all leisure spending. Together, books, magazines and papers were seven times as important, in cash nexus terms, and alcohol over 37 times as important. In 1969 only one single and one LP was sold in the UK per head of the population. What was also true was that the size of the record business in both the UK and the USA doubled in the period 1960–9, from £15 million to £32 million and from $600 million to $1,358 million respectively. That growth was not solely a 1960s phenomenon; between 1955 and 1959 the UK business had grown by 50 per cent; and between 1954 and 1959, that in the USA had quadrupled. Yet within these apparently relentlessly rising figures, we have to remember that growth was neither continuous nor guaranteed. The US industry lost ground in the general recession around 1960, as did that in the UK in 1965–6. Growth was sluggish in the USA in 1963, and comparatively stagnant in the UK between 1963 and 1968. In 1966 UK singles production slumped to 1955 levels, and then fell even further by 1969. In fact it was not until 1967 (in the USA) and 1972 (in the UK) that the popular music business began to take off again, but not on the basis of singles, by the Beatles or anyone else (Murrells 1978; *BPI Yearbook* 1977). What mattered in that process were LPs.

Of course, the Beatles were important to the popular music industry. In April 1964 they had 12 singles in the US Hot 100; and while it is very important not to over-estimate the weight of such achievements, given the problems with singles charts that have been explained elsewhere (Harker 1980: 54, 69–70, 84, 94–100; see also Beresford 1983), the accompanying boost to sales was important, for a while. For around three weeks, at this period, the Beatles accounted for about 60 per cent of all singles sold in the USA. In 1963–4 the turnover from Beatles records went from nil to £6 million; and by mid-1964 they were earning £500,000 a month. By 1968 they had received $154 million from worldwide sales (Chapple and Garofalo 1977: 70, 135, 249). And yet, in terms of the industry's favourite public assessment of success, the charts (Murrells 1978;

Gillet 1974), the Beatles' success both sides of the Atlantic was by no means total.

In the US singles charts the Beatles' longest-stayer at number 1 was not until 'Hey Jude' in 1968, which was there for nine weeks; but Percy Faith's 'Theme From "A Summer Place" ' had achieved that longevity in 1960. The Beatles' next-best, 'I Want to Hold Your Hand' in 1964, lasted seven weeks at number 1; but Bobby Lewis's 'Tossin' and Turnin' ' had done that in 1961, and both the Monkees' 'I'm a Believer' and Marvin Gaye's 'I Heard It Through The Grapevine' equalled that achievement in 1966 and 1968 respectively. In the UK singles charts the Beatles' record at number 1 was even less impressive. Their longest-lived number 1s were 'From Me To You' and 'Hello Goodbye', which stayed at the top for seven weeks in 1963 and 1967; but both Presley's 'It's Now or Never' (1960) and the Shadows' 'Wonderful Land' (1962) had achieved eight weeks, while the Everly Brothers' 'Cathy's Clown' (1960) was number 1 for nine weeks. Hegemony (even in dubious chart terms) this is not.

Similarly, the overall chart 'stamina' of the Beatles during the 1960s does not support Wicke's thesis. The longest-stayer in the US Top 20 singles charts, 1960–69, was Bob Rydell's 'Forget Him' (1963), which lasted 18 weeks. True, the Beatles' 'Hey Jude' came second (1968, 16 weeks), but only second equal with Jim Reeves's 'He'll Have To Go' (1960) and Louis Armstrong's 'Hello Dolly' (1964). On 15 weeks we find the Archies' 'Sugar Sugar' (1969), the Everly Brothers' 'Cathy's Clown' (1960), Percy Faith's 'Theme From "A Summer Place" ' (1960) and Bobby Lewis's 'Tossin' and Turnin' ' (1961). The Beatles' next-best, 'Something/ Come Together', was released as late as 1969, and stayed for 14 weeks; but Presley had done that in 1960 with 'It's Now or Never'. Once again, the Beatles' UK singles chart stamina wasn't any more overwhelming. Their longest-lasting single, 'She Loves You' (24 weeks in 1963), was third, behind Acker Bilk's 'Stranger on the Shore' (1961, 39 weeks) and Jim Reeves's 'I Love You Because' (1964, 26 weeks). Clearly, there must be other evidence for the Beatles' alleged prime significance.

The Beatles had the highest number of number 1 hits in the UK singles charts in the 1960s – 17 – but Presley had 11, the Rolling Stones 8, and Cliff Richard 6. Moreover, in terms of total numbers of singles to reach the UK Top 20, Richard had 38, Presley had 32 and the Beatles had 22. Totting up the aggregate number of weeks that these three had a single in the charts, we find the same running-order – Richard 315 weeks, Presley 240 and the Beatles 219. All this would be confusing, were it not the case that most consumers (if not all critics) understand that singles charts were always unreliable indicators, even of market popularity (Beresford 1983). In any one year in the 1960s, for example, there might be only 12 or as many as 24 number 1s; and so the ratio of any year's quota of number 1s to the total market sales could vary widely, from 1 to 2.6 million to 1 to 4.8 million. Over the decade there does seem to be some correspondence between the number of number 1s and total singles sales; but such patterns remain difficult to assess culturally. So, in the absence of any sustained empirical work on record consumers, we have to turn to aggregate sales figures in order to try to understand the relative importance of the Beatles' popularity.

Up to 1975 the Beatles' best-selling single, 'I Want To Hold Your Hand' (1963), had worldwide sales of 12 million. Ahead of them were Presley's 'It's Now or Never' (1960, 20 million), Bill Haley's 'Rock Around the Clock' (1954, 22 million), and two singles by Bing Crosby, 'Silent Night/Adeste Fideles' and 'White Christmas', both released in 1942, and both with sales of over 30 million. The Beatles' next best was 'Hey Jude' (1968, over 7½ million), which was 18th. At 24th we find 'Can't Buy Me Love' (1964, over 6 million), and at 39th 'She Loves You' (1963, over 5 million). None of their other singles achieved sales of over 5 million in this period (Murrells 1978: 395). And even the aggregate of these, their four best-sellers, could not reach the same number of sales as either of Crosby's hits – one of which, 'White Christmas', was still selling a million copies a year at the end of the 1960s (Murrells 1978: 27), when the artist was at least 65.

Until the work is done properly, we cannot generalize confidently about what the people who bought singles or LPs thought and felt about their purchases, or even what they did with them. And even the bare numbers pertaining to record purchases can sometimes be allowed to distort important economic and cultural trends, and to foreshorten historical changes. For example, it is a sobering thought that 100,000 shellac 78 rpm singles were produced in 1970 in the UK, and that 12 million had been produced in the previous decade. Then again, units sold do not correspond to either economic or cultural significance in an unmediated way. Between 1960 and 1969, for example, the value of singles sold in the UK rose from £17 million to £20 million, while numbers of units actually fell. In the same decade, the value of LPs quadrupled, from £30 million to £120 million; and the ratio of singles/LP value stretched from just under 2:1 to 6:1. It may be, then, that LPs became more important economically than singles in the UK in 1955. In the USA, 1955 did mark such a crossover; and by the end of the 1960s LPs accounted for over 80 per cent of the 'sales dollar' of the US music industry (Chapple and Garofalo 1977: 44, 76), and possibly more in the UK. Strangely, many critical histories of 'pop' and 'rock' music still concentrate unproblematically on singles. But LPs were already more important before the 1960s began, let alone so late as *Sergeant Pepper* in 1967.

In fact, in chart terms, *Sergeant Pepper* was not even the Beatles' most successful LP. Its 27 weeks at number 1 in the UK LP charts was not equal to their own *Please Please Me* of 1963; and its 43 weeks in the top 10 pales by comparison with the really hegemonic 'group' of the decade – Soundtrack, featuring Original Cast! In the UK, for example, the 1960 original cast and 1965 soundtrack LPs of *The Sound of Music* stayed in the Top 10 for an aggregate of 268 weeks – over five years – and the 1965 album alone was at number 1 for 69 weeks. In sales terms, by 1975, worldwide, these twin LPs had sold virtually twice as many units as the Beatles' best-seller, which was in fact *Abbey Road* of 1969 – over 17½ million compared to 9 million – and well over twice as many as *Sergeant Pepper*, which had shifted some 7 million units. Sandwiched between these two Beatles LPs was the soundtrack of *Mary Poppins* (1964, over 7 million); and ahead of both of them were five other albums. Three of these were the original cast and soundtrack versions of *My Fair Lady* (1956 and 1964, over 9½ million), *West Side Story* (1957 and 1961, 10½ million) and *South Pacific* (1949 and 1958, over 11 million). Next came the Harry Simeone Chorale's *Little Drummer Boy* (1958/63, over 14 million). And second only to *The Sound of Music* was, perhaps unsurprisingly by now, Bing Crosby's *Merry Christmas* (1947), the sale of which, in various formats from 78 rpm shellac onwards, is claimed to be the all-time best-seller up to 1975, when it was still selling 200,000 copies a year, without appearing in the UK top 10, let alone reaching number 1.

In US LP chart terms, the hegemony of soundtrack and original cast albums was virtually total throughout the 1960s. *South Pacific* (in one form or the other) was number 1 for nearly two-and-a-half years, and stayed in the charts for an aggregate of over 13 years. *The Sound of Music* lasted almost as long – over 12 years – and was kept from the number 1 spot for all but 14 weeks by its earlier-released rival. *My Fair Lady* lasted almost a dozen years, too. The Beatles' best, *Sergeant Pepper*, with 19 weeks at number 1 and just over two years in the charts, was about the same as *Mary Poppins*. Ahead of both of them was a longish list:

Johnny Mathis, *Johnny's Greatest Hits*(1958–68)	490 weeks
Van Cliburn, *My Favourite Chopin* (1966–73)	360 weeks
Carlos and Folkman, *Switched On Bach* (1968–74)	310 weeks
Van Cliburn, *Tchaikovsky Piano Concerto No 1* (1958–61)	
	297 weeks
Tennessie Ernie Ford, *Hymns* (1957–62)	276 weeks
Soundtrack, *2001* (1968–73)	271 weeks
Original Cast, *Camelot* (1961–68)	265 weeks
Soundtrack,*Oklahoma* (1955–64)	264 weeks

Presley's best had been *GI Blues* (111 weeks, 1961–2), and the Beatles never did much better. Even in the UK, their chart successes were far from overwhelming; *Sergeant Pepper* was at number 1 for 27 weeks and in the Top 10 for 43 weeks, compared, say, to *South Pacific*'s 46 and 178 weeks (Murrells 1978: 373, 378–9).

The popularity of Chopin, Bach and Tchaikovsky was not surprising. In 1965 what Shemel and Krasilovsky termed 'serious music' accounted for all but 10 per cent of all US LP sales, grossing nearly $60 million and forming over 60 per cent of all 'regular price' LP sales. That year, too, the same authors estimated a piano-playing population of 22 million, with 7½ million guitarists and 3½ million organists, not to speak of performers on other instruments. As a consequence, sheet-music sales of 100,000 for some songs were achievable (Shemel and Krasilovsky 1971: 15–17, 43, 50). The link to some stage and soundtrack musicals was not so far: *West Side Story* was not written by a lucky amateur, after all; and the further link to really popular commercial music was by no means much further.

It was *The Sound of Music*, however, that was the most popular commercial musical product of the 1960s. In the first two weeks of its release in the USA the soundtrack LP had sold 500,000 copies. By December 1966 over 7 million copies had sold worldwide; and by October 1968 over 2 million copies had been bought in the UK alone. There were large sales in Canada, Australia and Japan; while the film itself grossed rentals of $150 million worldwide by 1 January

1969, almost four times as much as the previous record-holder, *Gone With the Wind* (Murrells 1978: 185). Across the anglophone regions of the planet, and even beyond, *The Sound of Music* was the most popular music of the 1960s. How was it received? What pleasures did it offer? Who bought it, when and why?

FOREVER YOUNG?

There has been a remarkable amount of popular music criticism in English since the early 1970s, and some of it has been good; but we won't find a serious explanation (let alone an analysis) of *The Sound of Music* in any of them, even the best left-populist accounts. Richard Middleton finds no space for it in *Studying Popular Music* (1990). Peter Wicke ignores it, not only in *Rock Music: Culture, Aesthetics and Sociology* (1990), but also in his and Wieland Ziegenrucher's *Rock Pop Jazz Folk* (1985), which offers to be a *Handbuch der populären Musik*. Steve Chapple and Reebee Garofalo do not analyse its pleasures in *Rock 'n' Roll is Here to Pay* (1977), though their subtitle offers to engage with *The History and Politics of the Music Industry*; and they unaccountably claim (1977: 80) that Carole King's *Tapestry*, with sales of 13 million, was 'the highest selling album of all time'. Charlie Gillett, presumably, did not consider that the audience for *The Sound of Music* was urban (or urbane) enough for *The Sound of the City* (1971); while Dave Laing banishes the best-selling anglophone LP of the 1960s from *The Sound of Our Time* (1969). Whose time or city, we might wonder, was the world's commercially most-successful anglophone LP about? And while the more modish Street (1986), Chambers (1985) and Frith (1978 and 1983) might justify its exclusion because it was not 'rock' music, their failure to define that category leaves them open to the charge of failing to write about the popular because it does not suit their subjective, and perhaps not wholly representative, tastes, no matter what most people thought and felt.

Interestingly, a few liberal and right-wing populist critics do mention *The Sound of Music*. Greil Marcus, for example, writes (1977: 113) that such LPs typify what 'American' – by which he seems to mean US – culture can be, 'at its worst'; and he agrees with Pauline Kael when she characterizes its audience of over 17½ million people as uniformly exhibiting 'the lowest common denominator of feeling – a sponge'. (How many people did she interview to support such a remarkable proposition?) Hamm (1979: 462) takes a more radical-sounding perspective by implying that *The Sound of Music* is some-how legitimized when one of its tracks was recorded by black singers, The Four Tops. We have to do better than this.

Unfortunately, most popular music critics do not offer theoreti-cally clear or consistent justifications for their writings. Of the few that do, perhaps Professor Frith is most confident.

> We can make a distinction between music conceived with no reference to a mass market and music that is inseparable from the mass market in its conception. The former category includes classical music, folk music, and most jazz, the latter is pop.
>
> (Frith 1983: 6)

There are, however, some problems with this attempt at genre classification. First of all, Frith seems to be ignoring the existence of mass markets for printed and performed music prior to 1955 or 1956 – certainly before the application of electricity to the commodi-tization process of music. Second, he seems to imply that 'classical', 'folk', 'jazz' and other conversational terms are coherent and useful concepts, unlike recent work by, amongst others, Harker (1985) and Tagg (1989). Third, he seems to be saying that the term 'pop' is hegemonic for most purposes in Europe and North America in the twentieth century, whereas the term came into general use no earlier than the mid-1950s as an abbreviation of 'popular' (Cham-bers 1985: 7). Fourth, Frith seems to place an undue (and unar-gued) weight here on composers' intentions. Granted that many writers and performers do aim for market popularity, what would Frith's theory tell us about the market popularity of, say, Carlos and Folkman's *Switched On Bach*, which was number 1 for a record 102 weeks in the US LP charts between 1968 and 1973? What did Bach know of sound engineering by electronics; of his future performers' and conductors' skills, attitudes and intentions; or of what happens to cultural products in an era of almost total commod-itization? It seems disingenuous of Frith to claim that the fact that 'classical or folk music can be listened to on records is accidental for its form and content' (1983: 6). Unless he is contradicting a position he strenuously attacks elsewhere (1988: 94–101), isn't he assuming some 'authentic' essence of Bach-made texts that can miraculously survive a long and complex process of mediation untouched? As for 'folk' composers, what does Frith know of such people, especially since many 'folk' scholars define what they term 'traditional' songwriters as unknown and unknowable – wrongly,

as it turns out (Harker 1987; Pickering and Green 1987). In seeking
to elaborate a general theory of the popular in music, then, Frith
begins with his own legitimate personal tastes and then (illeg-
itimately) seeks to marginalize or even to exclude much really
popular music from his 'definition'. Within bourgeois culture, such
methods have a long and not very honourable history (see Harker
1985 and Scott 1989), and their results are, as ever, conceptual
vacuousness.

In order to shore up his argument, Frith has recourse to further
doubtful propositions (1983: 7, 10); 'there is a special relationship
between pop music and youth', and the 'history of British pop
audiences has always been a history of British youth styles'. But if
'pop' began in the mid-1950s, what do we call music popular with
'youth' before that date? Were there no 'British youth styles' before
the Teds? And what happens to this 'special relationship' when
originally youthful fans, and their favourite artists, age? Why is
Chuck Berry often central to non-racist popular musical criticism,
but Leonard Cohen not? They were after all, contemporaries – in
1991 Berry was 60 and Cohen 57. Evidently, the answer lies in the
separation of 'pop' music from something else, variously known as
'rock 'n' roll', 'rock and roll' or just plain 'rock'. But the conceptual
distinctions are rarely if ever made seriously, if they get made at all.
To Frith, 'rock' is 'music produced commercially for simultaneous
consumption by a mass youth market', and it differs crucially from
'pop' – the goal-posts shift once again – on intellectual grounds: 'In
rock, words mattered; in pop, it seemed, they did not'. Developing
this notion, Frith goes so far as to claim that 'pop' songs 'celebrate
not the articulate but the inarticulate' (1983: 34–5). How was this
knowledge produced? How does it help us explain Ray Davies of
the Kinks, or the early Beatles singles? And who does Frith leave
out of this unfortunate category, since not only are Dave Laing's
'television and light ale elders' (1969: 151) automatically excluded
from the 'rock' audience, but so are most working-class children
too. This majority is also ideologically excluded, according to Frith,
because of what he concedes is the 'essentially petit bourgeois'
ethos of 'rock' music; and what then happens is a form of cultural
expropriation, through 'the gradual middle-class adoption of the
trappings of working-class life' (1983: 79, 190). So, while 'rock is a
form of capitalist culture', Frith suggests (1983: 269) 'that capitalist
culture is what we're trying to understand and to use, to subvert
and to enjoy'. Who, precisely, are 'we'? What is 'our' point of

leverage in the struggle against capital when, as Frith seems quite confident, the conception of the working-class being its grave-digger does not square with his perception of the average inarticulate socially and politically unconscious 'pop' fan, in the 1960s or the 1990s?

Other critics have not swallowed André Gorz, Eric Hobsbawm and 'new realism' whole. Peter Wicke, for example, offers a more complex view of the consciousness of music consumers. He denies that 'everyday culture' can be 'reduced to the problem of "youth" ' and believes that the 'overall context' in which music consumption takes place 'owes its existence in equal measure to social and political relations as well as to the particular environment of its listeners' (1990: viii-ix). Even anglophone youth are not divided neatly on the basis of class, race, gender or sexuality; and anglophone musical products did not stop at national frontiers for a long time before the 1960s. Besides, performers have often been substantially older than their audiences – Paul Simon, at 50, appeared on BBC TV's *Top of the Pops*, while Dylan, at 49, had an LP in the UK Top 10 – and even dead stars can win new audiences. So Wicke is correct: we should not make a fetish of 'youth', even for 'rock'.

The key problem remains. Empirical research on popular music audiences is, to say the least, underdeveloped; but the little that is available is suggestive. Robinson (cited in Sullivan 1987: 324 note 15) found that the average age of US 'rock' fans in 1982 was 30.1, whilst those who disliked 'rock' were aged 49.3. If this is even vaguely accurate, 'rock' fans would have been born in the early 1950s, and so would be far too young for Haley's 'Rock Around the Clock', while 'rock' haters would have been old enough to be their parents, having been born in the early 1930s, and so just the age for mid-1950s 'rock and roll'. The 'rock' fans would have been late adolescents when West Coast white 'rock' was booming in the late 1960s, during the polarization induced by the Vietnam War, and the 'rock' haters of an age to make the draft an academic matter. Perhaps there are such correspondences, but what conceptual differences are there between these musical genre names?

There have been sporadic attempts to define popular music genres, too often in a journalistic fashion. Charlie Gillett believes that popular music, and especially 'rock and roll', is fundamentally 'black music'. Moreover, he claims that there was something essentially different about 'the generations of popular music audiences since 1956', who have 'quite different sensibilities from the preceding generations which were raised on sentiment and melo-drama' (Gillett 1971: vii); 1956 was evidently a watershed, a sea-change, that showed that

> audiences or creators can determine the content of a popular art communicated through the mass media. The businessmen who mediate between the audience and the creator can be forced by either to accept a new style. The rise of rock and roll is proof.
>
> (Gillett 1971: i-ii)

What clinches this theory, for Gillett, is that 'after 1956, at least one fourth of the best-selling records' in the USA were by black singers (1971: iii). The problem is that three-quarters of them were not, and those that were did not necessarily earn their makers equivalent rewards to those made by whites, even after Elvis Presley (Harker 1980: 51–65; see also Storey 1988 and 1990).

Gillett's is an argument long held by liberals and reformists from the black community. Paul Robeson, speaking in 1951, had no doubts:

> One great creation, modern popular music, whether it be in theatre, film, radio, records – wherever it may be – is almost completely based upon the Negro idiom. There is no leading American singer, performer of popular songs, whether it be a Crosby, a Sinatra, a Shore, a Judy Garland, an Ella Logan, who has not listened (and learned) by the hour to Holliday, Waters, Florence Mills, to Bert Williams, to Fitzgerald, and to the greatest of them all, Bessie Smith. Without these models, who would ever have heard of a Tucker, a Jolson, a Cantor? . . . This is very important to the Negro artists, because billions, literally billions of dollars, have been earned and are being earned from their creation, and the Negro people have received almost nothing.
>
> (Foner 1978: 299)

Economically, Robeson was correct (Harker 1980: *passim*). Cul-turally, his position is highly problematical. Peterson (1990: 113–14) has shown that the newness and coherence of so-called 'rock and roll' is open to doubt. As for its 'blackness', the problem is that if we assume with Gillett and Robeson that there is an essence of it in the music, it still remains notoriously difficult to separate out analytically the 'blackness' from the 'whiteness'. In fact, the attempt is fraught with dangers of inadvertently supporting soft racism. How does that 'blackness' correspond to the black people who make and consume music? Biologically? Psychologically? Via the 'phallus'? How, also, could Robeson resist the political pull of black nationalism, or even of separatism, in spite of his apparently inter-nationalist and anti-racist ideas?

Sadly, most popular music critics start from precisely such unten-able premises. According to Frith (1983: 15–17), 'rock' has a special relationship with what he terms 'black music', the 'essence' of which (we are plainly told) 'is the expression of the performers' feelings'. Do black people have a monopoly of feelings, or of their expression? Are black people, by implication, all the same, anyway? Frith is clear (1983: 20) 'rock 'n' roll faith is faith in the music's black elements'; and even Wicke adapts to this kind of vulgar essentialism: 'right from the start, rock 'n' roll was nothing more than black music performed by white musicians', so that 'the essential nature of Afro-American music is to be found in the collective presentation of emotions, postures and gestures' (1990: 19; cf Oliver 1990). The usual line of reasoning then regresses further. Since Wicke believes that 'rhythm and blues' is the basis of 'rock', then the latter 'largely retained the collective character of music which is part of all auth-entic folk music'. So, given the 'necessary collective character' of work in a recording studio, 'Rock is a collective means of expression' too (1990: 15–17). We are back, once again, to problems of genre, in the context of idealizing cultural work under traditional or state forms of capitalism, and powered by the ideology of 1960s 'collectiv-ism' and 'authenticity' so carefully nurtured by capitalist culture industries, then and now (Harker 1980: 103–11).

Those myths appeal most strongly, of course, to left-populists. Writing at the end of the 1960s, Dave Laing felt he had been part of the 'crystallisation of a fused group' of 'self-directed' young people operating 'on an international scale' (1969: 139). (Laing forgot that even liberals can experience a form of internationalist feeling, and can identify with the victims of certain forms of oppression.) It is important that we also understand that popular music critics have often prized 'black music' for negative rather than positive reasons – it is not white, not British or American, not bourgeois or 'Estab-lishment' – just as white Americans responded to the 'British invasion' led by the Beatles because that music was not American or as viciously imperialist, not petit bourgeois, not orthodoxly religious and patriotic, and, seemingly, not wholly 'white' either. We have to remember that this music was not from Harlem or Watts, any more than the soundtracks to the films allegedly about

Vietnam (Harker and Fair 1986; Storey 1988 and 1990). This nega-
tivity allowed populists of both left and right to celebrate that great
'fusion', 'rock 'n' roll', as adapted by white Americans, then white
Britons, and then white Americans once more in the later 1960s.
This was music that could plausibly be set against conservatism –
it was neither Macmillan nor Eisenhower, not obviously tainted by
declining British or rising US imperialism, and, most importantly,
neither Conservative nor Labourist (in either social-democratic or
Stalinist manifestations). The music didn't threaten capitalism one
bit, of course: in fact, from Chuck Berry to the Beatles to the
Beach Boys, it celebrated the products of capitalist industry. Its self-
appointed 'critics' still do.

One device for deflecting this analysis is the concentration by
people like Gillett on alleged cultural benefits arising from small
capital, entrepreneurs, working-class-kids-made-good. This highly
dubious proposition has been under challenge for some time now
(Chapple and Garofalo 1977; Harker 1980); and it seems to rest to
a large extent on a faith in young people changing the world through
consumption. This was not so much a serious political perspective
as an economic one; and its weakness – which was shared by the
reformist and Stalinist left in Britain and the USA – was its under-
estimation of the recuperative powers of postwar capital, and its
over-estimation of the possibilities of transforming the capitalist
mode of production through cultural practices such as buying
records, even if that did help, in Robeson's terms, to 'wilt' the 'Ivy
Curtain of conformity, which for a decade' had shaded US students
'from the sunlight of independent thinking' (Foner 1978: 403). As
consumers, the post-1945 baby boom cohort of 17-year-old Americans – the largest single age-group in 1964 – were offered, and took
(for a time), the Beatles. By so doing, as Chapple and Garofalo
note (1977: 70), they also took that 'clean, suited image that Epstein
built for the Beatles' that was designed to make sure they 'greased
their way into the hearts of parents, as well as teenyboppers'. In
fact, only the religious far-right were offended; and what upset those
people most was not simply the Beatles' irreligion but, crucially,
their perceived potential to weaken class-cultural divisions; Joseph
R. Gusfield lamented that 'Cultural values that emanate from the
national institutions of school, entertainment media, and even
the major churches are depicted as sources for the decay in the
status of the old middle class' (cited in Sullivan 1987: 316).

Yet they needn't have worried. As early as 1969 Dave Laing

noted with bemusement (1969: 149) that 'virtually all those involved
in "swinging London" ' in 1966 and 1967 'emanated from the
middle and upper classes'. But he didn't follow this insight through
to its logical conclusion. The key ideological component of the
mythology of (especially) the later 1960s 'fused group' of young
would-be internationalists was its apparent classlessness; and however much disillusioned popular music critics might wish to deny
it today, what held together this myth was the effective exclusion
of most people – that is, in class societies from the USA to the
Soviet Union, the working class – from the 'popular'. Not only that,
as Peter Wicke notes, 'Most rock musicians come from the *petit
bourgeois* middle classes, and have never experienced the everyday
life of working-class teenagers'. Yet Wicke continues to believe that
'rock' music 'is always both part of a commercial product *and* an
object of class-specific cultural use, whereby the one limits and
conveys the other', so that 'rock music is neither the expression of
a culture *for* the mass of working-class teenagers nor *their* musical
instrument of articulation' (1990: 87, 91, 179). Whose is it then?
And does consumption, however radical, threaten production
structurally? The pull of idealism remains very strong. Richard
Middleton seems to believe that 'musical action can be a model,
an action model, of social change' (1990: 292). Precisely how he
doesn't tell us; but he is sure that this 'model' supersedes old-
fashioned notions about the potential revolutionary power of the
working class. There are, Middleton revealingly writes, 'no revolutionary subjects to wheel onto the stage' (1990: 169). Only Stalin-
ists ever believed that working-class people were wheelable; Marx,
Engels, Lenin, Trotsky, Luxemburg and the revolutionary (not
the Eurocommunist parody of) Gramsci knew it was a bit more
complicated than that (Molyneux 1985). Besides, the composition,
power and culture of the working class in every nation-state has
changed through history (Callinicos and Harman 1987). But it is
not true that history is made for people, in the 1960s or now,
while they accept passively the role of victim (Callinicos 1987). If,
however, you believed that the 1960s – 1968, above all – represented
the highest point of development of revolutionary consciousness,
with students somehow appearing to be at the fore, then, of course,
the 1980s downturn in class struggle would demoralize you (Frith
1983: 190; Chambers 1985: 102) The problem remains that May
1968 saw 10 million French workers on strike, and a president in
a funk, as the combined and uneven economic and political crisis

rocked capitalist states east and west, rumbling on until the mid-1970s (Harman 1988; Birchall 1986). Why is it, then, that even left-populist music critics marginalize or even omit working-class people from history, too?

It may seem a paradox, but what most popular music critics have in common is not so much materialism – let alone historical materialism – as idealism. Like Joan Baez, who exhorted Berkeley students in 1964 to 'keep love in their hearts' as she sang them 'Blowin' in the Wind', immediately before they were clubbed and arrested by the police, so most critics fail to understand that, as John Street notes, a song, 'however powerful its performance, cannot win an argument' (Harman 1988: 38; Street 1986: 60). What is even more confusing is that the critics' idealism has its roots in what, until recently, was perceived as Marxism, but which was, in fact, Stalinism, and many of their assumptions can be traced to 1950s texts such as *The American Threat to British Culture* and *Britain's Cultural Heritage* (Communist Party of Great Britain 1951; Communist Party of Great Britain 1952), via the work of Althusser and Foucault (Cliff and Gluckstein 1988; Callinicos 1989; Williams 1990). This strange mixture of orthodox idealism and Stalinism could be called Stalinoid ideology, and in terms of cultural criticism it produced contradictory ideas such as 'cultural imperialism' and 'coca-colonization', in which Donald Duck and Elvis Presley or the Beatles took the place of what Lenin understood by the economic and political effects of imperialism (Harker and Fair 1986). That, however, is another story.

Meanwhile, those of us genuinely concerned to redraw the map of the musical field need what Peter Wicke terms 'an alternative *politics* of culture', which 'can hardly be developed in books' (1990: 183). Logically, as Wicke accepts, this requires a 'revolutionary praxis' to be effective; but even non-revolutionaries can make a contribution (Williams 1989). What critics and students have to acknowledge is that, so far, the musical practices and tastes of most people – the working class – are marginalized or ignored in even the better critical accounts of periods like the 1960s; most of the critics try to generalize from the experience of students and budding academics. Instead, it seems to me, we need to start with a basic respect for working-class people, and acknowledge that, with a few notable exceptions, we know virtually nothing about their musical culture. The people, in other words, have been left out of 'popular' music studies, and it's high time they were included.

BIBLIOGRAPHY

Beresford, Steve *et al.* 1983. 'Invisible Hits'. *Collusion*, 4, Feb./April 1983. 28–33.

Birchall, Ian 1986. *Bailing Out the System: Reformist Socialism in Western Europe 1944–1985*. London: Bookmarks.

Bradley, Dick forthcoming. *Beat Music in Britain*. Milton Keynes: Open University Press.

BPI 1978. Scaping, P. and Hunter, N. (eds), *BPI Yearbook 1978: A Review of the British Record and Tape Industry*. London: BPI.

BPI 1990. John, H. (comp.) and Scaping, P. (ed.), *BPI Yearbook 1989/90: A Statistical Description of the British Record Industry*. London: BPI.

Callinicos, Alex 1987. *Making History*. Cambridge: Polity.

Callinicos, Alex 1989. *Against Postmodernism*. Cambridge: Polity.

Callinicos, Alex and Harman, Chris 1987. *The Changing Working Class*. London: Bookmarks.

Chambers, Iain 1985. *Urban Rhythms: Pop Music and Popular Culture*. London: Methuen.

Chapple, Steve and Garofalo, Reebee 1977. *Rock 'n' Roll Is Here To Pay. The History and Politics of the Music Industry*. Chicago: Nelson-Hall.

Cliff, Tony and Gluckstein, Donny 1988. *The Labour Party: A Marxist History*. London: Bookmarks.

Communist Party of Great Britain 1951. *The American Threat to British Culture*. London: Communist Party of Great Britain.

Communist Party of Great Britain 1952. *Britain's Cultural Heritage*. London: Communist Party of Great Britain.

Foner, Phillip 1978. *Paul Robeson Speaks*. London: Quartet.

Frith, Simon 1978. *The Sociology of Rock*. London: Constable.

Frith, Simon 1983. *Sound Effects: Youth, Leisure and the Politics of Rock 'n' Roll*. London: Constable.

Frith, Simon 1988. *Music for Pleasure: Essays in the Sociology of Pop*. Cambridge: Polity.

Gillett, Charlie 1971. *The Sound of the City*. London: Sphere.

Gillett, Charlie 1974. *Rock File 2*. St Albans: Panther.

Hamm, Charles 1979. *Yesterdays: Popular Song in America*. New York: Norton.

Harker, Dave 1980. *One for the Money: the Politics of Popular Song*. London: Hutchinson.

Harker, Dave 1985. *Fakesong: the Manufacture of British 'Folksong', 1700 to the Present Day*. Milton Keynes: Open University Press.

Harker, Dave 1987. 'The price you pay: an introduction to the life and songs of Laurence Price'. In Avron Levine White (ed.), *Lost in Music: Culture, Style and the Musical Event*. London: Routledge & Kegan Paul. 107–63.

Harker, Dave and Fair, Alan 1986. 'US Imperialism and US Popular Music'. Unpublished paper given to the American Culture Association and Popular Culture Association, Atlanta.

Harman, Chris 1988. *The Fire Last Time: 1968 and After*. London: Bookmarks.

Kelly, Matthew forthcoming. *Pop Music in Boom and Slump*. Milton Keynes: Open University Press.

Laing, Dave 1969. *The Sound of Our Time*. London: Sheed & Ward.

Mackinnon, Niall forthcoming. *The British Folk Revival*. Milton Keynes: Open University Press.

Marcus, Greil 1977. *Mystery Train: Images of America in Rock 'n' Roll Music*. London: Omnibus Press.

Middleton, Richard 1990. *Studying Popular Music*. Milton Keynes: Open University Press.

Molyneux, John 1988. *What is the Real Marxist Tradition?* London: Bookmarks.

Moore, Alan forthcoming. *Styles of Rock*. Milton Keynes: Open University Press.

Murrells, Joseph 1978. *The Book of Golden Discs: the Records that Sold a Million*. London: Barrie & Jenkins.

Oliver, Paul (ed.) 1990. *Black Music in Britain*. Milton Keynes: Open University Press.

Peterson, Richard 1990. 'Why 1955? Explaining the advent of rock music.' *Popular Music*, 9/1, 97–116.

Pickering, Michael and Green, A. E. (eds) 1987. *Everyday Culture: Popular Song and the Vernacular Milieu*. Milton Keynes: Open University Press.

Scott, Derek 1989. *The Singing Bourgeois: Songs of the Victorian Drawing Room and Parlour*. Milton Keynes: Open University Press.

Shemel, Sidney and Krasilovsky, M. William 1971. *More About this Business of Music*. New York: Billboard.

Shepherd, John forthcoming. *Fighting the Menace: the British Sheet Music Industry*. Milton Keynes: Open University Press.

Storey, John 1988. 'Rockin' hegemony: West Coast rock and Amerika's war in Vietnam'. In Louvre, A. and Walsh, J. (eds), *Tell Me Lies About Vietnam*. Milton Keynes: Open University Press, 181–98.

Storey, John 1990. 'Bringing it all back home: American popular song and the war in Vietnam'. In Michael Klein (ed.), *The Vietnam Era*. London: Pluto.

Street, John 1986. *Rebel Rock: the Politics of Popular Music*. Oxford: Blackwell.

Sullivan, Mark 1987. ' "More popular than Jesus": the Beatles and the religious far right'. *Popular Music*, 6/3, 313–26.

Tagg, Philip 1989. 'Open letter: black music, Afro-American music and European music'. *Popular Music*, 8/3, 285–98.

Wicke, Peter 1990. *Rock Music. Culture, Aesthetics and Sociology*. Cambridge: Cambridge University Press.

Wicke, Peter and Ziegenrucher, Wieland 1985. *Rock Pop Jazz Folk: Handbuch der popularen Musik*. Leipzig: VEB Deutscherverlag für Musik.

Williams, Raymond 1989. *What I Came Here To Say*. London: Hutchinson.

Williams, Raymond 1990. *The Politics of Modernism: Against the New Conformists*. London: Verso.

FURTHER READING

There is no thoroughly worthwhile book on 1960s anglophone popular music. Someone should write it. Meanwhile, there are some kicking-off points in my *One for the Money* (1980), in Philip Tagg's excellent theoretical critique of 'Black music' (1989), and the works I critique here by Peter Wicke (*Rock Music*, 1990) and Richard Middleton (*Studying Popular Music*, 1990), which should remain useful throughout the 1990s. Otherwise the best single source is the journal *Popular Music*, which, in amongst the dross and the trendy careerism, contains many valuable items with a worldwide (though usually anglophone) perspective. Theoretically, however, most contributors to this journal seem mesmerized by forms of vulgar materialism, vulgar feminism, or vulgar psychologism, and sometimes all three.

Some serious work is currently being done in Britain; readers should look out for John Shepherd's *Fighting the Menace: the British Sheet Music Industry*, Dick Bradley's *Beat Music in Britain*, Allan Moore's *Styles of Rock*, Matthew Kelly's *Pop Music in Boom and Slump* and Niall Mackinnon's *The British Folk Revival*.

Chapter 13

Caro verbum factus est: British art in the 1960s

Stuart Sillars

IMAGING THE 1960s

There is a kind of folk image of British art in the 1960s, fostered by colour supplements then and fading memories since, in which a new generation of artists rejected the abstract expressionism, symbolic landscape and aristocratic portraiture of the 1940s and 1950s, and turned instead to imagery that was genuinely popular, free from establishment cant, and closer to American than European models. In this reading, Pop Art reached its climax in Peter Blake's sleeve design for a Beatles' LP,[1] and Op Art found completion when Bridget Riley's black and white rhythms were hijacked from the gallery by chainstore dress-designers. Art was at last owned by the people – or, at least, the younger people; firmly allied to popular values, it was to play its part in the new socialist state.

Like most popular views this has enough truth to be seductive but too little to be accurate. A lot of the art of the decade was popular, but not in the usually accepted sense. Optical prints on dresses, union flags on carrier-bags and wickerwork panels on Austin Minis were all part of a shift that made everyday objects visually striking, at the same time revealing a new freedom that matched social and political changes. But the quality and achievement of visual artists covered a wider range than this superficial view suggests and, whilst a lot was radically new, the older figures did not stop working overnight, nor should they be seen as quite separate from their younger contemporaries.

Barbara Hepworth, for example, not only revisited and completed many projects begun in the 1930s, but also developed new directions that may be seen as influential on younger sculptors. Works such as *Four-square (walk through)*[2] (1966) and *Three-piece Vertical (offering)*[3]

(1967) give a new sense of rhythm, insisting on the viewer's participation in their spaces; the linear forms of *Construction (Crucifixion)*[4]
(1966) take to their furthest limit the possibilities of bronze while
advancing a new sharpness of line and divided space, suggesting
the constructed sculptures of Caro and others. It is Hepworth,
rather than Henry Moore, who emerges as the major figure of the
older generation of sculptors of the decade; Moore's success with
the establishment and the art market, along with his romantic
landscape-humanism, made him very much a figure to be rejected
rather than followed.

Ben Nicholson, the most European British abstract artist, extends
and develops his practice of the 1930s in works such as *June 1964
(Valley between Rimini and Urbino)*[5] (1964), in an awareness of plane
and colour that perhaps underlies that of Robyn Denny. But Francis
Bacon was the older artist most admired by the young; the violence
of his forms and the moral ambiguity of their world seems quite at
one with many elements of the decade's thinking. *Crucifixion*[6] (1965)
denudes the Christian myth of its sentimentality, leaving it with all
of the agony of the passion and none of its redemptive energy. *Lying
Figure with a Hypodermic Syringe*[7] (1963) is both a rejection of the
emerging drug culture – the psychedelic sixties – and an assertion
that we are all somehow part of it.

The new departures had a bewildering range of form, and of the
many kinds that were emerging at the time, some were to prove of
less significance than others. At the opening of the decade the
'Situation' show at the RBA Galleries presented large canvases of
pure colours with abstracted, often symmetrical, geometric forms.
The artists who produced such work, notable among whom were
Robyn Denny and Richard Smith, have been seen (Hewison 1986)
as the start of a British Hard Edge school, taking from the abstract
expressionism of Kenneth Noland and Ellsworth Kelly the elements
of porcelain texture and sharply defined spaces to produce another
version of Colour Field painting. Yet there seems little to support
a view that Hard Edge in itself was an important style in British
art of the 1960s. Instead it becomes subsumed into other forms.
The smooth textures can be seen in Hockney's acrylics; Noland's
attenuation of forms and the use of monochrome are taken up by
Bridget Riley; Leon Polk Smith's shaped canvases perhaps influence
Allen Jones, as well as Hockney in some early images; Kelly's
movement from canvas to low-relief to sculpture perhaps reflects
the interest in space seen in many British artists through the decade.

The art form that baffled, outraged and excited so many at the time, the happening, also seems not to represent the true course of British art of the decade. Begun in the Reuben Gallery, New York, by the artist Allan Kaprow, the happening was a coming together of objects, people and some kind of roughly-outlined scenario. Its essence was its spontaneity and the involvement of those who would normally be seen as the 'audience', as well as the use of everyday materials. Cars, garbage, crowds and random actions were brought together in an effort to avoid conventional art categories, eschew bourgeois narrative and elide the space of onlooker and participant. There were happenings in Britain, most notably those of Richard Hamilton; yet once again the influence seems to be greater on other kinds of art. The use of the everyday object is something that British Pop Art adopted, but in a very specific way, quite different from its American counterpart, as the next section will make clear. Perhaps the happening lived on in Britain in the resurgence of street theatre and mime, albeit in rather institutionalized form. It had little influence on what might seem its successor, the performance art of the following decades; the ritualistic obsessive movements of, for example, Gilbert and George, are rigidly defined to exclude the onlooker, and indeed the pair frequently 'performed' to completely empty galleries. Yet the elision between art and onlooker at the basis of the happening is something underlying a lot of other art of the decade; the 'Situation' show's catalogue stressed the need to experience art as a total environment; Bridget Riley's work makes the viewer participate by defining shapes and movement within surfaces; and the new sculpture of the decade only defines its forms and mass when the onlooker moves around it and shares its space.

One of the most obvious signs of newness was the popularity of the screenprint, which became for a while an essential medium; it was a way of linking 'popular' and 'fine' art that was accessible to a far wider audience than the more traditional engraving or etching, both because it was cheap to produce in largish quantities and because its subjects were often taken from mass culture. Richard Hamilton's *My Marilyn*[8] (1965) and *Adonis in Y-Fronts*[9] (1962–3), for example, draw their imagery respectively from the popular cinema and the advertiser's storyboard-pantheon. But even these are atypical. Ron Kitaj's titles reveal a deliberate distancing from popular immediacy: *Mahler becomes Politics, Beisbol*[10] (1964–7). Hockney's prints include a cynical and allusive series updating Hogarth (*A Rake's Progress*,[11] 1961–3) in a medium that is traditional, refined and expensive. What synthesis there is between these two extremes – the 'fine' and the 'popular', to use the awkward distinction that the decade did a lot to explode – comes in Paolozzi's prints, including the wonderfully titled *Wittgenstein at the Cinema Admires Betty Grable*[12] (1965).

Perhaps the complicated relationship between the popular vision of Pop Art and its reality is best suggested in the title of a series of Hamilton's works, the most celebrated of which is based on a press photograph of two members of the Rolling Stones seen through the window of a police van, shielding their faces from the public and so revealing that they are handcuffed together; it is called *Swingeing London*[13] (1967–9). There was a link between the imagery of the everyday and that of the Pop artist; but it is a complicated and selective one, which needs careful and detached observation before it reveals itself. London, whether swinging or swingeing, was only one part of the country; and Pop Art – whatever the term means – was only one of a number of separate strands of aesthetic activity.

What, then, are the strands of British art of the 1960s that are most significant? I think there are three main ones: the way in which British Pop Art extends a long tradition of iconographic reference by embracing everyday visual imagery; the work of separate artists who, like so many earlier British painters, are both eclectic and highly individualistic; and the re-definition of space, ranging from optical effects through the use of extreme impasto to the great reawakening of sculpture in the work of Anthony Caro.

POP ART, THE ARTIST AND THE TRADITION

It is generally held that Pop Art in Britain had its origins at the RCA in the early 1950s, in an effort to rid British art of its ruminant concern with the natural world and bring it into direct awareness of an urban popular environment. In fact it goes back still further, to the collages Eduardo Paolozzi had made in the late 1940s like *I was a Rich Man's Plaything*[14] (1947); a montage of images, including a Coke bottle, a cover girl from a pulp magazine, and an American warplane, this was probably as near as British Pop ever came to the American version, with its direct presentation of popular images – billboards, packages, automotive and consumer goods – in pure, vibrant colours, flat textures and large formats. In the 1960s British Pop – if, indeed, the work of a range of artists can be lumped together under its banner – developed in a manner quite different from its transatlantic equivalent; that it did so was largely because of the work of Richard Hamilton.

Hamilton had been involved in the Independent Group at the RCA from its foundation in the 1950s, and had shared its interest in the visual elements of popular culture. This resulted in a famous manifesto (1982: 28):

Pop Art is:
Popular (designed for a mass audience)
Transient (short-term solution)
Expendable (easily forgotten)
Low cost
Mass produced
Young (aimed at youth)
Witty
Sexy
Gimmicky
Glamorous
Big business

This is a key statement about British art in the 1960s, but not perhaps in the way one might expect. Hamilton is saying that the world of the consumer society is already an art form in itself; there is no need for the artist to produce images or representations of it because it already has its own identity. To Hamilton, Pop Art is the real Campbell's soup can on the supermarket shelf, not a painting or sculpture of it in unreconstructed form along the lines of Jasper Johns, Andy Warhol or the other leading American Pop artists.

This is the key difference between American and British Pop. Whereas the American form presents images of the consumer society in an unmodified form – save for its scale, and the statement that this is 'art' – the British kind sees the consumer products as already an art form. This acceptance allows the British Pop artist to use and refer to the imagery of the everyday in a subtler fashion; it becomes a new source of allusion, a new kind of iconography for use in a range of new ways. Thus it is that British Pop Art subsumes elements of contemporary visual reality into the pantheon of high art iconography, rather than simply celebrating the new forms without comment. Where the American celebrates, the British cerebrates; and this difference accounts for the fact that Pop Art in Britain is extremely various, since each artist uses what he or she needs of the new visual reality to form part of his or her own stylistic, moral or political purpose.

How this works in practice can best be shown by looking at some key works by the two major artists involved. Hamilton himself is the most elegant of British Pop artists, absorbing elements from everyday visual experience into canvases of near-abstract play of mass and space. *She*[15] (1958–61) brings together elements of a vacuum cleaner, the hose of which elides into a streamlined electric toaster; the interior of a fridge; a double-image eye printed on plastic, which appears to wink at the onlooker; and a stylized treatment of a backless dress. The use of low-relief and a silky airbrushed texture mimics the technique of the advertising hoarding and the glossy sales-brochure. All this creates an image of sensuous rhythm and form that both states and comments on the exchange between the erotic and the mechanical in so much consumer-goods marketing and design. The visual pun of the title suggests and amplifies the painting's theme – the exploitative equation between marketing and female sexuality, most obviously in the USA. As if to stress the traditional use of iconographic reference that the reader must decode, Hamilton's own gloss on the painting runs to four pages (1982: 51–5), but this is not essential to an experience of the painting; its sensuality offers a unity between the human and the mechanical that is subtle and satisfying, something quite different from the glorious raucousness of a lot of American celebrations of machine-sex.

These themes, begun in his *Hommage à Chrysler Corp*[16] (1957) continue in other work. *Pin-up*[17] (1961), according to the artist, uses the imagery of 'girlie pictures', which are both 'vulgar and unattractive' and 'sophisticated and often exquisite' (1982: 40) – an explanation that betrays perhaps the artist's real attitude to popular culture as well as to images of women as more ambivalent than his earlier, more explicit, espousals would have us believe. In *Aah!*[18] (1962) a steering column gearshift becomes a sexual orgasmic object; it is as if the erotic nature of the car-driver relationship exploited by Madison Avenue and celebrated by e e cummings in 'she being Brand/ -new' (1963: 15–16) has been re-created in the iconographic tradition of British art.

Peter Blake uses Pop imagery of another sort and to different ends. In the 1950s Blake had produced paintings in a personal extension of a loosely anecdotal tradition in English figure painting. These grew into paintings using pop images – often stuck on to the canvas in untreated form – such as badges, comics, magazines, postcards and photographs of the Royal family. An image such as *Self-Portrait with Badges*[19] (1961) shows the central figure wearing canvas shoes, jeans and a denim jacket covered with the circular badges that were then beginning to be a fashionable way of expressing political dissent or devotion to a pop singer. The latter idea is continued in the magazine cover in the artist's right hand, which has the large title 'Elvis' above a picture of the singer. Clothes, stance and accompanying detail are all clearly of a popular nature; the artist seems directly to espouse the new classless youth culture of the age.

Yet the image also makes use of traditional figurations in the very way that it rejects them. The technique of revealing characterization through setting or emblematic objects, familiar in the sixteenth and seventeenth century, is carried on, but now we have badges and not heraldic emblems, a pop pin-up instead of a staff of state. The setting helps continue and reject tradition, too; the artist stands in front of a wooden fence, before which a single tree can be seen and behind which there are suggestions of other vegetation. This suggests a suburban back garden, not the rolling acres owned by the patriarch in Gainsborough and Reynolds; but it also continues that older tradition. The tree is short and thin, but it offers a new version of the tree as emblem of inherited ownership in eighteenth-century portraits, and the fence also stresses personal, not shared, space.

Blake went on to produce paintings of popular stars – 'personalities', in the language of television promotion – and then turned to strippers, wrestlers and people from the same subcultures that had fascinated earlier British artists as diverse as Laura Knight, Augustus John and Edward Burra. This perhaps shows his roots in the anecdotal tradition; he is often compared to Stanley Spencer and, although the spiritual basis of the two artists' work is poles apart, there is the same desire to present the human figure as a species seen anew. The tree and the garden are perhaps more revealing than at first sight they seem; in the 1970s Blake became a founder member of the Brotherhood of Ruralists, a kind of late twentieth-century reinvention of William Morris's arcadian craft guilds.

It is perhaps too early to decide whether there really was British Pop Art, or whether a series of individuals chose to make use of the imagery of mass culture in their own ways. Probably the title will remain because of its sheer convenience to the art historian, like the frequently flabby use of the label 'pre-Raphaelite'. Hamilton and Blake are individual artists, not members of a movement, and since this is true of the two other artists most often labelled as Pop, it is sensible to discuss them as figures in their own right.

YOUNG CONTEMPORARIES: HOCKNEY AND KITAJ

Older than his fellow-students at the RCA, and American by birth, R. B. Kitaj adopted pop imagery for more complex purposes. His canvases have to be read with as much care as a Hogarth morality, encompassing as they do references to contemporary life, history, politics, literature and the artist's own life and relationships. Kitaj is often regarded as the most rigorously intellectual painter of that time, but this is only half the story; his images are certainly full of allusions to be decoded, but they also have a sensual immediacy in the use of paint that marks them off from Hamilton and Blake.

Dismantling the Red Tent[20] (1964) shows this well. The red tent was used by polar explorers as both a haven and a beacon, and Kitaj uses this as both a literal and a moral point of orientation; the painting was completed after Kennedy's assassination, to show the need for a new beacon of this sort. According to the artist himself the male figures of the foreground are political men – 'some hollow, some not' – who 'hover about the tent for warmth after regicide' (Livingstone 1985: 148). In the background a real etching by Alphonse Legros is included, broadening the painting's reference by suggesting the same search for moral sustenance in an earlier time. Kitaj goes on to say: 'Twenty years later, I wish this little mystery-picture had been more perfectly painted because I like its terms even more deeply now than I understood then' – a revealing comment, showing that the iconography of his paintings grows and shifts with the passing of time, something that the artist himself stresses.

The same breadth is evident in all of Kitaj's work of this period. References to recent history, political philosophy and *film noir* coalesce with experiences and personages from the artist's youth in a mixture of the personal and the philosophical – a simultaneous exposure and concealment of self – that surfaces, in a quite different way, in the art of David Hockney. The contemporary reality of Kitaj's art is always an intellectual one, yet it is also compassionate; and the web of allusion is united by a compelling visual directness that is both immediately personal and conscious of tradition. At Oxford, Kitaj was deeply impressed by the iconographical analyses of Edgar Wind and Aby Warbourg; his achievement is to embody this kind of scholarly complexity in a visual language that is both sensually immediate and the common property of his age.

Perhaps the most characteristic feature of David Hockney's work is its refusal to be characterized or to follow any single stylistic line, to the bewilderment of critics then and now. At first it seemed that there were in his work clear leanings towards Pop Art. *Tea Painting in an Illusionistic Style*[21] (1961) uses the form of an opened packet of Ty-Phoo tea both as its subject and as its outline, the canvas being shaped to follow its isometrically-projected form. Within this shape the figure of a seated male nude holding a teacup is inserted. The 'illusionistic style' is in part created by the uncertainty of space – is the man sitting within the packet or are the images merely superimposed? This is far from the glossy style of American representations of commercial packaging; even though the brand name and printed instructions are clearly legible, the precision of the printing is deliberately broken – by the misspelling 'Ty-Phoo TAE' on the side, the smudged '2d off' on the square above the open lid, and the overlapping of broad brush strokes of transparent flesh-tone that give mass to the nude figure. It becomes apparent that this is far more a consideration of balancing and conflicting spatial schemes than a statement about the surrounding visual environment. It is almost a personal reworking of Bacon's *Figure in a Landscape*[22] of 1945. Its significance is clarified by the title of the series in which it is a part – *Demonstrations of Versatility*,[23] four paintings shown at the RCA's 'Young Contemporaries' show of 1962. In these paintings Hockney set out to show his own versatility, yet all concern the basic issue of presenting objects in a flat space. This is a far more traditional concern than that of the 'super-realist' pop painters; as the artist himself said, 'This is as close to pop art as I ever came. But I didn't use it (the tea packet) because I was interested in the design. . . . These paintings were my first attempt to put recognizable images into paintings' (1978: 14).

Evidence of his versatility is provided by another important image of the 1960s, *We Two Boys Together Clinging*[24] (1961). The forms of the two boys are childlike and imprecise, two torsos with stick legs linked by an arm depicted only in outline, contrasting strongly to the bodies, which are broad masses of colour, and the simple child-distorted heads. A broad band of blue rises at the left of the canvas, with various versions of the word 'boy', a red heart and the figures 4.2 at the foot. The title is written around the outlines of the boys in crude nursery lower-case, and to the right another heart is placed above some barely-legible lines of verse.

The free use of vivid colours and forms defined by mass, not outline, is significant in foreshadowing a later stage of Hockney's art in the California landscapes, but it has a more insistent function; it is as if the deliberate espousal of childlike style is a rejection of the formalities of high art. This rejection is made stronger by the way in which the apparently representational elements of the painting – the words and figures – seem to defy interpretation. In fact they are strongly personal; the '4.2' is, in Hockney's alphanumeric code, the letters DB, standing for Doll Boy, the nickname of Cliff Richard; Hockney had seen the headline 'Two boys cling to Cliff all night long' and read it as an embodiment of a homosexual fantasy about the singer and not a saga of mountain isolation. The lines to the right are from Walt Whitman's *Leaves of Grass*, and celebrate male friendship; in some versions the two figures bear the numbers 4.8 (= DH = David Hockney) and 16.3 (= PC = Peter Crotch, Hockney's lover) to continue the homosexual theme and also make the painting more personal.

Overall, the painting is a rejection of establishment values in its form and its content; by using the idiom of a child's painting it deliberately rejects notions of high art sophistication, and by its references, which are at once private and homosexual, it turns its back on traditional portraiture showing a man and woman in a relationship at once heterosexual and material – a rejection of the Gainsborough gentry portrait, which we might see repeated (though this time by much closer reference) in the later *Mr and Mrs Grant and Percy*[25] (1970–1).

Hockney's portraits of the 1960s are of two main strands. First there are the drawings, in which taut lines contain loose spaces, very much in a personal extension of the linear economy of Picasso. *W. H. Auden*[26] (1968) succeeds not only in revealing the poet's craggy face – a wedding-cake left out in the rain, as someone said – but also in removing it a long way from the rhetoric of the Victorian portraits of poets as great and good. Here the intimacy is as great as that with the drawings of Hockney's male lovers of the period – a world of liaisons, which, of course, Auden shared with Hockney – and this lays further stress on the importance of the personal and the sexual in the decade of the Wolfenden Report and the explosive growth of individual freedom.

Then there are the more painterly portraits, the porcelain-smooth acrylics in which rhetoric and rank are alike rejected, and wealthy American patrons are treated with the same insouciance as intimate acquaintances. *The Room, Tirzana*[27] (1967), with its balance of cool tonalities and what must be for Hockney, both here and in the swimming-pool paintings, an intense homo-eroticism – a male version of Boucher's sprawling nudes,[28] showing again the fine art references – shares its style with *American Collectors (Fred and Marcia Weisman)*[29] (1968). There are signs of a greater looseness, and hence greater intimacy, in *Christopher Isherwood and Don Bachardy*[30] (1968) – intimacy of many kinds, for not only does it have the usual connotations of character-revelation in portraiture, but it also hints at levels of sexual intimacy between the subjects, and possibly their painter, in the curious blend of the personal and the public, the simultaneous effacement of private doings and their outward trumpeting that is a part not only of Hockney's art but of a lot of the other cultural and social shifts of the decade.

All these works show Hockney as a major figure of the time, although it is not until the next decade that his screen prints begin to make him genuinely popular in the sense of being accessible. His direct rejection of many fine art conventions makes him paradoxically far more a part of the mainstream of European art than a figure standing outside it. As a character in N. F. Simpson's *A Resounding Tinkle* says: 'It takes an educated audience to appreciate a non-sequitur'. It was to this audience that Hockney's work appealed. Even his stage designs continue a practice common for popular Romantic and Victorian Painters; and they are for work that could hardly be called populist – the Royal Court's *Ubu Roi*, not Stratford East's *Oh, What a Lovely War!*

THE MOVE TO THREE DIMENSIONS

Despite the splashings of the press about the all-new all-populist nature of Pop Art, probably the most exciting and significant development of British art in the 1960s can be described as a new awareness of the three-dimensional nature of the art object. This took many forms, some to do with an extension of painting – literally and conceptually – into new kinds of space, others to do with new definitions of sculpture. Yet it would be a mistake to see them as all variants of a single impulse, despite the convenience of grouping that this view offers; they owe their origins to different ideas of the artist's media, the space of the artwork and the notion of sculpture.

Take, for example, the paintings of Leon Kossoff and Frank
Auerbach. In the 1960s both produced portraits that use an unprecedented amount of paint, often squeezed straight from the tube
(lots of tubes) to produce a texture akin almost to the broad deep
corduroys that were fashionable at the time. This was seen by some
as a move towards sculpture, to create a greater illusion of depth
within a portrait, with the aim of showing a figure within a setting.
Not so: it was a concern for the textural tactile qualities of paint
that had not been seen in England for a long time, perhaps since
Turner. This can have complex effects on the spaces within paintings, as well as on their ostensible subjects, as in Auerbach's *The
Sitting Room*[31] (1964), where the figures emerge slowly from the vast
depth of impasto and, once discerned, seem to vibrate from within
the picture's recessive depths to the surface of the picture's plane,
almost as does the figure in Hockney's *Tea Painting*.

This last work is one of a few examples of Hockney's use of the
shaped canvas, a device exploited more fully by many other 1960s
artists. Although in a sense this is a move towards a kind of realism,
as the shape of the painting is based on its subject, it is also a move
to greater abstraction, since the shape forces us to remember that
this is a painting, not the object itself. The bus paintings of Allen
Jones,[32] for example, use the shape to convey a dynamic movement
that is an aesthetic recreation of the experience of a bus passing, not
a photographic presentation of it; the package-paintings of Derek
Boshier[33] use canvases that follow the shapes of their subjects to
present the world of the supermarket consumer with a new freshness
– sometimes sinister, always challenging – rather than simply to
state it in the manner of American Pop at its most forthright.

Another kind of spatial awareness is provided in the best Op (or
optical) art of the 1960s. At its best, in the work of Bridget Riley,
this drew on the whole history of visual representation of receding
space to create images that depended on a partnership between art
and the perceiver. *Current*[34] (1964) is one of many works in which
black lines on a white ground follow a similar movement with
minute variations in spacing to create in the eye of the onlooker an
illusion of wave motion. Perhaps this was related to stroboscopic
lighting used in the newly-emerged discotheques; perhaps it was
part of a fascination with black and white that paradoxically followed the explosion of colour made possible by developments in
paint technology. Now that monochrome was no longer an endemic
state of the external world – in dark and drab cars, clothes and

consumer goods – it became something to be explored and exploited. At its finest, Riley's work has a chaste astringent quality that places it far more in a tradition of abstract exploration than at the centre of a new tricksy popularism. That it suggests movement within a surface, both still and planar, is a development of that older tradition in a conceptually new and striking way, more than an indication of some larger underlying move towards three-dimensionality. Here, as elsewhere in the work of the decade, artist and beholder are engaged in a partnership to generate a text that is both personal and dynamic.

If a single concrete embodiment of 1960s thought is to be found at all in the visual art of the period, it would be in the sculpture of Anthony Caro and the New Generation artists. Caro's transformation from a follower of the romantic-humanist tradition, fostered when he briefly assisted Henry Moore in the early 1950s, began with a meeting with Clement Greenberg and a subsequent visit to the USA where he encountered for the first time the work of David Smith.

Instead of the traditional forms and media of his earlier work – figures in clay developing Moore's linkage of figure and landscape – Caro moved to work of a kind that was at first sight wholly new. This was most obvious in the medium – metal plates, girders and tubes, some bought off the shelf as standard industrial sections, others found by chance in scrapyards. These elements were assembled by welding and bolting, with no preparatory sketches or maquettes; it was a three-dimensional re-invention of the immediacy and risk of the great period of watercolour in English art. That comparison is in a sense absurd, as Caro's works were often 20 feet in length; but in others it is quite fitting. The forms grew as self-defining structures that often had a lyricism of form and rhythm that seemed quite at odds with the nature of the material from which they were constructed – a paradox aided by the surface coverage in pure primary-coloured gloss paint and the titles of the works, often precisely suggestive of times or situations.

The parallel with a Romantic watercolour holds good, too, in that a work by Caro is as directly experienced by the onlooker – more so, in fact. The traditional rhetoric of placing a sculpture on a plinth is abandoned, removing the spatial separation between it and the beholder. And what space does the sculpture itself occupy? An assemblage of strut, tube and plate – does it exist only in the masses of its metal shapes or does it occupy the cube of space that its extremities define? The three-dimensionality so strongly stressed by the apertures in the work of Moore and Hepworth is made more strongly present as we walk around these works, as we must; individual shapes change, rhythms compress and elongate, and the whole comes to dominate our senses in the manner of a gestalt perception, a whole unity of experience rather than a single element within a larger visual clutter. Once again, a compact is struck between artist and onlooker to generate an experiential dynamic work.

Early one Morning[35] (1962) is a fine example. Composed of plate, tube and industrial I-section girder, the whole is some 20 feet in length and 10 in width and height. Its bright red colour is often regarded as a sign of optimism appropriate to the title, but it is also, in a literal sense, suggestive of an intense sunrise. As we move around the structure its form and rhythm change so that it at once suggests both the shapes of some ancient farm-implement and the inner structure of a contemporary building. Indeed, it is significant that Caro's imagery has much in common with what we might call the deep structure of the system-built office towers that were rising with alarming speed throughout the cities during the decade; it suggests a new version of the ancient artistic theme of a relationship between the inhabitant and the environment, but one that is new, incisive, urban and metallic.

Yet the forms are strangely organic too. Often the rectilinear sections are bent into elegant curves, which, taken with the tubular components, both offset and merge with the rigid rectangles and straight lines of other components to produce a totality suggesting a new kind of organism. Graham Sutherland's paintings of blasted city buildings[36] in the 1940s have something of this quality; it is as if the built environment is serving as yet another metaphor of the human and organic world. Certainly the horizontality of the sculpture emphasizes this; Caro's departures from Moore's reclining biomorphs may not be as total and as revolutionary as they seem, although this is in no way to deny the exhilarating originality of vision and medium they represent.

Other sculptors exhibiting at the 'New Generation' show of 1962 – pupils of Caro or his colleagues at St Martin's School of Art – approach spaces and textures in different ways. Phillip King's use of metal or one of the newly-available thermoplastics to produce forms of sweeping curves and enameled glosses[37] reveals a mindset that was new, exciting and wholly the product of its decade. His works have titles that are witty and allusive, yet their significance reveals an intellectual excitement quite inseparable from an innately practical awareness of form – 'blood, intellect and imagination running together', as Yeats said about probably the most-studied poet of the decade, John Donne. To call this sculpture metaphysical is confusing, since it suggests that its physicality is not important, and the term has been used for the work of others; but with King, and also with other figures such as William Turnbull, William Tucker and William Pye, there is a feeling that the beautifully wrought form has a significance indivisible into idea and shape. The New Generation sculptors offered a new way of thinking and being in metal and hard gloss paint that was insistent and exuberant, a great, elegant thrust of inventiveness into a medium gone flabby with convention. For a while, too, this thrust became part of a wider visual environment; the New Generation sculptors both benefited from and helped to create the new patrons of sculpture – the large companies and institutions which, along with the state in the enthusiastic new Arts Council, replaced the private patrons of earlier times.

The work of Eduardo Paolozzi in the 1960s is often seen as the link between the new sculpture and Pop Art, and in a way this is a valid view. Certainly, the exuberance of Pop Art and its confrontation of a culture predominantly urban can be found in abundance in his sculpture; but the nature of its invention is more broadly based. It also rests on a tradition that, in a sense, separates it from the art of Hamilton, Blake or Kitaj – the European surrealist outlook and frame of reference that stems from Ernst and dada.

Paolozzi's work frequently uses popular imagery to reveal the absurdity of a great deal of contemporary life. If Hamilton's paintings show the harmony between humanity and the mechanical, Paolozzi's collages and sculptures satirize it by showing the ridiculous and sometimes the sinister within it. His *Mr Machine* drawing[30] (1959–60) is based on a children's toy robot, in a combination of human and mechanical elements; it shows a move from the Pop collages of the 1950s to something more ironic and detached.

Later sculptural work becomes more exuberant. The two *Diana as an Engine*[39] (1962 and 1963) sculptures present the goddess with a triangular body and a circular head reminiscent of a rotary aero-engine; *City of the Circle and Square*[40] (1963) is a series of rectilinear aluminium casts painted in brash primary colours, supported on a pedestal and an elegant wheel – something from a Victorian barrow, perhaps, or a treadle machine – to celebrate the new forms of the urban setting.

Yet however forthright his use of popular images, Paolozzi in the 1960s is essentially an artist whose work is, like Hamilton's, an extension of the fine art lexicon – in his case a projection of the European modernist-surrealist axis. There is also a pronounced streak of 1920s neo-classicism, in say, *Towards a New Laocoon*[41] (1963) or his 'fables in sculpture' like *Hamlet in a Japanese Manner*[42] (1966). The stress on cylinders and engines is an echo of futurism, in theory if not form; and the screenprints, including *As Is When* (1965), use images to suggest collages in the manner of those Max Ernst made in England from old copies of *The Illustrated London News*. Were these perhaps the source of the animations punctuating *Monty Python's Flying Circus*? This is another of those imponderable links between popular mass-consumption art forms and the work of the 'fine' artist that result in a practical blurring of distinctions between the two – an extension of the continuum of which Hamilton spoke – which makes it so pleasingly difficult to define the true limits of Pop Art in the decade. Whether Paolozzi set out to celebrate the new establishment of the tower block and the machine, or to undermine it, he seems to have succeeded in both: at the end of the century he is a respected cultural knight, whose links are more with the Underground than the underground, in the mural produced for Tottenham Court Road tube station.

LARGER SIGNIFICANCES

What was the lasting impact of the art of the decade? Before attempting to answer this question, it is worthwhile examining briefly the superstructure of art in the 1960s – the galleries and institutions that organized and displayed the new work, the educational bodies that produced new artists, and the dealers and auction houses who both followed and directed public taste.

Whatever the lasting effects of the artworks produced in the decade, the 1960s certainly saw major changes in the way that the art world organized itself. In this the fortunes of the Royal Academy have both a symbolic and a literal importance. At the start of the decade, under the presidency of the sculptor Charles Wheeler, it found itself close to bankruptcy and was saved only by putting up for auction its Leonardo cartoon of the *Virgin with St Anne and St John*. It spent some of the money, not on contemporary art, but on restoring works by West, Kent and Kauffmann, emphasizing a belief in tradition shown also in its exhibitions of Wilkie, Landseer and Lawrence. True, it did also have shows of more recent painters, but for British artists these only got as far as Gerald Kelly and Matthew Smith; its 'Primitives to Picasso' show was out of place amidst the more comforting 'Age of Louis XIV', 'Age of Charles II' and 'Italian Art in Britain'. Yet there was still a strong demand for this kind of historical survey; the 'Goya and his Times' exhibition had 350,000 visitors in 1963–4, whereas other shows averaged between 60,000 and 100,000. At the end of 1968 there was a show of work related to the Bauhaus, but this closed early, as the official history of the RA remarks (Hutchison 1986: 189) because of 'threats of trouble connected with some demonstrations in London'. The decade ended on safer ground with the RA's 'Bicentenary Exhibition' of work by distinguished earlier Academicians. If I close this paragraph with the remark that dry rot was then discovered in the basement, it should be taken only at a purely literal level. The RA had always had a shaky grasp on developments in the contemporary art world, but in the 1950s it had seemed closer than at many other times to work being produced; in the 1960s, however, it seemed to have little to do with the business of being a contemporary artist. This was probably to have a greater effect 20 years on, with both Hockney and Kitaj as members and a very strong bias towards the new orthodoxy, to the disquiet of many more cautious onlookers (see Fuller 1989).

The art establishment was, however, flourishing in the auction rooms. Sothebys had taken over the New York house of Parke Bernet in 1964; its glossy hardback record of sales changed its name from *The Ivory Hammer* to *Art at Auction* in 1967, which showed at least that the business ethic was openly acknowledged. The volume makes an intriguing guide to the values – financial and aesthetic – of the year. Its section headings assert the continuity of traditional connoisseurship: 'Old Master paintings'; 'Impressionist paintings and works of art'; and, quaintly, 'The photograph as object d'art'. The last talks of 'the work of Julia Margaret Cameron, that wonderful eccentric'. Clearly the traditional art market was a long way from the actualities of Pop and New Generation. The conventionality is shown, too, in the auction records. A Cézanne watercolour was sold for £145,000 and Picasso's *Maternité au bord de la mer* for £190,000, 'by far the highest sum yet given anywhere for a work by a living painter'. Taste in British painting was still respectable and cautious;

£5,000 would have bought a canvas by the Victorian classicist John Frederick Lewis, slightly more a Samuel Palmer, but Sickerts were to be had for little more than £1,000, a Ben Nicholson abstract for £1,800 and a David Jones watercolour for an absurd £250. These figures must be read with care; even to take normal inflation into account, we probably need to multiply them by 10 or 20. But it is clear, nevertheless, that the use of paintings as investment objects was not at the feverish level it attained in the 1970s and 1980s.

There was, of course, another art market – that created by large institutions, both commercial and public. Robert Sainsbury was beginning the collection eventually to be housed in Norman Foster's new gallery at the University of East Anglia; Sebastian de Ferranti and Alistair McAlpine were like-minded patrons who used institutional funds to encourage the work of younger artists and sculptors. Perhaps more surprisingly, the John Moores organization had funded a biennial exhibition, with substantial cash awards, from 1957 onwards; the Peter Stuyvesant Foundation sponsored the 'New Generation' shows between 1964 and 1968. Public institutions were similarly eager. The Arts Council's spending on contemporary British art rose to £21,000 in 1967–8, the first year of its new charter; criticized for not doing enough to encourage new artistic media, it founded a New Activities Committee the next year, which itself came under strong attack from the avant-garde. The British Council bought works, including Hockney's *We Two Boys Together Clinging*, the Tate sculpture by Caro and a fine collection of Pop prints; the Contemporary Art Society, in mounting the 'British Painting in the 60s' show, announced that a large sum had been set aside from its budget to acquire important works for permanent display.

This last show was split between the Tate and Whitechapel Art Gallery; the 'New Generation' show was held wholly at the latter. This is part of an important shift in the display of art work in the decade, as galleries outside central London grew in stature. The Bond Street gallery circuit was still important – indeed, new names like Victor Waddington, Mateus Grabowski, Robert Fraser and John Kasmin all opened galleries that were important shop windows for younger artists. But there were other centres. The John Moores biennial shows were held at the Walker Art Gallery in Liverpool; the Whitworth in Manchester also hosted important shows for younger artists. The Stockwell Depot and the St Katharine Docks community were examples of a new kind of display – artists working together and organizing their own shows in their own spaces. The

Department of Education and Science encouraged the foundation and growth of regional arts centres, perhaps the finest example of which was Camden, which, under its director Peter Carey, mounted shows like its 1969 'Survey 69: New Space' that was influential in the growth of installation art. There were educational shifts too. St Martin's became the focus for sculpture, the RCA for a new breed of painting that seemed in direct rejection of the painstaking drafts-manship for so long the hallmark of the Slade. The growth in university education during the decade created new departments for the academic study of art history, laying the ground for the critical debate that was to produce the 'new art history' of the next two decades.

All of this meant that there were new places to study art, and new spaces in which to display it. In terms of sheer activity in the arts – production, exhibition, sale – Britain certainly took pre-cedence over European and American cities. Chronicling this is one thing; explaining it is another. Was it that the energy had gone out of abstract expressionism? Had American art ironically become too provincial in its celebration of popular culture only wholly accessible to its own citizens? Perhaps Europe was in decline, with Picasso and Miró, its presiding masters, seen as in their declining years – a heresy maintained until fairly recently. Perhaps London's success as the new art centre was the result of its shameless self-publicity, along with some sound commercial acumen – the swinging and the swingeing, you might say. But this doesn't explain the presence of so many outstanding and original artists; and the reasons for this are probably just as complex and arbitrary as those that created the Florentine Renaissance.

What of the art itself? Did Pop Art really succeed in eliding the barriers between the fine and the popular? For a time it might have seemed so, but the answer is probably 'No'. The use of popular imagery was important, not because it showed a lurch to the left in producing a genuine art of the people, but because it was a further expression – in gloriously energetic and sensual terms – of the anecdotal and ironic so dear to English art, which had in large measure been rejected by the romantics of the 1940s and 1950s. Hockney's *Rake's Progress* suite provides a touchstone in its reference to Hogarth, an earlier incarnation of the artist who makes a personal language out of popular iconography.

Pop Art did have another significance, even though it was not too clear at the time. It was a powerful, and largely practical, stimulus to the study of semiotics and popular culture that was to explode in the 1970s and 1980s; before it there had been only Orwell and Hoggart, the former moralist, the latter sniffy at what the people did with their aesthetic impulses. The fact that this book discusses the Beatles instead of Maxwell Davies and Boulez is perhaps further testimony to a lasting shift of focus to which the Pop Art of the 1960s contributed.

Changes in sculpture were probably the most important; the use of metal, fibreglass and plastic, as well as a range of other inorganic materials and found objects, is now an essential part of the language of the sculptor. In the longer term the work of the New Generation figures can be seen as a crucial point, where sculpture turned from the romantic landscape-humanist tradition of Henry Moore to embrace elements of a new built world and its detritus. Yet, paradoxically, the open rhythms of Caro and the awareness of spaces defined by the exchange between onlooker and artwork led to the organic sculptures and installations of Richard Long; the line from Sutherland and Moore runs still through Caro and Long.

The involvement of the onlooker was important elsewhere, too: in the work of Bridget Riley in terms of perceptual psychology; in the 'Situation' shows in terms of defining and sharing a space; and in recognizing the use of pop images in a way that was often a kind of witty collusion of artist and beholder, as in the winking eye of Hamilton's *She*. All of this was to have echoes later in new concepts of the exact nature and permanence of an artistic 'text'.

Despite Paolozzi's references to Ernst, the main overseas link was with the United States. Kitaj provided a type of the mid-Atlantic artist, as Hockney was later to do in reverse. Hamilton's imagery is frankly transatlantic; Blake's figures wear American-style clothes and read American-style comics; Caro's work owes much to David Smith. But British Pop Art never quite achieved the instant thrust of its American equivalent; there was nothing that quite matched Oldenburg's soft typewriter or Lichtenstein's comic strips.

At its best, the art of the 1960s was energetic and genuinely witty; if it didn't quite get out of the galleries, at least it got the wind of change blowing anarchically through them. If at the end of the decade art was still the property of the gallery-going classes, at least there had been an extension of this franchise, due not only to the Butler Education Act but also the use of the mass imagery of contemporary life. And this had its effect in an awakening of interest in design and fashion, the visual furniture of the everyday.

Probably the decade's greatest achievement was not only in making art accessible, but in making it enjoyable; intellectual wit and spatial awareness made English art once more vigorous and amusing, and also the focus of raging argument and dissent that was a very powerful dynamic. At the time, before its role in expanding a traditional iconographic strand became clear, it was deeply exciting in its seeming rejection of a centuries-old view of art; just for a while, before the art establishment took control and ownership once again, as the big auction-houses realized the potential of Pop and its allies, art was no longer something to be worshipped with cathedral silence in stuffy galleries, or explained to a grateful public by stuffy connoisseurs.

NOTES

Sizes of paintings are given in inches, with height preceding width; the dimensions of sculptures are likewise given in inches, with height followed by width by depth.

1 *Sergeant Pepper's Lonely Hearts Club Band*, 1967.
2 Bronze, height 13 ft 11½ in; Churchill College, Cambridge.
3 Marble, height 7 ft 7¾ in, the artist.
4 Bronze, height 12 ft, width 15 ft 8 in.
5 Oil on canvas on board, 25½ × 27⅛, private collection.
6 Oil on canvas, triptych, each panel 77⅝ × 57⅞, Staatsgalerie Moderner Kunst, Munich.
7 Oil on canvas, 78 × 57, private collection, Switzerland.
8 Screenprint on paper, 27⅛ × 33.
9 Screenprint on paper, 26 × 33.
10 Series of screenprints, each 32 × 21⅞.
11 Series of 16 prints, zinc etching and coloured aquatint on paper, each 12 × 16.
12 From *As Is When*, folio with 12 sheets, 1 poster and texts; screenprint on paper, 31½ × 21⅝.
13 Silkscreen and pastel on paper, 28 × 34⁶/10.
14 Collage 14 × 9¼ on card 16⅞ × 13⅞, Tate Gallery, London.
15 Oil and mixed media on board, 48 × 32, Tate Gallery, London.
16 Lithograph with pastel, gouache and collage, 15 × 20⅞, private collection.
17 Oil, cellulose and collage on panel, 48 × 32, private collection.
18 Oil on panel, 32 × 48, Mr and Mrs Max Wasserman, Chestnut Hill, Mass., USA.
19 Oil on hardboard, 68 × 47½, Tate Gallery, London.
20 Oil on canvas, with an original etching by Alphonse Legros, 48 ×

48, Michael and Dorothy Blankfurt Collection at Los Angeles County Museum, California.

21 Oil on canvas, 78 × 30, Bruno Bischofberger, Zurich.

22 Oil on canvas, 57 × 50½, Tate Gallery, London.

23 The others were *A Grand Procession of Dignitaries in the Semi-Egyptian Style*, oil on canvas, 84 × 144, private collection, Los Angeles; *Swiss Landscape in a Scenic Style*, now known as *Flight into Italy – Swiss Landscape*, oil on canvas, 72 × 72, Galerie Zwirmer, Cologne; and *Figure in a Flat Style*, oil on canvas, 36 × 24, private collection, Germany.

24 Oil on board, 48 × 60, the Arts Council of Great Britain, London.

25 Acrylic on canvas, 84 × 120, Tate Gallery, London.

26 Ink on paper, 17 × 14, private collection, London.

27 Acrylic on canvas, 96 × 96, private collection, USA.

28 For example, *Reclining Girl (Mademoiselle O'Murphy)*, 1751, oil on canvas, 23½ × 28¾, Walraf-Richartz Museum, Cologne.

29 Acrylic on canvas, 84 × 120, present whereabouts unknown.

30 Acrylic on canvas, 83½ × 119½, private collection, London.

31 Oil on hardboard, 50½ × 50⅜, Tate Gallery, London.

32 For example, *Second Bus*, oil on canvas, 48¾ × 60¾, Granada Television, Manchester.

33 For example, *First Toothpaste Painting*, oil on canvas, 54 × 30, Sheffield City Art Galleries.

34 Synthetic polymer paint on composition board, 58⅜ × 58⅜, Museum of Modern Art, New York.

35 Painted steel, 114 × 244 × 132, Tate Gallery, London.

36 Most particularly, *Devastation, 1941, City: Fallen Lift Shaft*, 1941, gouache, 25½ × 44, Imperial War Museum, London; and *Devastation, 1941, City: Twisted Girders (1)*, 1941, gouache, 26 × 44, Ferens Art Gallery, Kingston-upon-Hull.

37 For example, *Genghis Khan*, 1963, purple plastic and fibreglass with steel supports, 84 × 108 × 144, Peter Stuyvesant Foundation, London; and *Rosebud*, 1962, pink and green plastic, 60 × 72 (cone), Museum of Modern Art, New York.

38 Pencil on paper, 15⅛ × 11⅝.

39 I, 1962, aluminium, 102 × 47⅝ × 51, private collection; II, 1963, aluminium, 63¾ × 41 × 18⅛, private collection.

40 Aluminium, 80⅜ × 39¾ × 26⅜, Tate Gallery, London.

41 Aluminium, 78 × 50 × 36, M. R. Vanthournout-T'Kint, Belgium.

42 Aluminium; three elements, 43 × 43¼ × 38⅛; 60⅝ × 72⁸⁄₁₀ × 70⅞; 65 × 68⁹⁄₁₀ × 43¼, Glasgow Art Gallery Museum, Kelvingrove, Glasgow.

BIBLIOGRAPHY

Adams, Hugh 1978. *Art of the Sixties*. Oxford: Phaidon.

Amaya, Mario 1965. *Pop as Art: A Survey of the New Super Realism*. London: Studio Vista.

cummings, e e 1963. *e e cummings selected poems 1923–1958.* Harmondsworth: Penguin.
Fuller, Peter 1988. *Theoria.* London: Chatto & Windus.
Fuller, Peter 1989. 'RA: Has it lost its way?' *Sunday Telegraph,* 25 June 1989.
Hamilton, Richard 1982. *Collected Words.* London and New York: Thames & Hudson.
Hewison, Robert 1986. *Too Much: Art and Society in the Sixties 1960–75.* London: Methuen.
Hockney, David 1978. *David Hockney: Travels with Pen, Pencil and Ink.* London: Petersburg Press.
Hoggart, Richard 1957. *The Uses of Literacy.* London: Chatto & Windus.
Hunter, Sam 1970. *Modern American – Op, Pop and the School of Colour.* New York: McCall.
Hunter, Sam 1973. *American Art of the Twentieth Century.* New York: H. N. Abrams.
Hutchison, Sidney C. 1986. *The History of the Royal Academy 1768–1986.* London: Robert Royce.
Kaprow, Allan 1966. *Assemblage, Environment, and Happenings.* New York: H. N. Abrams.
Kirby, Michael 1965. *Happenings: An Illustrated Anthology.* New York: Dutton.
Konnertz, Winfried 1984. *Eduardo Paolozzi.* Cologne: Du Mont Buchverlag.
Lippard, Lucy (ed.) 1970. *Pop Art.* London: Thames & Hudson.
Livingstone, Marco 1981. *David Hockney.* London: Thames & Hudson.
Livingstone, Marco 1985. *R. B. Kitaj.* Oxford: Phaidon.
Mahsun, Carol Anne (ed.) 1989. *Pop Art: The Critical Dialogue.* Ann Arbor, Michigan: UMI Research Press.
Orwell, George 1961. 'Boys' Weeklies' (1939) and 'The Art of Donald McGill' (1942). In *Collected Essays,* London: Secker & Warburg.
Robertson, Bryan, *et al.* 1985. *Masterpieces of the Avantgarde: Three Decades of Contemporary Art.* London: Annely Juda Fine Art and Juda Rowan Gallery.
Rose, Barbara 1967. *American Art since 1900.* London: Thames & Hudson.
Russell, John and Gablick, Suzi 1969. *Pop Art Redefined.* London: Thames & Hudson.
Sothebys 1967. *Art at Auction 1966–67.* London: Macdonald.
Sillars, Stuart 1991. *British Romantic Art and the Second World War.* London: Macmillan.
Spalding, Frances 1986. *British Art since 1900.* London: Thames & Hudson.
Whitechapel Art Gallery 1968. *The New Generation: 1968 Interim.* London: Whitechapel Art Gallery.

FURTHER READING

British art of the 1960s is placed in a larger historical context by Spalding (1986); Sillars (1991) explores the kinds of romanticism against which it might be seen as rebelling. Hewison (1986) has much to say about contexts, but little about texts; Adams (1978) offers a general view of the work of the period. Lippard (1970) and Russell and Gablick (1969) offer various readings of Pop Art, although Mahsun (1989) is deeper and more wide ranging, especially in coverage of critical theory. Rose (1967) and Hunter (1970) are useful when attempting to define relations with American art; more specific US strands are documented by Kirby (1965) and discussed by Kaprow (1966) and Hunter (1970). Insights into the art establishment of the time are provided by Sothebys (1967) and Hutchison (1986) and, in a different way, by Robertson (1985). The volumes on individual artists all provide valuable introductions, and should be supplemented by the catalogues of the main exhibitions held by each during the decade. Similarly, exhibition catalogues from the Tate, Whitechapel and other galleries will give a clear indication of contemporary stances about arts of other kinds or earlier ages. Fuller (1988) offers a splendidly splenetic view of postwar British art as a process of shoddy betrayal, and his 1989 article is a useful antidote to Hutchison's stately progress. As so often, the writings of the artists themselves are helpful; the reticent lucidity of Hockney (1978) and the precision of Hamilton (1982) are especially valuable.

Index